CRACKING UP

CRACKING UP

AMERICAN HUMOR
IN A TIME OF CONFLICT

PAUL LEWIS

THE UNIVERSITY OF CHICAGO PRESS
Chicago and London

PAUL LEWIS, professor of English at Boston College, is also the author of *Comic Effects: Interdisciplinary Approaches to Humor in Literature*.

The University of Chicago Press, Chicago 60637
The University of Chicago Press, Ltd., London
© 2006 by The University of Chicago
All rights reserved. Published 2006
Printed in the United States of America

15 14 13 12 11 10 09 08 07 06   1 2 3 4 5

ISBN-13: 978-0-226-47699-5 (cloth)
ISBN-10: 0-226-47699-5 (cloth)

Library of Congress Cataloging-in-Publication Data

Lewis, Paul, 1949–
    Cracking up : American humor in a time of conflict / Paul Lewis
        p. cm.
    Includes bibliographical references and index.
    ISBN 0-226-47699-5 (cloth : alk. paper)
        1. American wit and humor—20th century—History and criticism.
    2. American wit and humor—21st century—History and criticism. 3. United
    States—Civilization—1970– I. Title.
    PS348 .L49 2006
    817'.509—dc22

                                                        2006005612

I am grateful to Mouton de Gruyter for permission to use materials that in an earlier version appeared in "Killing Jokes of the American 1980s," *Humor: International Journal of Humor Research* 10, no. 3 (1997): 249–81; to Darryl Cherney for permission to include the full text of "Spike a Tree for Jesus," words and music ©1988, 2004 by Darryl Cherney; and for images from "Batman" #1 ©1940. DC Comics. All Rights Reserved. Used with Permission; and *The Killing Joke* ©1988 DC Comics. All Rights Reserved. Used with Permission.

FOR WENDY AND CLARA

Bartender what is wrong with me?
Why am I so out of breath?
The captain said, "excuse me, ma'am,
This species has amused itself to death."

ROGER WATERS, *Amused to Death,* 1992

Isn't It Time You Laughed Again?

Billboard in front of the Radiant Megachurch in Surprise, Arizona,
featured in Jonathan Mahler, "With Jesus as Our Connector,"
New York Times Magazine, March 27, 2005

Contents

Illustrations

Introduction

Divided We Laugh: Humor in a Time of Conflict

Imagine for a moment that you're a member of an improv comedy troupe performing a skit called "185 Blanks" and someone in the audience has shouted out "terrorists" as the subject for the improv. Your mind is racing to come up with a punch line in an instant. Once the subject is chosen, the setup goes like this: "185 terrorists go into a bar and the bartender says, 'Sorry, we don't serve terrorists in here.' And the terrorists say . . .'" This is your part: what could they say? Well, they could say something like: "Guessed we bombed out tonight," or "Knock me over with an airplane," or "Sheesh, and all we wanted were Bloody Marys." In the post-9/11 world, an improv artist working with this material faces multiple challenges. In addition to finding a word or phrase with more than one meaning to build a joke around, she needs to worry about audience responses to this no doubt explosive subject: how easy it would be to cross a line and offend members of the audience. Say the wrong thing and "I was only kidding" might just not do the trick.

Or imagine that you're a small fifteen-year-old girl—a young woman really, though you don't look it—in for a major operation at a hospital that specializes in children's diseases. Though the surgery is likely to be successful, there will be a long period of recovery, with some pain. The afternoon before the operation you're lying in bed, contemplating your own mortality, the chance that you might not survive, that if you do, which seems probable after all, you may not be quite as active, as athletic, as independent as you were prior to the operation. Reaching into yourself for whatever you have in the way of faith, anger, and grit, you're interrupted, surprised to find that a clown in a doctor's suit has come to Patch Adams you up: make you laugh about your situation. "Hey, little girl," he begins, smiling but also pushing a button that leaves you thinking, "Get this guy out of here"!

Or imagine that you're a politician in the early weeks of a race for election to a high office, say, senator. Your advisers are trying to come up with a strategy for dealing with a weakness or vulnerability in your past life or public work that just broke as a news story. Perhaps you were caught inflating your achievements; perhaps you used to do drugs or drink to excess; perhaps one of your best friends is a corrupt corporate executive who has just been indicted. You can't simply deny or disown the matter because (unfortunately) it's true and (even worse) everyone who follows these things knows it. The obvious alternative is humor: craft a joke or two about the issue to show that you concede the point, think it's a problem but not that serious, and are big enough to laugh at yourself. If the strategy works, the issue will shrink in importance. Impressed by your seeming wit and modesty, your supporters will be heartily amused. When your detractors point out that what you've displayed is not the ability to criticize and reform yourself but to manage public opinion through a performance as pat as that of any stand-up comic, their point, you hope, will be drowned out in laughter.

The paradox of American humor since 1980 appears in just such moments of conflict or perplexity: during years in which the country has been drawn together in ever larger audiences via new technologies of communication, the jokes we've told and our responses to them suggest that we are deeply divided. We think about humor in contradictory ways. Split into subgroups, we are delighted and outraged by the comic treatment of different ideas. Like Tonto in the old joke about the time when he and the Lone Ranger were surrounded by "Indians," the fractious quality of humor appreciation in our time leads us to question the existence of a unified American audience, asking along with the scout, "What you mean, *we*?"

Divided responses to the particular attempts to amuse above, the distance that can open up between joke tellers and listeners, suggest something else about U.S. humor today: that much of our joking has serious objectives that can elicit acquiescence or resistance. For the most part, when jokes are exchanged around the stereotypical water cooler, when friends share jokes they remember over drinks, no lasting impact is desired. It may be, as early humor theorists noted, that these situations allow tellers to take fleeting pleasure in a sense of superiority (Thomas Hobbes);

the venting of hostile impulses or insinuation of sexual images into discussions (Sigmund Freud); the ridiculing of deviations from established norms (Henri Bergson); or puzzling incongruities and problem solving (James Beattie, Arthur Koestler). Still, since the experience of joke sharing tends to be brief and transitory, the images, ideas, or emotions jokes evoke often fade even before the laughter dies down.[1]

But then there are jokes that linger, joke tellers who intend to do more than amuse or who find that, without intending to, they have done more, sometimes to their peril. Increasingly over the past thirty years, strains of U.S. humor have achieved a range of effects, becoming more purposive while also working at cross purposes. At one end of our intentional humor spectrum we find a New Age movement devoted to bringing mirth and laughter into our schools, hospitals, workplaces, and homes—not just to amuse but to improve learning, healing, working, and living in general. At the other end we find killing jokes that not only amuse but also affect anxiety levels through the excitation or relaxation of fear. A common element uniting these caring and cruel humor clusters with much joking in between is a sense of purpose beyond the momentary flash of amusement, a sense that joking can have serious and lasting consequences.

The purposive and embattled state of American humor comes into focus as soon as we attend to conflicts between the attempt to amuse and resistance to it—between ridicule and resentment, satire and outrage—rife in the land. By way of preliminary examples, consider a few such controversies that erupted during a six-month period beginning in the autumn of 2003. One concerned unamused executives at Fox News who in late October revealed a less-than-cool affinity to Queen Victoria by taking umbrage over an episode of the animated *Simpsons* TV show called "Krusty for Congress" that featured a political debate on Fox News. According to *Simpsons* creator Matt Groening, Fox News threatened to sue in an effort to force him to cut out the segment. The real Fox News apparently objected less to being called "your voice for evil" than to the parodic "news crawl" at the bottom of the screen during the debate that read: "Do Democrats cause cancer? Find out at Foxnews.com. . . . Rupert Murdoch: Terrific Dancer. . . . Dow down 5000 points. . . . Study: 92 percent of Democrats are gay. . . . JFK posthumously joins Republican Party. . . . Oil slicks found to keep seals young, supple. . . . Dan Quayle: Awesome." What added spice to this conflict was the fact that these antagonists—the *Simspons* and Fox News—are products of the same network that in effect was chasing its own tail by threatening to sue itself.[2]

In early November, within a week or two of when the Fox-*Simpsons* story broke, another controversy made news. When the Merriam-Webster

Dictionary included the word "McJob" and defined it as "low paying, dead-end work," McDonald's CEO Jim Cantalupo was far from amused. In a letter to the lexicographers, he insisted that the term was "an inaccurate description of restaurant employment" and "a slap in the face to the 12 million men and women" who work in the restaurant industry. Of course, as a variation on the company name and an allusion to its mascot Ronald McDonald, the word McJob expresses a tendentious point directed not at undercompensated employees but at a corporation that serves billions and billions of hamburgers while maintaining high profit margins and low product cost. Cantalupo's protest, no doubt to his frustration, had the inevitable effect of publicizing the very word he deplored, "the kind of corporate strategy," observed, Jan Freeman, the Boston Globe's language columnist, "you'd expect from the clown, not the CEO."[3]

Also around this time, similarly outraged senses of humor were on display in the Republican-controlled Senate Judiciary Committee where frustrated members of the majority were trying to advance the confirmation of Janice Brown, a conservative nominated by President Bush to the DC Court of Appeals. As a frequent dissenter during her time as a California state judge and a fierce opponent of affirmative action, Brown, though an African American, raised the ire of organizations like the NAACP for, in the words of Democratic New York Senator Charles Schumer, wanting "to turn back the clock . . . by a century or more." In addition to defending Judge Brown, who, according to detractor Representative Diane Watson (D-CA), made "Clarence Thomas look like Thurgood Marshall," Republican senators railed against a cartoon (fig. 1) drawn by Khalil Bendib and distributed by the on-line progressive Web page, www.BlackCommentator.com.

Waving the cartoon during a hearing, Chairman Orrin Hatch (R-UT) declared, "It's . . . filled with bigotry that maligns not only Justice Brown but others as well: Justice Thomas, Colin Powell and Condoleezza Rice. It's the utmost in bigotry . . . I hope that everyone here considers that cartoon offensive and despicable." Although Democratic senators were quick to deplore the cartoon, an editorial posted on BlackCommentator argued that "the Republican's purpose in making a fetish of the cartoon was to disrupt the hearing, itself. Orrin Hatch staged an utterly cynical, perverse assault on a nomination process that occasionally frustrates the GOP's relentless packing of the judiciary with Hard Right lawyers."[4]

The most conspicuous feature of these examples is not just that they are political but that they come from the political right and look very much like similar moves associated with earlier left-of-center politically correct critiques of jokes and joke cycles deemed insensitive and harmful in their

treatment of racial, ethnic, or gender-based materials. Although political correctness was put down in the late 1980s and early 1990s by a backlash based to some extent on the charge that its critiques revealed a lack of humor (as in, "Hey, lighten up. It's only a joke!"), in its wake partisans on all sides of the culture wars are likely to cry foul when a particularly pointed or edgy joke crosses what they see as a line of good taste by conjuring painful associations that reveal raw emotions and beliefs.

When the 2004 Super Bowl half-time show featured not only the "malfunctioning" of Janet Jackson's costume but also ads for Bud Light that showed flatulent horses, a crotch-biting dog, and a talking chimpanzee flirting with his owner's girlfriend, responses varied. While media blogs and college student newspapers offered varying rankings of the best and worst ads, and MSNBC media writer Jane Weaver opined that, though tacky, "there were no [2004] embarrassing candidates for the Super Bowl commercial hall of shame," George Konig, writing on his Christian Internet Forum, was outraged: "As bad as that [nipplegate] may be, some of the Super Bowl commercials were actually worse, especially the suggestion of bestiality in a beer commercial, where a monkey asks a human women to go upstairs and have sex with him. Another beer commercial has a horse passing gas in a woman's face. Now in a short period of time during the Super Bowl, women have been degraded at least three times, with the monkey, the horse, and Jackson's peep show." Similar humor controversies bubbled through the run-up to the presidential campaign. For reminding the audience at a John Kerry fund-raising event of the association between the president's name and female genital hair in May 2004, Whoopie Goldberg lost her lucrative role in Slim-Fast advertising. Similarly, Teresa Heinz's jokes about the president ("George Bush is like Forrest Gump with an attitude") and his supporters (who seemed to be voting for "four more years of hell") drew predictably partisan responses divided between "You go, girl" and "She's Howard Dean in a dress." We have reached a point where the edgy-jokes-lead-to-angry-criticism-and-countering-defensive-moves dance has become a ritual of public discourse, where careers rise and fall on a celebrity's use of humor, where dueling political insult books (for instance, Al Franken's *Rush Limbaugh Is a Big Fat Idiot* and David T. Hardy and Jason Clark's *Michael Moore Is a Big Fat Stupid White Man;* Ann Coulter's *Treason: Liberal Treachery from the Cold War to the War on Terrorism* and Clint Willis's *The I Hate Ann Coulter, Bill O'Reilly, Rush Limbaugh, Michael Savage, Sean Hannity . . . Reader;* Rush Limbaugh's *The Way Things Ought to Be* and Steven Rendall, Jim Naureckas, and Jeff Cohen's *The Way Things Aren't*) and radio talk networks (Limbaugh's Excellence in Broadcasting Network vs. George Sorros's Air America) struggle to shape public perception of individuals and issues.[5]

The eagerness to provoke and be provoked operative in these exchanges suggests that they are rooted in sharp disagreements over the specific issues involved, with the jokers highlighting the inadequacies of some butt and the objectors insisting that the butt targeted is unfairly being seen as inadequate. In the cases considered above, the focus is on the objectivity of Fox News's reporting and analysis, the quality of work at McDonald's, the qualifications of a judicial nominee, the morality of humorous TV ads, and the appropriateness of comments about political figures. And each side has its own take on the underlying issues: fair and balanced reporting versus propaganda disguised as news; the poor quality of an increasing number of jobs in the United States versus opportunities in the service sector; the far-right opinions of a judge versus unfair or racist attacks on legitimate organizations and individuals; the use of what can be seen as comic and/or crude images in advertising; and the limits of political mockery. The language of derisive humor—including put-*down* and send-*up*—suggests the directional energy of these butt wars: how jokes can seek to achieve or contribute to a butt shift, defined as (1) a change in how seriously a person or idea is taken, and (2) the successful attachment of a negative trait to an individual or idea through comic association. The accumulation of examples from the past twenty-five or thirty years to be discussed here will suggest that butt wars—intentional humor and resistance to it—have become habitual.

To see the fault lines in our humor culture, to locate and evaluate intentional humor, we need to move beyond the predictable and safe joking of the most widely consumed comic genres: network sitcoms, romantic comedies, the nightly monologues, and most stand-up routines. By establishing a static situation around a set group of family members, co-workers, or friends, and by sustaining it up to the series finales at which point real changes can occur, sitcoms provide multiple variations on familiar themes, security through repetition. By snuggling up to taboo violation but never making a commitment to it, romantic comedies seek to draw large audiences by providing easy affirmation. By exploiting only the most widely shared knowledge (familiar news stories and celebrity character traits) and by steering clear of provocative, unexpected ideas, the monologists reassure audiences, preparing them for slumber. What's new in recent humor is discernible at the margins where one is more likely to be surprised, shocked, or offended: in our response to national disasters and embarrassments; in stories about humor controversies and laughter clubs; in the deliberate use of humor in political conflicts; in on-line jokes and parodies; in gross-out horror films and TV reality shows; in the rants of Internet blog masters and talk show hosts. This book invites you to trek these and other cultural backstreets in pursuit of insights into the ever-morphing, opportunistic, oppositional, and purposeful nature of American humor today.[6]

Cracking Up proceeds from the view that Americans tend to have strong attitudes about humor and that these attitudes are in need of adjustment. Though many of us are likely to be offended when an idea, person, or group we esteem is subjected to harsh ridicule, we tend not to see or think much about the most harmful uses of humor. Widely regarded as a potent force for good, humor is valued and celebrated first as a source of pleasure in a world of stress and second as an antidote to (indeed, a panacea for) what ails us, including the stress. You've watched reality TV; here's some reality prose: if you have a serious illness and humor is the best treatment available, you're probably in big trouble. Not all humor reduces anxiety and not all anxiety-reduction is beneficial. Humor can help us cope with problems or deny them, inform or misinform, express our most loving and most hateful feelings, embrace and attack, draw us to other people who share our values or fallaciously convince us that they do when they don't. Beyond this, a joke can highlight a point or blow smoke on it, call attention to a problem or cover it up. Especially at times when what we're joking about is important, the good news about humor (that it is absorbing, delightful, relaxing, and dismissive) is frequently also the bad news.[7]

Stop, You're Killing Me! Abu Ghraib and American Humor Today

While comparatively minor skirmishes about right-wing media, fast-food jobs, and edgy TV ads flickered into and out of national consciousness in the winter of 2003–4, the makings of a full-fledged humor scandal were under construction at the Abu Ghraib prison in Baghdad, Iraq. With the insurgency against the U.S. occupation intensifying, in April 2004, America was shaken by news that guards at the prison had tortured and humiliated prisoners a few months earlier. As photographs taken by soldiers appeared on CBS's *60 Minutes* and on-line showing naked Iraqis being walked like dogs, piled up on top of each other, hooded and connected to electrical wires, the story could not be suppressed, and it became an instant public relations disaster for the United States and the Bush war on terrorism. All kidding aside: in the very prison where the dictator Saddam Hussein had brutalized his own people, the forces of democracy and human rights had picked up where he left off. But in addition to this central irony, other features of the story make it a microcosm of U.S. humor today: at the same time that ridicule and satire were deployed in arguments about what the scandal meant, different ideas about what humor is and should be figured in the process of understanding how it played into the behavior of the American guards whose seemingly giddy amusement was a particularly unsettling feature of the photographs.

Unsurprisingly in the run-up to the 2004 presidential election, the Abu Ghraib debate unfolded as a political contest, with the revelation of legal memos prepared for the White House defending the president's right to engage in some kinds of torture or equivocating about the meaning of torture serving as evidence against the claim that only low-ranking enlisted men and women were morally or criminally culpable. On May 26 Al Gore railed against Bush and Co. for dragging us into an avoidable war and sanctioning prisoner abuse. In June the Supreme Court granted legal standing to all U.S. prisoners, regardless of citizenship status, in part to halt the excesses that were occurring in Iraq, Cuba, and Afghanistan. By July, an ongoing investigation by the U.S. military conducted by Lt. Gen. Paul T. Mikolashek had uncovered ninety-four instances of prisoner abuse in these countries.

As the nation processed the horrifying images, political debate about the scandal deployed all forms of serious and comic rhetoric. Had we become oppressors, an occupying power no better than the torturers we had displaced? Were these the images of a fledgling democracy? How would the rest of the world, especially the Muslim world respond? Were we fighting terrorism or spending billions of dollars to help our enemies recruit new suicide bombers? With great earnestness, on May 11, Senator James Inhofe (R-OK) declared that he was "more outraged by the outrage than . . . by the treatment" of prisoners at Abu Ghraib. With habitual bombast, on his May 4, 2004, program Rush Limbaugh insisted that the abusive guards were having "a good time," enjoying a much-needed "emotional release"; two days later, Limbaugh made news by declaring that "the people who executed [the abuse] pulled off a brilliant maneuver," that the infamous torture photographs were just "good old American pornography," and that what happened was "no different than what happens at the Skull and Bones [Yale fraternity] initiation." And political humorists of every persuasion (and of none) went to town. Former *Saturday Night Live* "anchorman" turned conservative comedian Dennis Miller offered the following observation on his June 6 CNBC show: "I'm sorry, those pictures from the Abu Ghraib. At first, they, like infuriated me, I was sad. Then like, a couple days later, after they cut his [abducted American contractor Nick Berg's] head off, they didn't seem like much. And now, I like to trade them with my friends." Jay Leno quipped, "The Bush administration renewed its call for a constitutional amendment to ban gay marriage. So I guess they feel the only time that guys should be on top of each other naked is in an Iraqi prison," while Conan O'Brien joked, "Donald Rumsfeld made a surprise visit to Baghdad where he visited Abu Ghraib prison. Apparently, the visit was going well until Rumsfeld took out his camera and said, 'Hey, how about a few pictures?'"

The July 2004 issue of *Funny Times,* a monthly collection of progressive humor writing and cartoons, also focused on the scandal. In it, a cartoon by derf shows naked figures of Dick Cheney, Donald Rumsfeld, Colin Powell, and Rush Limbaugh in sexual poses described as "Acceptable Tortures," a cartoon by Kevin Siers shows a Rumsfeld doghouse with the secretary inside on a leash held by the infamous Private Lynde England, and a Ward Sutton cartoon has Bush, Rumsfeld, Limbaugh, and Inhofe explaining how "everything's hunky-dory." The Bush comment is typical: "Torturers do not represent the America I know. The America I know is represented by filthy rich corporate criminals and right wing Christian fanatics."

Positions on both sides of this butt war were shaped by contrasting views of the core problem. On the one hand, this was a publicity problem that needed to be handled. Limbaugh's claim that these acts were "brilliant" was of a piece with President Bush's claim that embattled Defense Secretary Rumsfeld was doing a "superb job." Implicit in both is a detachment from the victims of cruelty. On the other hand, the war in general or the way it was being waged was the problem. Jokes were used to highlight the absurdity of an army of peace-and-democracy bringers reduced to brutality. Either as an exception to generally higher standards or as a lurid example of the entire Iraq War, the prison abuse scandal provided opportunities for satirists to foreground the wounded humanity of Iraqi victims. Given the intensity of the images and the anti-American rage they were igniting around the world, virtually all of the jokes told about the torture were purposive: meant to do more than amuse.

Lost in the framing of the conflict along partisan lines and in the give and take of intentional joking was the potentially more alarming and, therefore, revealing fact that the abusive U.S. prison guards used sadistic humor as part of their strategy of humiliation:

In one of the most striking images to surface, a detainee jokingly referred to as "Gilligan" by the MPs was forced to stand on a box of food, with wires connected to his fingers, toes, and penis.

Spec. Sabrina Harman said she attached the wires to "Gilligan" and told him he would be electrocuted if he fell off the box.

"Why did you do this to the detainee 'Gilligan'?" a military investigator asked.

"Just playing with him," Harman said."

According to Private Jeremy Sivits, who took some of the soon-to-be-infamous photos and was the first participant to be convicted in a military court, "soldiers [were] laughing and joking as they beat, stripped and sexually humiliated [Iraqi] detainees." At one point, naked prisoners were heaped into a pile, and guards, pretending it was a pile of leaves, jumped on top laughing. At another time, guards posed with broad smiles on their faces and their thumbs up over the body of a dead detainee (fig. 2). One of the guards in particular, Military Police Corporal Charles A. Graner, Jr., acted as a ringleader, Sivits said, "joking, laughing, . . . acting like he was enjoying it. [Once,] Graner said in a baby-type voice to an injured detainee, 'Ah, does that hurt?'" Watching these kidding torturers, Sivits was torn: "I was laughing at some of the stuff they had them do," he said, "[but] I was disgusted at some of the stuff as well."[8]

Graner's trial in January 2005 briefly recalled attention to what should have been the greatest humor controversy of our time: no, not the coming out of Ellen DeGeneres or SpongeBob SquarePants, but the role of sadistic joking in the torture of Iraqi detainees. Along with the criminal

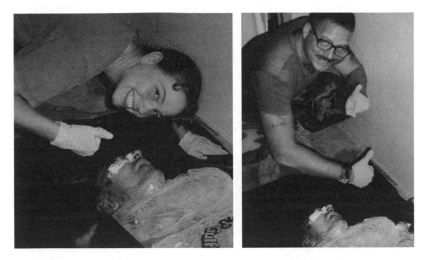

FIGURE TWO. American guards, Specialists Sabrina Harman and Charles Graner, pose over the dead body of Manadel al-Jamadi, a prisoner in the Abu Ghraib prison, Iraq, November 2003 (http://en.wikipedia.org/wiki/Abu_Ghraib_prisoner_abuse).

activity and self-destructive violence that characterized the scandal, the abuse of humor was for the most part ignored and smoothed over in American media coverage. But it is interesting to note that during closing arguments, both prosecution and defense attorneys appealed to then-familiar American ideas about humor function. Recalling the testimony of witnesses who characterized Graner as the "'primary torturer' who merrily whistled, sang and laughed while brutalizing detainees," prosecution lawyer Captain Chris Graveline insisted that Graner operated as a sadistic joker who enjoyed his work. Showing the military jury the infamous pictures, he said that what Graner did "was for sport, for laughs." But, when it came time for the defense to close, Graner's lawyer Guy Womack argued not only that the guards were under orders to "soften up detainees" but that they were under extreme pressure to do this and that the pictures they took were, therefore, "gallows humor."[9]

The question for the jury would seem to have been, was Graner more like Freddy Krueger or Norman Cousins? Was he a sadistic murderer who took pleasure and found amusement in the suffering of others or a stressed-out employee who sought relief through laughter, hoping to access the healing power of humor? A question for the rest of us concerns the odd proximity in this case of two kinds of humor generally thought of as distinct, even incompatible.

Americans who were particularly shocked by the use of joking as a component of torture might well be excused on the ground that a good deal of popular writing about humor looks, in the words of Monty Python's Brian, "on the sunny side." Indeed, even as the Abu Ghraib scandal unfolded, the Humor Project, the most successful U.S. center for the promotion of humor, was preparing for its annual conference in Saratoga Springs, New York. Focusing on "The Positive Power of Humor, Hope and Healing," the conference enticed participants by insisting that "what the world needs now is laughter, sweet laughter." Drawing on New Age optimism, the Humor Project and the consultants it trains assume that it's possible to teach people how to be more effective and get more out of life through joking and laughing.

And yet humor backfired when President Bush attempted to deflect criticism by joking about the failure to find evidence to support his primary reason for going to war against Iraq: that Saddam had stockpiles of lethal weapons of mass destruction (WMDs) and that the dictator was developing nuclear weapons. Though the U.S. right had labored mightily to ridicule Hans Blix and other United Nations inspectors for taking "just one look" and not finding weapons in the run-up to the war in the winter of 2003, months of searching by occupying forces also failed to locate the stockpiles. When the president joked about the fruitless search for WMDs at a dinner for the Radio and Television Correspondents' Association on March 24, 2004, by showing pictures of himself looking around the Oval Office and saying such things as, "No, no weapons over here," and "Maybe under here?" he was blasted by both adversaries and allies. Since the president stopped joking about WMDs immediately after this effort failed, his advisers must have realized that he had crossed a line.

Meanwhile, as the prison scandal faded into the background of the presidential race, butt wars were raging on the World Wide Web. Limbaugh (on the radio and on-line) was joined by scrappleface.com in leading the comic assault on John Kerry—mocked as a flip-flopping liberal—while such Web pages as Topplebush.com, TooStupidToBePresident.com, Theworriedshrimp.com, and BushFlash.com were providing regularly updated anti-Bush parodies, jokes, and cartoons including animated productions like "Doctor Bushlove," "Rock against Bush," and "The Idiot Son of an Asshole." According to Daniel Kurtzman, the editor of About .com's popular political humor Web site, October 2004 saw a massive increase in traffic as millions of surfers checked out the latest moves in the feverish run-up-to-the-election sparring. The opening of Michael Moore's anti-Bush "mockumentary" in June provided an assault on the president's Iraq policy that brought hilariously ironic and deadly serious points to the attention of millions of filmgoers whose political affiliations correlated with whether they were amused by the film and what outraged them in it: the president's behavior and policies or Moore's depiction of them. And the effort to define a political opponent through humor made news again just after the Democratic Convention nominated John Kerry in July 2004 when the *New York Times* reported that Mr. Bush's advisers were planning to reduce Mr. Kerry to "an object of humor and calculated derision" at the Republican Convention in New York.[10]

Dying Frogs and Killing Jokes: Not Just a Laughing Matter

Though necessarily selective, this snapshot of joking during a six-month period starting in October 2003 suggests that these are tough, competitive, complex times in U.S. humor production and consumption, times in which the significance and nature of jokes is a matter of debate and in which the effort to shape public opinion by way of ridicule and satire has become a serious project shared by professional writers and amateurs with access to mass audiences via television, radio, and the Internet. On the assumption that opinions can be influenced and policies affected by the exchange between jokes and antijokes, combatants deploy humor in an effort either to make light of particular subjects or to take them seriously. By calling attention to facts or images excluded from or contradicted in jokes, antijokes ask a laughter-silencing question—What's so funny about that?—and the "that" can be anything from starving Ethiopians to tortured prisoners, from frigid JAPS to beer-selling dogs in TV ads. In the give and take of our butt wars—the struggle between can't you take a joke? and what's so funny about that?—antijokes are deployed in an effort to turn thoughtless mirth into grim reflection by insisting that the subject treated humorously in a joke, joke cycle, comment, cartoon, or commercial is too serious, too dangerous, too depressing, or too urgent to laugh at perhaps because laughing at it could intensify the danger or undermine attempts to deal with the matter seriously. Just as intentional humor seeks to effect change by cajoling those exposed to it over a line, antijokes push back, expressing the determination not to be kidded into attraction, affiliation, or conviction.[11]

Antijokes remind us that humor can present listeners with a choice: take a joke seriously and it dies; fail to take it seriously, and it might kill. The first claim requires little in the way of supporting argument. E. B. White made essentially the same point decades ago when he noted that "humor can be dissected, as a frog can, but the thing dies in the process and the innards are discouraging to any but the pure scientific mind." An intuitive sense of this probably inspires the lapse in attention that frequently greets attempts to explain why a failed joke really is funny.[12]

The second claim—that humor can be harmful, even deadly—is likely to encounter more resistance. Of course, many jokes are positive, innocuous, innocent, or at least benign. Children tell jokes to test or demonstrate their mastery of new words and concepts; adults joke to break the ice in uncomfortable social situations; comedians serve up monologues meant to entertain and tickle audiences. As an intellectual, emotional, and physical experience, humor rewards cognitive effort with moments of delightful discovery and massages of laughter. Still, because jokes rely on the playful association of ideas or images, engage the listener's mind in brief, largely unconscious spurts of problem solving, and dismiss their subjects (however troubling) in amusement, joke sharing is fraught with the potential for harm highlighted in the rhetorical question asked by someone who refuses to join in laughter: "Is everything a joke?"

When jokes do harm it is, ironically, their most shining features—their cleverness and playfulness—that make this possible. Jokes not only bring together familiar ideas in surprising ways, their cleverness is related to the surprise, and their emotional impact is based on their sense of unseriousness, the permission they provide to relax, laugh, and move on quickly to the next joke or back to a serious discussion of another topic. Combined with potentially unwelcome ideas, this seductive and playfully nudging permission is exactly what can trigger resistance, as a listener steps back from the implied assertion that it's okay to laugh about the subject at hand. Associating terrorism with Borscht Belt stand-up (as in Take 9/11. Please, somebody . . .) or Jesus with a guest on a trash-talking TV show (as in the hit London musical *Jerry Springer—the Opera*) could—depending on such variables as the listener's politics, taste, and frame of mind—seem outrageous. In these cases, a resisting listener or viewer could wonder whether such jokes are likely to contribute to the development of sensible antiterrorist policies or the spread of Christian piety.

Wait a minute, I can hear you thinking, doesn't this critique miss the key point: that, far from dealing with ideas seriously, humor not only can but should provide relaxation and distraction? Don't questions about how jokes function risk, in White's terms, killing the frog? Perhaps, but forgoing the pleasure of some jokes at some times may be a small price to pay for what is gained by taking particular subjects at particular moments seriously. Chapter 2, on the positive humor movement, will explore implications of (and the industry that has developed around) the idea that humor appreciation can reduce stress; here I want to accept the premise but suggest that in some situations reducing stress can be harmful, that relaxing about a given subject or problem is, even in the context of a stress-ridden culture, not always wise.

This observation extends ideas developed by Thomas E. Ford and Mark A. Furguson whose "prejudiced norm theory" seeks to explain findings in recent research on the social impact of disparaging humor that targets subgroups. Pending a return to this body of research in a discussion of humor controversies in chapter 3, here I will briefly note that it supports the conclusion that being exposed to disparaging jokes about disadvantaged subgroups can move listeners already prejudiced against these groups toward a greater tolerance of discrimination. Empirical data suggest that this effect is the result of the way jokes tend to shift the disparagement of target groups into a "nonserious mindset" that can weaken external norms against discrimination. Depending on the subject and context, this shift into the nonserious, the playful, the relaxing is both the best and worst effect of humor. In the flow of everyday life, one often benefits from the way humor can make obstacles and problems seem less daunting; in extreme situations, as Private Sivits found at Abu Ghraib, this function can, by mingling revulsion with amusement, weaken one's sense of moral purpose or restraint.[13]

In a 2002 study of humor, stress, and coping strategies, Millicent H. Abel confirmed earlier experiments that found correlations between having a high sense of humor and a reduced perception of problems as well as reduced stress and anxiety. "These results," Abel noted, "support the view that humor positively affects the appraisal of stressful events and attenuates the negative affective response." Still, though at its best humor can aid in (re)solving problems by helping us calm down, lighten up, and think clearly and creatively, at its worst it can facilitate a process of "positive reinterpretation" or distancing. If the problems are real (rather than imagined), humor can support denial and evasion, drawing observers, like three-card Monty, away from urgent issues by enticing them to enjoy a little laugh about a subject and dismiss it from consciousness. Even if the arousal and anxiety associated with stress are generally unwelcome and virtually always unpleasant, there are surely times when they are more useful and adaptive than a good laugh.[14]

For instance, though professionals familiar with operating rooms know that by reducing stress, humor can help solve problems, not all jokes told in stressful situations are beneficial. Imagine a joke spasm that begins when a protective cover slips off and members of a surgical team about to perform a coronary bypass notice potentially funny features of the anesthetized patient's body. It starts when a nurse sees that a prominent tattoo has a misspelled word ("sweethart" for "sweetheart") and starts laughing. Catching the contagion, the anesthesiologist, noting that the patient's toenails have been bitten to the quick, picks up a foot, and, touching one toe at a time, says, "This little piggy is a piggy." And then the surgeon, joining in, grabs hold of two large belly rolls of fat, and shaping them into a form that resembles a butt crack, says, "Look, look, it's mooning us." These jokes would be disturbing not just because they are mean-spirited and cowardly, and not just because we might wonder whether the unconscious patient might hear and remember them. Even worse is the suspicion that such derogatory mirth might negatively affect the team's performance by reducing empathy. Caring just a bit less, might they be more likely to let their concentration drift to an unfinished chore or upcoming round of golf?

By way of an unwelcome but rhetorically useful coincidence, according to the Center for Biological Informatics of the U.S. Geological Survey, the very animals White compared to jokes "are in decline in many areas of the world. In cities and the countryside, in rainforests and wetlands, countless areas which previously hosted a range of healthy amphibian populations now have fewer—and even no—frogs, toads, and salamanders." Genetic deformities—including extra legs, misplaced legs, legs growing out of legs, and tadpole tails that were never absorbed, initially discovered by school children in Minnesota—are now common in frogs throughout the United States. Although no definitive proof has been offered, it seems likely that these effects are related (not to humor analysis but) to environmental changes, including such things as industrial pollution, UV radiation, habitat loss, and global climate change. To many who regard these potential underlying causes as serious problems facing not only the U.S. government but the human race, we have arrived at a crucial decision point: one that will require the mobilization of forces, innovative technologies, financial resources, and energetic political leadership.[15]

As evidence has accumulated over the past decade, the possibility that we are in the midst of global climate change has struck some environmentalists as presenting us with a modern, secular version of Pascal's wager. Just as Pascal began with the proposition that either God exists or he doesn't, this argument begins by noting that either we're faced with an environmental crisis or we aren't. Following Pascal's logic, if we ignore the problems and do nothing, and the crisis is real, we will plunge into catastrophe. If, in contrast, we take major, even drastic, steps to deal with the situation, and it isn't a crisis, the worst thing that will result from our wager (that the crisis was real) is an improvement in the quality of life for those who are most affected by pollution (for example, children in the Northeast exposed to mercury from Midwestern power plants, and the dying frogs). At best, taking strong preventive action could moderate climate shifts, improve health worldwide, and lead to a new era of global cooperation. In Pascal's sense, we should act as if we are threatened, as if we are facing a crisis, by gearing up to solve it—betting that this is the sensible response.[16]

If we are facing a crisis, then we need to act perhaps by first taking it seriously. But humor is relaxing, the most dismissive verbal tranquilizer available in the give and take of public disputation. This is why when an antienvironmentalist like Rush Limbaugh launches an attack, lacking sound science, he is likely to resort to ridicule, calling those he opposes "environmental wackos" and "tree huggers," laughing and joking about how the earth is too massive for any merely human activities to change its operations radically. Repeated constantly, along with similar comic assaults against "feminazis" and "lib-er-als," the attempt to label and mock progressives is intended to support antienvironmental, procorporate politicians. When conservative satire seeks to highlight the failures and excesses of progressive leaders and policies, it can be constructive. But to the extent that humorists of any political bent use humor to minimize serious risks, as I will argue in chapters 3 and 4, they align themselves with the sadistic jokers of recent U.S. horror. Just as these villains employ humor to undermine empathy for their human victims, so the use of humor to lure potential victims of unsound policies away from a serious contemplation of the subject at hand encourages relaxation when action is needed. If we're on the *Titanic,* joking about the wisdom of properly maintaining the lifeboats and lifejackets can be murderous. As we shall see, over the past twenty-five years, the yearning for detachment from seemingly unsolvable and yet inescapable problems, seen in the popularity of both killing jokes and healing laughter, has contributed to the rise of a politics of denial.

Beyond their impact on denigrated individuals and groups (the point at issue in debates about humor and political correctness), jokes can affect public policy by providing answers to questions about whether particular facts or situations are problematic or no big deal. Unlike the lethal joke in the Monty Python sketch, it is probably true that no joke (that is, as a text) is intrinsically hurtful or beneficial. And yet, even when they are not particularly hostile, in a world fraught with danger (and in which different groups regard different threats as more or less dangerous), jokes that tend (and that can be intended) to increase or decrease anxiety can cut to the throbbing core of our most pressing concerns either by whispering "relax and forget about this" or by shouting "wake up and deal with THIS"! Is nuclear power a menace or a blessing? Should we be worried about species extinction? Or the torturing of detainees in the war on terror? Issues like these trouble some, while others are more concerned about a decline in traditional religious, social, familial, and patriotic values: the rise of sexual promiscuity and gay culture, philandering and dishonesty in the White House, the absence of prayer in public schools. And what about abortion? Should we take it seriously because it is murder or because denying access to it places women's lives at risk? The point is not that joking about such subjects is necessarily destructive or in poor taste but that in a given context someone is likely to object and that the objection may be valid.

Though cultural movements can rarely be traced back to a specific originating moment, 1980 provides an approximate starting point for the trends followed here. Falling between the appearance of Norman Cousins's first book on humor and healing in 1979 and of Freddy Krueger in the first *Nightmare on Elm Street* movie in 1984, the year in American politics climaxed in the election of Ronald Reagan. Over the following decades, as Freddy's way of joking became a staple of pop horror and Cousins's ideas attracted widespread acceptance, Reagan's philosophy and style—the smiling, jovial face that accompanied his avoidance of problem solving and indifference to pain—have blossomed into George W. Bush's "compassionate conservatism," the oxymoronic but nonetheless triumphant slogan of recent elections.

Cultural and political value clashes during these years suggest another essential element in humor appreciation: that how we respond to jokes depends not only on how clever they are but on our relation to their subjects and butts as well. In our divided culture, progressives are likely to wince at Bill O'Reilly's and Dennis Miller's idea of comedy, conservatives at Jim Hightower's and Al Franken's. The more we identify with a particular leader (say, Hillary Clinton or Dick Cheney), the less we are going to enjoy jokes at her or his expense. For this reason, as both individuals and members of social subgroups, we are more or less likely to think that not all but only some joke-telling losers (for instance, Trent Lott or Whoopie Goldberg) get what they deserve and that only some butts (Bill Clinton as lecher or Rush Limbaugh as drug addict) merit the ridicule heaped on them.

For those who believe that in the early years of the twenty-first century the United States made ruinous political, military, economic, and environmental decisions—alienating itself from the rest of the world while bankrupting its treasury, squandering natural resources, and ill-serving its citizens in areas of domestic security broadly defined—underlying questions concern the role of humor in these catastrophic developments. Where and how has it functioned deceptively as one of several fallacious appeals? Have we been laughing our way to disaster, amusing ourselves, in Neil Postman's memorable phrase, "to death"?

Though many people take humor for granted, preferring to enjoy and not think much about it, the jokes we tell, the jokers we admire, and the subtle influence of comic rhetoric have never mattered more. As the examples above begin to suggest, far from monolithic or uniform, the strands of post-1980 American humor considered here are frayed, in tension, purposeful. Sometimes nurturing, more often tendentious, combative, and contested, they both follow and help shape cultural fault lines, revealing and affecting anxieties, hostilities, and desires during years in which widely shared attitudes and convictions in the United States have had and are continuing to have unprecedented global impact.

Since no one can be objective in matters of politics, culture, and taste, at this point I'm going to put down some identity markers. So brace yourself. I am (among other things and in no particular order) a secular, Jewish, Northeastern progressive, an unabashed (which means I don't break up the syllables and sneer when I say the word) liberal, and an academic. Like Al Gore and Anthony Giddens, I very much believe that the Earth is in the balance, indeed that we are teetering on the edge of multiple disasters and that the sooner the human race joins in a common effort to ward off the worst of them, the less likely we are to bring on the ruination that people of another outlook believe God has planned. If you reject much or all of this, you probably enjoy different jokes and support different politicians than I do.

Growing up in the 1950s and 1960s on the West Side of Manhattan in a family that dealt with calamity early and often and in which rough joking was a primary mode of communication, I was drawn to irreverent comics like Groucho Marx and W. C. Fields, to camp horror films, and to writers like Edgar Allan Poe and H. P. Lovecraft, whose stories move from comedy to terror with the flick of a trowel. These interests led eventually to a dissertation on gothic mystery and later explorations of dark humor. For several years beginning in the mid-1980s, I regularly taught a course on humor. Because I wanted my students to write responsibly, the course led them to study the social and psychological functions of humor, required them to write about controversies and gaffes, and introduced them to thoughtful comedians like Jonathan Katz and Barry Crimmins, who appeared as guest speakers in my classes. At that time I began following trends in U.S. humor culture, noting, in particular, both a growing self-consciousness about jokes and joke cycles and an emerging belief in their potency. Since then, my work has been shaped by the organization and accessibility of comic materials on the World Wide Web. While studies of American humor by historians, folklorists, and sociologists have tended to treat jokes as anonymously created and circulated texts, my focus in recent years has been on humor that—by virtue of its known and often reachable creators, clearly defined and characterized targets, and/or context-specific purposes—barely conceals its serious intent behind a veneer of play.[17]

The period covered by this book, 1980 to the present, has seen two developments important to its argument and perspective: the increasing subtlety and validity of empirical humor research and the mixed-voiced discourses of creative nonfiction. While the former has been providing insights into humor function that can clarify cultural practices, the latter has licensed stylistic shifts between levels of engagement, including ethnographic and more detached modes of observation. Remembering Thoreau's famous assertion that "it is always the first person that is speaking," I am going to move between seemingly more and less personal approaches, depending on such variables as whether I am commenting on materials I experienced as a member of a large audience or in more individual contexts and situations, private or professional. Through these shifts, my purpose will remain constant: following trends in intentional humor and holding particular examples up to both practical and ethical scrutiny.

Combined with a sense that individuals and groups have been using jokes to achieve different objectives, a fascination with provocative, offbeat, dark, and destructive humor has prepared me both to follow the comic eruptions of our times and to question ideas widely taken on faith. For instance, people often say, or at least imply, that humor should be free, as free as court jesters and fools were (presumably) to speak the truth with impunity. This sounds okay and would be, in a world of honest and ethical jesters, but here's the rub: how do we know that ideas advanced humorously are true? That particular jesters are guided by good will, that they have the best interests of their listeners or of humanity at heart? Like Web surfers who happened onto pictures of the Abu Ghraib torturers, or like stand-up comics trying to deal safely with risky material, many of us have complex feelings about the state of American humor today. By describing ways we have been not just enjoying but also deploying humor, taking note of boundaries crossed, highlighting moments of comic contestation, and speculating about the needs and values buried in banter,

Cracking Up aims to explore and clarify this complexity. The process begins with a meeting of humor subcultures: the juxtaposition of our generally upbeat assumptions about the positive functions of humor with jokes that seem not to ameliorate but to celebrate human misery and pain. Norman, take a moment. Heeeeeer's Freddy.[18]

1 | "One, Two, Freddy's Coming for You"

KILLING JOKES OF THE 1980S AND 1990S

FIRST TEENAGE GIRL: Freddy, no question.

SECOND TEENAGE GIRL: You're crazy. Jason just chops your head off and it's finished, but Freddy makes you *suffer* first.

FIRST TEENAGE GIRL: I know. That's the whole point. If I have to be murdered, I'd rather be murdered by a guy with imagination.

SECOND TEENAGE GIRL: You're crazy! Jason or that Halloween guy, they just kill you and you're *dead*. . . . Freddy makes you a nervous wreck and *then* kills you and *then* turns you into a face sticking out of his chest!

FIRST TEENAGE GIRL: Yeah, but he's so *funny*.

Conversation overheard in a video store, reported in the Youthanasia column of *Premiere Magazine,* August 1990

In the late summer and fall of 1991—as the story of Jeffrey Dahmer's cannibalistic serial murders ran its course and before much was known about his personality—jokes about Dahmer started to circulate. A typical and much-varied one about a dinner party attended by the killer's mother just prior to her son's arrest constructed Dahmer as a sadistic humorist. "I don't like your friends," his mother says during the meal, and he replies, "Try the vegetables."

On June 18, 1994, following a televised chase on the Los Angeles freeway system, O. J. Simpson was arrested for the double murder of Nicole Simpson and Ronald Goldman. Within hours the first O. J. jokes began to appear on the Internet, on talk shows, in comedy clubs, and in private conversations across the Unites States. In the context of earlier joke cycles about Dahmer, Polly Klass, Lorena Bobbitt, Michael Jackson, and Tanya

Harding—the O. J. jokes were predictable. Indeed, joking about violent crime had become so much a convention of folk culture that sensational stories about child molestation, murder, rape, or kidnapping raised the expectation that humor would follow, as in the question asked across the country on the morning after Simspon was apprehended: "So, have you heard any O. J. jokes yet?" How did these expectations—that violent criminals tend to joke about their victims and that crimes will inspire jokes—develop?

For an answer to this question, we might turn to March of 1981, when, at the dawn of the contemporary horror film, reviewer Roger Ebert had an experience that alarmed him. At a showing of United Artist's *I Spit on Your Grave,* Ebert was disturbed to find the audience supporting the film's killer, applauding and cheering as one victim after another was tortured and/or murdered. What appalled Ebert most was his sense that "the audience seemed to take [the film's many acts of cruelty] as a comedy," as there were "shouts and loud laughs at the climaxes of violence." In 1983, looking back over recent horror films, Philip Brophy argued that the work of such filmmakers as George Romero, Wes Craven, John Carpenter, David Cronenberg, and Tobe Hooper is defined by a repudiation of "social realism, cultural enlightenment or emotional humanism." Audience response to contemporary horror films, Brophy noted, follows a series of shocks in which one moves through a set of emotions including frozen terror and screaming laughter. Far from random or coincidental, the audiences observed by Ebert and Brophy were reacting to early examples of what would become a strain of sadistic humor, of killing jokes, in the American 1980s, the decade of Freddy Krueger, Ronald Reagan, and the Vampire Lestat.[1]

Frequently accompanied by twisted facial expressions and cruel laughter, these jokes invite us to be amused by images of bodily mutilation, vulnerability, and victimization. That a line of such humor can be traced through the 1980s and 1990s in American horror films, comic books, joke anthologies, advertising, cartoons, reality TV, and political discourse—from Freddy Krueger to Hannibal Lecter, from Blanche Knott to Mike Judge, from Ronald Reagan to Abu Ghraib, and from Robert Chambers to Old Joe Camel—must be significant. The apparent intensification of cruel humor over the decade—the increasing popularity and acceptability of killing jokes and jokers—suggests that they constituted an evolving and resonant humor convention, one that both revealed and supported a widely shared desire or need.

Unbridled and extreme cruelty distinguishes these jokes from such milder forms of potentially aggressive humor as tickling and teasing. The tickler, often an overpowering adult, can hover or tower Freddy-like over the person being tickled, often a child; the teaser can use ridicule to reprimand, embarrass, even humiliate the target of derision. In such situations, kidders dance up to and even cross the line between play and seriousness, friendliness and enmity. But only if they charge across this line, combining physical violence and pain with their wit, moving beyond teasing or tickling to torture and attack, do they start to resemble killing jokers. For, with killing jokes, though the attacker adopts a playful pose and often seems to be having fun, the accompanying violence bars the butt/victim from joining in the laughter and puts the viewer in the awkward position of laughing with a monster, refusing to do so, or sustaining an uneasy ambivalence.

Most striking about these jokes are the mixed responses they are meant to evoke. Beyond mere humor but built around it, killing jokes assume socio- and/or psychopathic values and defy standards of decency not only to amuse but to shock, terrify, and appall as well: shock by amusing, amuse by shocking. A reading of these jokes based on established work on humor appreciation and audience disposition toward butts will demonstrate that as a group they provide (and therefore must appeal to a need for) an antisentimental detachment from their human targets and, by extension, from the human race broadly considered. This observation will lead to speculation, based on the work of Anthony Giddens and Joanna Macy, about the rise of the killing joke in a decade of increasing anxiety about (and denial of) global risks and dangers that seemed to threaten the survival not just of nations and groups but also of mankind. But, before this point about the appeal and function of killing jokes can be developed, an overview of their evolution is called for, if only to bring readers who have never seen a *Nightmare on Elm Street* film, or read a Splatterpunk story, or watched a Bumfights video up to speed.

Insofar as no cultural motif rises full blown, many antecedents of the sadistic humor that rose to prominence in the 1980s can be identified. Shakespeare put killing jokes into the mouths of several villains—including Richard III and Lear's violent relatives—and Poe allows Montresor, the murderous narrator of "The Cask of Amontillado," to enjoy a few. Examples in the pre-1980 American context include the slapstick violence of the Three Stooges, the horror comics of the early 1950s that led to the imposition of the Comics Code, the joking of such romantic film enforcers as James Bond and Dirty Harry, the work of Stephen King and Stanley Kubrick, and the popularity of sick (for instance, "mommy, mommy" and Helen Keller) jokes. Still, the following review of representative killing jokes in a number of 1980s and 1990s pop works and genres is offered as preliminary evidence of the increasing popularity and intensity of this humor through these decades, a progression apparent in the movement from, say, mommy, mommy to dead-baby jokes, from the Joker of the 1940s, 1950s, and 1960s to the Joker of 1980s, and from the Freddy Krueger of the first *Nightmare on Elm Street* (*NES*) film to the Freddy of the sequels.

Nightmares on Elm Street

Englund has been quoted as saying that what Freddy stands for is the idea of killing the future. He elaborates: "This is the first time in the twentieth century that kids will probably not live as well as their parents. You can imagine what it is like to be seventeen or eighteen today and enter a world with a drug culture and hardly any jobs on the horizon, and AIDS and racial unrest. . . . Freddy represents all of these things that are out of kilter in the world, all the sins of the parents that are being passed on."[2]

A sense of the mainstreaming of sadistic humor in American culture over the past two decades can be gathered from the changing response to Freddy Krueger (fig. 3), the dream stalker of New Line Cinema's *NES* series. Although the first of these films was widely panned and marginalized as a derivative slasher, Freddy found wider and wider acceptance, a phenomenon on display when Mayor Tom Bradley declared September 13, 1991, Freddy Krueger Day in the city of Los Angeles. Diminutively named from the outset, Krueger became the Fredster, the Fredmeister, the Freddytollah . . . making (not copies but) corpses. As it entered its second decade of prominence in 1994, the *NES* industry could look back at its six commercially successful feature films, a syndicated TV show called *Freddy's Nightmares,* five LPs, and $15 million in merchandise, including a board game, Halloween costumes, and a Freddy doll, complete with plastic razor fingers.[3]

The most puzzling feature of this horror cult is not the interest in horrific violence to which it appeals. This interest, as the Marquis de Sade observed, has underpinned the popularity of gothic fiction since its first great outpouring following the excesses of the French Revolution. What is most intriguing is the popularity of Freddy himself, a relentless and savage, but also an imaginative and witty, murderer. A cutup in both senses, Freddy set the standard for humorous treatments of violence and sadism in the American 1980s.

Conceived by Wes Craven, who wrote and directed the first *NES* film, as a laughing sadist, Krueger evolved in sequels into a one-line comic who

FIGURE THREE. Freddy Krueger, *A Nightmare on Elm Street 4: The Dream Master*

both figuratively (in the comic's sense of slaying an audience by making it laugh) and then literally kills people. The first of the *NES* films (1984), established the conventions for the series and characters: a group of teenagers residing on Elm Street in Springwood—that is, in suburban America at the present time—are haunted in their dreams by a boogey man who is able to not only torment them psychologically but also attack them physically. Even though these kids are being brutally murdered one at a time (because what Freddy does to them in their nightmares actually happens to them)—no adults believe their desperate complaints about a disfigured man who wears a red and green sweater, lures them to a boiler room, and attacks them with razor claws. It is worth noting that the very parents who refuse to believe in Krueger's existence are implicated in his crimes by way of their earlier vigilante violence against Krueger: released by a judge on a technicality, Krueger was hunted down and executed by Elm Street parents who now want to forget about the whole business. What Craven developed was a gruesome enough situation for a slasher film, but it was also rather original in its use of sleep and awake states to shift back and forth between a normal and apparently safe world and a deviant and dangerous one.

In spite of the metaphysical and psychological oddities of this situation, Craven's original conception of Freddy's sense of humor was morally conventional insofar as Freddy in the first film is often (perhaps always) amused but rarely amusing. The opening credits are covered by demonic laughter, but we are not allowed to share the gag. This use of humor in establishing the relation between an audience and a villain is familiar to students of Shakespeare's depiction of an Iago or Shylock as villains whose sense of humor defines their deviation from moral norms. But with hindsight it is possible to see that Freddy's few jokes in the first film point toward his later development into a fiendish comedian (as opposed to a laughing fiend). In this way, when one of his potential victims takes a bath and briefly falls asleep, Freddy's claws pop up out of the water and then drop back down when she wakes up. Similarly, in the film's final sequence, the teenagers who think they have beaten Krueger at last are startled to be caught driving in a Freddymobile, a convertible that first traps them inside and then bolts down its own top, which we may be amused to see is striped green and red just like the dreaded sweater. And, in his one verbal quip in this film, Freddy appears as a female hall monitor in the local high school, turns into himself, and advises the terrified Nancy not to run in the hallway.

Beginning with the second film, *NES 2: Freddy's Revenge* (1985), this line of joking becomes central to the character, contributing richly to audience interest in and even identification with Krueger by inviting a gleeful participation in his otherwise obscene crimes. In trying to account for audience enthusiasm for the villains of cruel horror films, Roger Ebert pointed to the odd camera work, which follows the attacker's point of view, displacing the "lust to kill" from a "depraved character" (where it is located in older horror films) onto the audience. The *NES* series gives us a depraved enough character, to be sure, but it also intensifies this process of displaced vision by plunging us at regular intervals into the thrilling, vulgar, menacing, and hilarious fantasy landscape Freddy controls. Once in that landscape, if we are amused it is because Freddy is amusing us with the perversely witty allusions, puns, and visual (special effect) gags that serve as both foreplay to and climax of his sensational violence.[4]

Freddy's lethal, wicked, and playful sense of humor expresses itself in three notable ways: (1) in one-line jokes that intimidate his victims by ironically reminding them that they are at his mercy, (2) in clever manifestations of his form or presence, and (3) in assaults and murders that have a twisted relevance to the interests and/or problems of his victims. A few examples will both capture the tone and spirit of these comic moves and reveal how they give Freddy his special charm. In *NES 3: Dream Warriors* (1987), Freddy attacks the last of the old Elm Street kids while they are being treated at an asylum for, among other things, sleep disorders. Assuming the form of a gorgeous nurse, Freddy lures one of the kids, a mute named Joey, away from the others and starts to seduce him. This adolescent male fantasy darkens when the nurse's tongue elongates into a hideous cord that binds the terrified boy to the four corners of the bed. Reverting to his true form, Krueger taunts his captive, saying, "What's wrong, Joey, feeling tongue-tied"?

Although Joey survives this film, he is murdered in *NES 4: The Dream Gate* (1988) through a similar sexual assault in which his mattress suddenly fills with water and drowns him, as Freddy jokes "How's this for a wet dream?" In the same film, Freddy sits down next to his chief antagonist, Alice, in a nightmare restaurant and orders a pizza, saying, "If the food don't kill you, the service will." When his pizza arrives it is topped with the tiny, tormented human heads of his past victims. As he picks up the meatball-shaped heads and swallows them, he cracks, "I love soul food, bring me more." And in *NES 5: Dream Child* (1989), Freddy attacks Alice's boyfriend Dan by taking control of his truck. As Dan drives off to save Alice, an unusual talk show comes over the air:

CALLER (Dan's mother's voice): I'm calling about my wayward ex-son Daniel who's been acting like an ungrateful, unmanageable dickweed ever since he was seduced by that bimbo, whore, slut Alice.
FREDDY (as host): If I were you, lady, I'd kill the ungrateful piggy.

Freddy indulges a sense of whimsy in his clever appearances. Typically he assumes his human shape with a burned face, wearing his famous sweater, his brown hat, and his right claw glove. But before taking this shape, he can appear in any number of potentially comic forms. In *NES 3*, for instance, he first animates a bathroom faucet, turning its prongs into attacking claws, and later manifests himself by appearing in a small doll hanging on a wall. In *NES 4,* when Kristin tries to imagine herself on a calm tropical beach, Freddy appears as shark-fin claws in the water. In *NES 5,* when a boy named Mark resists Freddy by turning into a super-hero, Freddy also appears in a costume and says "Faster than a bastard maniac, it's Super Freddy." And, after he kills Mark, he says, "I told you comics were bad for you" and laughs. In these characteristic instances, Freddy uses humor both to change the mood of the dreamer/victim and to assert his murderous will.

As the films evolved, particular murders became both more appropriate for individual victims and, perhaps, more predictable. In attacking a re-formed drug addict named Taryn in *NES 3,* Freddy turns his fingers into syringes, jabs them into the terrified girl, and says "What a rush" as she dies. In *NES 4,* he approaches a girl named Debby while she is working out in a gym. First he rips out her arms, saying, "No pain, no gain"; then he turns her into an insect, traps her in a roach motel, says, "You can check in but you can't check out," and crushes the hotel/box. And in *NES 5,* Freddy murders Dan while the teenager is riding his motorcycle. Assuming control of the vehicle, Freddy makes wires grow out of it and puncture Dan's body everywhere, saying, "Fuel injection, power drive, fast lane," and, after Dan is dead, "Hey, Danny, better not dream and drive." By forcing us to observe the metamorphosis of victims from attractive people into ruined and revolting creatures (bug/person and wired skeleton)—both Debby and Dan's deaths can evoke conflicting feelings. Our sympathy for them as victims can give way, at least in part, to a sense of revulsion, a sense that under the circumstances they would be better off dead.

At the end of these movies, the surviving hero or heroine usually has a moment of imperfect triumph over Freddy, imperfect because the monster's survival into sequels is soon after foreshadowed. In *NES,* Freddy is defeated when his victim drains him of power by turning her back to him; in *NES 2,* Freddy is banished from the body he has taken over through the power of love; in *NES 3,* Freddy's bones are covered by sanctified soil, and his demonic form seems to dissolve; in *NES 4,* Freddy is overwhelmed by forces drawn from the positive dream gate; in *NES 5,* Freddy is destroyed by the mother and fetus/child he had been using as pathways for his violence. But in spite of these setbacks, Freddy has endured both in retellings of his story and as a model for and engine of an evolving humor tradition.

The popularity of the *Nightmare on Elm Street* movies, produced by independent New Line Cinema, startled the industry. According to a story that ran on September 16, 1991, in *Business Wire,* NES grossed $26 million on a production budget of $1.7 million; *NES 2* grossed $30 million on a budget of $2.5 million; *NES 3* earned $45 million on a budget of $4.5

million; *NES 4* set a new box office record for independent films by grossing $50 million on a budget of $6.5 million; and *NES 5,* produced for $7.5 million, grossed $25 million. On September 5, 1988, *Time* reported that "the first three Nightmares [had] sold half a million videocassettes." And the increasing fascination with cruel jokers suggested by these figures gains additional support from the even more impressive triumphs of Tim Burton's 1989 release *Batman,* with its gross dometic box office take of $251 million, and Jonathan Demme's 1991 *The Silence of the Lambs,* with its gross domestic box office of $131 million.[5]

The Joker

For a sense of Freddy's influence, consider the evolution of the DC Comics Batman series in the 1980s, especially the treatment of the Joker, Batman's principal enemy and alter ego. When the Joker first appeared in Batman Comics in the early 1940s, he was not a joke teller but a practical joker, a sadistic murderer who announced his crimes in advance, pulled them off under the eye of the police, and left his poisoned victims' faces (fig. 4) twisted in fixed smiles. Under the sway of the self-imposed Comics Code, the Joker of late 1950s and 1960s comics, like the Joker of the camp TV series played for laughs by Cesar Romero, was a pathetic clown— more foolish than malevolent—himself rarely more threatening than a joke. But the Joker of the 1980s (in both comics and the 1989 film) is a psychopath and jokester, or rather, like Freddy, a joking psychopath.[6]

In Tim Burton's 1989 film *Batman,* the Joker dominates much of the action, as Jack Nicholson prances his way through a stylized performance. Consistently sadistic, this Joker moves from laughing at his own mutilation (in the accident that twists his face into an unchanging grin) to laughing at his victims. As he kills a defiant mobster by burning him up, the Joker sings lyrics from "Hot Time in the Old Town Tonight," and then asks his literally smoking enemy whether he is feeling "a little hot under the collar." When another mobster says, "You're crazy," the Joker quips, "Haven't you heard about the healing power of laughter?" Later, after killing with poisoned ink, he says, "The pen is truly mightier than the sword." And, when he breaks into the Gotham Museum of Art, gassing the occupants and vandalizing the paintings, he invites his gang to get into the spirit by saying, "Gentlemen, let's broaden our minds." The use of these jokes came as a surprise only to viewers unfamiliar with contemporaneous Joker comics.

In *The Killing Joke* (1988), Alan Moore tells the story of the Joker's origin, insisting that before he became a master criminal, Batman's foe was a struggling stand-up comic. Tempted into crime by poverty, the Joker is maddened by what he later comes to think of as just "one bad day," a day in which his pregnant wife dies and he falls into a disfiguring vat of chemicals. Early in this comic the Joker tries to drive Gotham City police commissioner Gordon insane by breaking into his house and shooting his daughter Barbara. "Barb," the commissioner cries out, rushing to help her, and the Joker, developing his idea that the wounded librarian is like a coffeetable book, quips: "Mind you, I can't say much for the *volume's* condition. I *mean,* there's a *hole* in the *jacket* and the *spine* appears to be damaged."[7]

In *Arkham Asylum* (1989), Grant Morrison tests Batman's sanity by plunging the dark knight into a lunatic asylum ruled by the Joker. As inmate-turned-keeper, the Joker kids about putting out the eyes of a hostage, equates the "duty" of a hospital administrator with a load of excrement "someone's just done . . . on the floor," and taunts Batman to the edges of insanity.[8]

Brought close to madness in these dark comics, the hero (Batman) discovers his own pollution, pain, and violence, a point rendered clearly by an illustration on the back cover of *The Killing Joke,* which shows a single

FIGURE FIVE. Batman and the Joker share
a laugh. From *The Killing Joke* ©1988 DC
Comics. All Rights Reserved. Used with
Permission.

royal card with two heads: one Batman's, the other the Joker's. And this
comic book builds toward just this image—the union of villain and
hero—joined by way of what Freddy has taught us to expect: a shared
joke (fig. 5). In spite of the archfiend's crimes, the Joker remains an object
not only of Batman's contempt but also of his pity. But when the Joker re-
buffs Batman's offer of help in being rehabilitated and, thus, determines to
wallow in pointless cruelty, the two apparent opponents join in the bi-
zarre enjoyment of a joke:

See, [the Joker says] there were these two guys in a *lunatic asylum* and *one* night they
decide they don't *like* living in an *asylum* any more. They decide they're going to
escape. So, like, they get up onto the *roof,* and *there,* just across this narrow *gap,* they
see the rooftops of the *town,* stretching away in the *moonlight.* Now, the *first* guy, he
jumps right across with no problem. But his *friend,* his friend daren't make the *leap.*
Y'see, y'see, he's afraid of falling. So then the *first* guy has an *idea.* He says "*Hey!* I have
my *flashlight* with me, I'll shine it across the *gap* between the *buildings.* You can walk
along the *beam* and *join* me!" B-but the *second* guy just shakes his *head.* He says . . . he
says "Wh-what do you think I *am*? *Crazy*? You'd turn it *off* when I was half way *across!*"

The irony of this moment looms in the way the Joker spurns Batman's
offer to join in a common healing effort by creating a fleeting moment of
shared humor, an act that confirms the Joker's incurable distrust and,

therefore, serves to support future acts of violence and sadism. Batman's willingness to laugh with the Joker reveals a need (perhaps quite transitory) not to take the suffering of present or future Joker victims seriously, a desire to surrender and—at least for a moment—stop feeling what the Batman should feel.[9]

Splatterpunks and Serial Kills

The quest for the outrageous that is one impulse of popular culture has seen 1980s horror and crime fiction—frequently written by people (for instance, Clive Barker and James Cameron) who also work in the comic book and/or film industry—reaching for ever more startling humor: jokes associated with corporeal decay or acts of aggression. The stories of extreme horror collected in the *Splatterpunks 1990* anthology, edited by Paul M. Sammon, are perhaps representative of 1980s horror fiction that goes beyond the comparatively restrained work of Stephen King and Anne Rice. According to Sammon, splatterpunk writers are renegades and outlaws who use black humor as "stand-up comics for the apocalypse. . . . Within every evisceration," Sammon suggests, "you will find humor's dark entrails."[10]

A few examples will capture the spirit of the splatterpunk version of the killing joke. In Joe R. Lansdale's 1988 story "Night They Missed the Horror Show," an innocent African American named Scott is murdered by two rednecks. After they watch him writhe in death agonies—"There was a snap like a bad knee going out and Scott's feet lifted in unison and went to the side and something dark squirted from his head and his feet swung back . . . and his shoes shuffled"—the killers observe, "Ain't that something . . . the rhythm is the last thing to go." In Edward Bryant's 1988 "While She Was Out," "a housewife's trip to the mall terminates in an attack by a group of homicidal boys. At one point in the chase, the pack leader takes the woman's driver's license out and notices that the picture on it looks "lousy." With a "ghastly laugh," he says, "I think maybe we're gonna make your face match it." And, in J. S. Russell's 1990 "City of Angels"—a nauseatingly cannibalistic postholocaust fable—a group of deteriorating nuclear war "survivors" wanders through a radioactive landscape killing and eating weaker people. Between snacks, they indulge in puns about literally eating a vagina and both figuratively and literally "nailing" a woman.[11]

Speaking of cannibals, any survey of killing jokers needs to consider Thomas Harris's brilliant serial murderer Dr. Hannibal (the Cannibal) Lecter. An upscale version of Freddy or the Joker, Dr. Lecter draws on his impressive intellect and vast store of knowledge in both committing crimes of great brutality and in coming up with witty accounts of them. This mingling of humor and violence characterizes Lecter both in the 1988 novel and in Jonathan Demme's 1990 film version of *The Silence of the Lambs*. When Clarice Starling of the FBI urges Lecter to submit to psychological testing early in the novel, the killer discourages her by saying, "A census taker tried to quantify me once. I ate his liver with fava beans." Later, in response to a question about why he served a murdered flutist's thymus and pancreas (sweetbreads) up to the president and conductor of the Baltimore Philharmonic, Lecter quips, "Haven't you ever had people coming over and no time to shop? You have to make do with what's in the fridge." The film ends with the escaped cannibal telling Starling that he is about to murder his former warden, Dr. Frederick Chilton: "I'm going to have an old friend for dinner." When Starling discusses Dr. Lecter's motivation with Jack Crawford, her FBI superior, at the end of the novel, he offers an interesting analysis. Starling wonders what Lecter wanted to happen as a result of his providing suggestions about the identity of a second serial killer. "'He wanted to amuse himself,' Crawford said. 'He's been amusing himself for a long, long time.'" Crawford may be correct about Lecter's long-standing interest in cruel humor, but it is interesting to note that Lecter does not indulge in killing jokes in the earlier novel by Harris, *Red Dragon* (1981), in which his relationship with FBI investigator Will Graham is more purely rooted in hostility than is Lecter's relationship with Starling in *Silence of the Lambs*. Like both Freddy and the Joker, Dr. Lecter developed into a killing joker as the 1980s advanced. Moving beyond these famous screen villains, one gets a sense of how obligatory killing jokes became in the construction of 1980s and 1990s Hollywood villains by considering such works as *Sleepwalkers* (1991), *Dr. Giggles* (1992), *Cape Fear* (1992), and *Lethal Weapon 3* (1992)—all of which feature this humor. In Stephen King's *Sleepwalkers,* the moment at which the villain (a vampire) loses whatever psychological and moral complexity he had displayed occurs precisely when (in his graveyard attack) he starts to crack killing jokes.[12]

Images of Violence in "Tasteless" Joke Books and Stand-up Routines

Structural and cognitive analyses of humor based on notions of incongruity resolution or script opposition tell us that particular jokes draw their comic impact from ideas or images retrieved after a moment of puzzlement. We understand and are amused by a joke when we call to mind the association that explains what we have heard. For example, in appreciating a joke about a sadist who opens a Cajun restaurant that features blackened bluefish as the specialty of the house, we need to see that *blackened blue*fish (a method of cooking) overlaps phonetically with *black and blue* (the appearance of wounded flesh) and, therefore, conceptually with sadism. Because the appreciation of this joke requires the adoption of a playful detachment from imagined acts of violence or suffering, it might not amuse an animal rights activist or people who have no interest in or tolerance of violent images. Insofar as the jokes discussed above are not only about violence but accompany it, they invite listeners simultaneously to retrieve images of enacted violence (in resolving joke incongruities) and laugh. Rather than venting aggression for the killing joker, then, this humor serves as foreplay to it while it works to distance viewers from victims by encouraging them to join in the amusement of violators.[13]

Inviting readers to laugh at images of bodily mutilation was—along with racial, gender, ethnic, and gay stereotypes—a focus of the "tasteless," "outrageous," and "gross" joke collections of the 1980s. As such, these books give us killing jokes without killing jokers, violence imagined without agents. The first, trend-setting volume, *Truly Tasteless Jokes*, appeared in 1982 and foregrounded jokes about the killing of babies in its opening pages:

Q : What's red and hangs from the ceiling?
A : A baby on a meathook.

Q : What's red and bubbly and scratches at the window?
A : A baby in a microwave.

And these murderous joke resolutions (punch lines that require the reader to conjure up images of criminal violence and physical torment in order to be amused) are applied to such different targets as nuns and the handicapped:

Q : What's black and red and has trouble getting through a revolving door?
A : A nun with a spear in her head.

Q : Who was the meanest guy in the world?
A : The guy who raped the deaf-and-dumb girl, then cut off her fingers so she couldn't yell for help.

It is worth noting that the group most often targeted in violent jokes in the tasteless collections is African Americans, usually called niggers. *The*

Worst of Truly Tasteless Jokes, published in 1985, presents selections from the first three volumes, including jokes about the murder of Martin Luther King, Jr., about a black man found at the bottom of a lake wrapped in chains, and about the opening of the "hunting season on blacks" in Alabama. And the idea of such a hunting season is implicit in jokes about white Baptists who drown blacks in baptism services and an angel who "hates black folks" so much that she returns to earth to murder a homeless black man.[14]

While "tasteless" joke books were achieving unexpected popularity in the 1980s, extremely hostile humor was grabbing a piece of the stand-up comedy market. Beyond the level of misogyny and homophobia underlying the work of many obscure comedians, both the late Sam Kinison and Andrew Dice Clay made rage and resentment their definitive moods. Most of the work of these comics—even when they are screaming or sneering in Kruegeresque tones—is only analogous to the explicit violence of the killing joke, but the intensity of underlying hostility at times carries them into clear examples of this comic strain. In the 1989 video *The Diceman Cometh,* for instance, Clay glories in anger that seems to threaten violence both to himself and to the butts of his humor, as when he talks about singeing a woman's flesh with a cigarette, or rapping a woman on the head during intercourse, or kicking a homeless man in the street. Clay's outrageous and rebellious anger attracted a horde of fans and curiosity seekers to performances that struck many critics not so much as "making fun of others [as] making war on them."[15]

Son of Freddy

Noting the way the ending of *Child's Play* (1988) "walks the line between horror and humor," in his review for the *Boston Globe,* Jay Carr highlighted the connection to the *NES* films: "Look out Freddy," he wrote, "Here comes Chucky." The central incongruity of a serial killer operating inside the body of a "Good Guys" doll is enough to infuse the *Child's Play* series with moments of incongruity and humor. In this way, Chucky (fig. 6) can simultaneously amuse and alarm by shifting between his two identities: on the one hand he's a talking doll who presents himself as your best friend always asking if you "wanna play" and laughing; on the other hand he's Charles Lee Ray, the dead and reembodied voodoo-practicing serial murderer whose seemingly unending supply of hostility keeps him cursing and killing.

In the first of these films, Chucky for the most part refrains from cracking killing jokes, though (perhaps because Freddy had made such quips in-

FIGURE SIX. Chucky, *Child's Play,* 1988

evitable) he unleashes one: before hitting a victim with a baseball bat, he leaps up and shouts, "Batter up." More often one senses that the screen-writers resisted the temptation to have Chucky joke, perhaps because they sensed that a homicidal toy might undercut its potential horror just by virtue of how it looks and moves. Perhaps for this reason, when he sur-prises his intended victim, a six-year-old boy named Andy Barclay, by dropping down the chimney into the fireplace, Chucky makes no allusion to Santa Claus; similarly, when he electrocutes a psychiatrist by way of an excessive dose of shock therapy, Chucky steers clear of obvious puns by not asking the previously incredulous and dying shrink if he is "shocked to see me, doc?" and by not exclaiming "quite a jolt!" Nonetheless, Chucky provides moments of dark comedy. Early in the film during an attack he switches from playful to hostile and calls his victim, Andy's mother's sympathetic friend Maggie, a "bitch"; later, after an older woman sees him in an elevator and calls him an "ugly doll," he says, "Fuck you" in a tone of angry and adult irritation. Near the end of the movie, after he has been cut up into pieces and set afire, his charred and melted head looks up, smiles, and reverts to a Good Guy asking the assembled people if they "wanna play." For all the tricky camera work that frequently projects the world as Chucky sees it, the doll does not so much stalk as scamper, taking quick but still tiny baby steps. He does not so much capture victims in his controlling gaze as he squints at them through his little rubbery eyeballs. And once his identity is known to his victims and they are engaged in hand-to-tiny-hand combat with him, the disproportion in sizes can also be hilarious. When the person he attacks gets a good hold on his arm or torso, he or she generally has no trouble flinging the wee monster across the room, flights that surely undercut not just his dignity but also his stature as a villain.[16]

In the inevitable sequels Chucky frequently laughs while killing but rarely jokes. In *Child's Play 2* (1990), he taunts a victim by tying him up, shooting him with a water pistol, and saying, "Bang, you're dead"; then he actually suffocates him with a plastic bag. Later, he murders Andy's teacher, Mrs. Kettlewell, by beating her with a schoolroom ruler and saying, "You've been very naughty." In *Child's Play 3: Look Who's Stalking* (1991), Chucky murders the CEO of the toy company that has just decided to reintroduce the Good Guy doll by hitting him with a golf club, then throwing darts at him, and finally strangling him in his executive chair. When the first dart hits, Chucky exclaims, "Bull's eye." Later, after slitting the throat of a sadistic barber, he says "Presto, you're dead. It's definitely you."

In *Bride of Chucky* (1998)—the fourth entry and the one that managed to breathe a bit of vitality into an increasingly pointless plotline by casting Jennifer Tilly as Tiffany, Chucky's homicidal partner in crime—the tone became more ironic, self-referential, and darkly comedic. Just before she murders a cop who peeks into a garbage bag that contains the burned-up remains of Chucky, Tiffany says, "Curiosity killed the cat." Rebuilding Chucky by stitching together doll parts and clothing fragments (in keeping with the *Bride of Frankenstein* motif), she ends up with a punk version of the killer doll and says, "Chucky—he's so 1980s." Later she urges Chucky to follow Martha Stewart's advice and be more improvisational in his murders. When he plays along by murdering a sheriff by driving enough nails into his head that he ends up looking like Pinhead, the franchise monster from the *Hellraiser* series, Chucky asks, "Now why does this look familiar?" and Tiffany responds, still thinking of Martha Stewart, "Now that's homicidal genius." As the mayhem spreads, leading to exploding cars and multiple murders, Tiffany captures her addition to the Chucky legend by commending her diminutive lover. "Well," she all but cackles, "at least you haven't forgotten how to show a girl a good time."

Gallows Humor, Gothic Nihilism, and Transhuman Detachment

"Vampires are killers," he said now. "Predators. Whose all-seeing eyes were meant to give them detachment. The ability to see a human life in its entirety, not with any mawkish sorrow but with a thrilling satisfaction in being the end of that life."

ANNE RICE, *Interview with the Vampire*

In *Nightmare on Main Street: Angels, Sadomasochism, and the Culture of the Gothic* (1997), Mark Edmundson sees in U.S. popular culture an uneven struggle between a potent nihilistic gothicism and a feeble because "facile transcendence." In Edmundson's view, the apocalyptic gothicism of a culture fascinated with defeatist horror films and repetitive crime stories thrives on a sense of doom and victimization: "Gothic is the art of haunting . . . in two senses. Gothic shows time and again that life, even at its most ostensibly innocent, is possessed, that the present is in thrall to the past. All are guilty. . . . Gothic shows the dark side, the world of cruelty, lust, perversion, and crime . . . hidden beneath established conventions. . . . Unsentimental, enraged by gentility and high-mindedness, skeptical about progress in any form, the Gothic mind is antithetical to all smiling American faiths." At the other end of U.S. culture Edmundson sees urges toward transcendence and regeneration that can be temporarily satisfied (or at least massaged) through experiences of a "therapeutic sublime [that] focuses on the inner self and provides an upbeat alternative to the interior Gothic mode. . . . Treatises on the therapeutic sublime show us how we might be transformed from our current unsatisfactory selves to paragons of wisdom, strength, sensitivity, and what have you." Of interest here, and largely untreated by Edmundson, is humor, specifically how different views, uses, and kinds of humor operate on both sides of this cultural divide.[17]

Leaving positive humor (the form of facile transcendence most relevant here) for the next chapter, it is interesting to see how killing jokes support (and verify the presence of) the nihilistic defeatism Edmundson associates with the apocalyptic gothic. In the purest form of the killing joke, featuring a criminal speaking while attacking someone, neither the speaker nor the creator of the joke is only kidding. On the contrary, they are using humor not as comic relief but as comic intensifier: heightening interest in the attacker (with whom the joke invites us to laugh) and, perhaps, detachment from the victim (at whom the joke encourages us to laugh). No doubt the creators of films, novels, stories, comic books, and joke collections that prominently feature these jokes were following their muse, crafting jokes to startle, gross out, and amuse; no doubt they were motivated by various desires including wealth, self-expression, fame, and success. More interesting than their motives and aesthetic objectives is the question raised by the rapid development and acceptance of the killing joke convention: why did it catch on?

Although, as we have seen, these jokes appear in a number of popular genres, no genre is defined by their presence. Horror films like *Friday the Thirteenth* and stand-up routines by most mainstream comedians were free of them. As Jim Collins has argued, popular culture and particular popular genres are neither consistent nor monolithic. Still, the diffusion of killing jokes throughout pop culture and the increasingly familiar appearance of the killing joker in horror films and fiction suggest that this humor has its own sources of appeal, sources that a consideration of both humor research and theories of pop culture should help us understand.[18]

Axiomatic in the analysis of jokes is the importance of context, the idea that we cannot derive the function(s) of a joke from its text alone because the same joke told in different situations will affect both listeners and tellers differently. In the analysis of joke cycles, we need, therefore, to distinguish between shared and distinctive features of particular illustrative examples. Given killing jokes can, by way of their specific materials, draw force from their treatment of any theme or issue: for instance, female revenge (*I Spit on Your Grave, Thelma and Louise*); drug use, motorcycle riding, teen sex (to take just a few of the *NES* examples discussed above); racial and religious stereotypes (*Truly Tasteless* collections); contempt for homosexuals, the homeless, librarians, and so on. Still, after we have observed the diverse content of these jokes, their common features—the use of images of lethal violence and of the agents of violence as joke tellers— deserve attention. In their purest form, killing jokes depict not only death but a more or less total destruction of the recognizable human identity (shape, form) of their victimized butts. Driven to hitherto impossible (or at least unlikely) images of mutilation by special effects technology (fig. 7), this humor explodes, penetrates, or transforms the human body, reducing it to the level of protoplasmic filth splattered onto the sides of microwave ovens, squeezed out of roach motels, or deposited as waste in ashtrays.[19]

The history of humor theory—while pointing here and there to the hostile, even satanic, nature of amusement—does not quite prepare us for this extreme set of jokes. In his adaptation of superiority theory, Charles Baudelaire sees humor as an expression of our fallen state. Compounded

of wretchedness and grandeur, caught between the divine and animal, we enjoy laughter, Baudelaire argues, because it confirms our sense of superiority, a sense rooted firmly in anxiety about being inferior. Because he regards amusement as a defect inherent in our psyches, Baudelaire sees the self-hating and misanthropic villain of Charles Robert Maturin's 1820 gothic novel *Melmoth the Wanderer* as the definitive laugher. But Melmoth's laughter—which tears and burns his own lips—is inner-directed, an expression primarily of self-mockery and scorn.[20]

In a later refinement of superiority theory, Freud argues that jokes often express hostile impulses. Unable to "love our enemies" but restrained from striking out physically, we employ humor as an acceptable "technique of invective," one that allows us to make "our enemies seem small and inferior." But, insofar as the notion of joking as a playful and therefore acceptable form of hostility underpins Freud's argument, none of Freud's examples come anywhere near the graphic violence of killing jokes. If such jokes have become common, then the range of subjects deemed appropriate for humorous treatment has expanded. An attacker who first puts down and then knocks down his victim can hardly claim to have been only kidding.[21]

The explicit violence of these jokes makes them seem pathological from a psychoanalytic perspective. Freud's notion of joke work includes both the partially concealed images and ideas in the joke text that need to be retrieved and the cognitive processes involved in retrieving them. As such, hostile impulses are seen as making their way past both the internal repression of the joke teller and the external social censorship or condemnation of listeners by a slight of hand that only belatedly allows violent or insulting images to become clear in a surprising and transient burst of amusement. With killing jokes, as we have seen, violence is neither concealed nor surprising and jokers operate without inhibition or repression.

Other points of contrast (to situations involving sentimentality and anxiety) can help position killing jokes in wider cultural and psychological frames. In a fascinating essay, Elliott Oring historicizes Freud's take on humor as a venting mechanism for hostile and sexual impulses by arguing that jokes can "disguise and express" any motives that "become problematic" or are "tabooed" at a given time. By way of example, Oring shows how the suppression of sentimentality in twentieth-century America led to the creation of covert comic outlets including greeting card texts and roasts—both of which use put-downs to seemingly insult while actually praising their butts. But, to the extent that they are similar, killing jokes are like comments made at a roast in hell: though they can be personally focused, they always torment, never praise, celebrate, or embrace their targets. Studies of humor and anxiety generally distinguish between two kinds of stimuli, exposing subjects to comic material (for instance, a video of stand-up comics) before or after they are exposed to anxiety-provoking material. Because this research tends to show that both pre- and post-stress humor can reduce anxiety responses, it suggests that killing jokes (which combine humorous and distressing material), though never tranquilizing for their targets, can provide some kind of relief for audience members.[22]

While James B. Twichell's work on the appeal of preposterous violence to young men maturing into cultures that seek to regulate their potentially destructive urges helps to explain why killing jokes first started to accumulate in transgressive popular genres marketed to and consumed disproportionately by preteen and teenage boys—Thomas Doherty's *Teenagers and Teenpics* (1988) provides a model for understanding how these genres have come to have a broader impact on American culture. But even in a society undergoing a process of juvenilization (Doherty's term), not all things that appeal to teenagers catch on. How, then, can we explain the evolution of the killing joker from the snarling (and not very clever) model provided by Freddy in the first low-budget *NES* film released in 1984 to late 1980s and early 1990s pop icons including not only the wittier Freddy of *NES 2–5* but even more celebrated comic murderers like the Alan Moore/Tim Burton Joker and the Thomas Harris/Jonathan Demme Dr. Lecter?[23]

Because the jokes considered here draw much of their impact from taboo violation, because they are meant to be shocking—many people have found them offensive. Indeed this sense of revulsion is built into the process of response they invite, either of amusement or contempt. Like the characters most closely associated with them—from Freddy Krueger to Beavis and Butt-Head—killing jokes mean to gross us out. The audience they seek to reach/construct—in the seductive, winking way of all transgressive humor—wants to be grossed out. But out of what?

Noting the transgressive nature of a set of jokes only begins to explain their appeal, insofar as we need to consider why the particular concerns (more or less conscious anxieties, desires, and/or fears) associated with them need to be humorously vented. Like the man in the Monty Python sketch who violates privacy norms by repeatedly nudging a stranger and asking him if he has done "*it*"—a popular set of jokes can highlight an "it" in need of venting. The notion that jokes draw on taboo violation is, of course, central to Freud's work on humor; the more interesting question, as Oring has suggested, is why particular taboos seem to cry out for humorous treatment at a given time in the life of a person or culture.

Instead of joking about his victims, Freddy Krueger might have violated other taboos—say against public urination or having sex with dead marsupials. Such acts could have lent themselves to nauseatingly comic/horrific treatments, but would they have been compelling, resonant? Would such acts have been imitated in films? Would they have moved out into the wider culture (Hannibal Lecter as the psychiatrist who jokes about peeing in restaurants; Blanche Knott as the compiler of jokes about sleeping with dead kangaroos)? Possibly, but if so, this would have suggested that inappropriate urination and roo-necrophilia had become (or were associated with) widely shared concerns. It is clear that killing jokes violate norms against decency and kindness and that they draw much of their power from their outrageousness; the question is why audiences responded positively to the violation of these norms: how humor about exploding, mutating, and dehumanizing the human form has massaged and can, therefore, highlight a widely shared "it" in recent American culture.

The structure and content of these jokes (narrative patterns of attack, murder, and ridicule; images of human destruction) point strongly toward a significant function. Just as critics of early American fiction such as Philip Fisher and Jane Tompkins see, in sentimental novels like Susanna Roswon's 1791 *Charlotte Temple* or Harriet Beecher Stowe's 1852 *Uncle Tom's Cabin,* a cultural project that involves the extension of humanity to groups or classes of people then widely regarded as subhuman (for instance, seduced women, slaves, prisoners), so killing jokes seem part of an antisentimental impulse that works to deny humanity—in the sense of moral value or worth—to the human race. Not only are these jokes an affront to the sentimental mood of moral seriousness and determined kindness (charity, respect, affection, and, above all, sympathy), they assail the foundations of sentimental morality by degrading/reducing their human butts to the level of charred bone, oozing slime, and mutated flesh.

Approaching these jokes from the perspective of research on humor appreciation should help explain their appeal. While some killing jokes target particular subgroups (African Americans, nuns, cripples) as butts, many others are more broadly aimed at "normal," sympathetic, average human beings (e.g., Barbara Gordon in the Batman comic, the familiar teenagers in the NES films). As a cycle, these jokes ratchet up the level of violence—images of human figures subjected to an array of destructive attacks (explosion, combustion, metamorphosis, murder)—associated with humor. Any told joke presents hearers with challenges of interpretation (getting it) and response (finding it amusing, silly, irritating, offensive). Strikingly over-the-top in their inventive transgression of the norms of tasteful humor, killing jokes intensify these challenges.

Studies suggest that teenagers both fear becoming targets of ridicule and are profoundly affected by watching someone else being ridiculed. Janes and Olsen found that these effects, results of what they termed "jeer pressure," include increased conformity and fear of rejection, both of which would seem to be based on a desire not to identify with (or assume the position of) the ridiculed butt. The activation of these responses may contribute to the amusement of killing joke appreciators. But killing jokes go far beyond ridicule. Rather than conveying a potentially useful correction or reprimand, their aggression and cruelty are unbridled and their targets generally do not deserve to be criticized, much less attacked.[24]

Considering the level of unconcealed hostility implicit in these jokes, Joanne R. Cantor and Dolf Zillmann's disposition theory of humor suggests that they would fail to amuse because audiences would identify with victims and, therefore, refuse to take images of their suffering, their victimization, indeed their loss of recognizable human identity lightly. Studies of the role of disposition in humor appreciation demonstrate an inverse correlation between disposition toward butts and amusement: that the more one is positively disposed toward a particular individual or group, the less one will enjoy jokes at his or their expense. A study by Patrice A. Opplinger and Dolf Zillmann of adolescent responses to disgusting (for the most part scatological) humor suggests that it would be a mistake to attribute the rise of the killing joke to the general rebelliousness of teenage male audiences. Though disgust-sensitive respondents liked both high and low disgusting *Beavis and Butt-Head* clips less than disgust-tolerant respondents, and though females tended to like disgusting humor less than males, no correlation was found between rebelliousness and appreciation of disgusting jokes. At the same time, studies of responses to cruel jokes indicate that there are limits beyond which hostile humor generally ceases to amuse. And yet, like the girls quoted at the beginning of this chapter, the audiences I joined for *NES* sequels in the late 1980s and early 1990s were filled with laughing teenagers many of whom appeared to be enjoying Freddy's increasingly spectacular and barbed wit.[25]

Taken to extremes, we might expect that this movement, which goes beyond teasing and ridicule to brutal violence, would distance viewers from killing jokers, and it undoubtedly does just this for many. But those who get into these jokes, at least in the moments of amusement, find themselves laughing with aggressors while distancing themselves from butts. By suspending the species identification that would otherwise support sympathy for victims, the sudden shift involved in getting and enjoying a killing joke would appear to provide moments of freedom from empathy broadly understood, that is, from the human as a component of identity.

This hypothesis helps explain the popularity of these jokes, especially among the teenage consumers of comics and horror films, by suggesting why audiences have laughed, why they have wanted to laugh, at images of their own annihilation. For, in a culture of rising teen suicide rates, killing jokes blur the distinction between homicide and suicide, inviting identification with cruel jokers by offering a temporary indulgence of the impulse not to be human or simply not to be. It is certainly true that members of particular groups (for instance, African Americans, Jews, women, Wasps) often find jokes about their own group amusing, but disposition theory suggests that when this is so, any or all of the following conditions may be operative: (1) the amused person may have a low level of affiliation with the group; (2) a narrowed definition of the group is involved (e.g., orthodox vs. secular Jews; African Americans who never completed high school vs. African Americans who hold PhDs, women who work outside the home vs. stay-at-home moms; Unitarians vs. Southern Baptists); (3) the negative disposition toward the butt group may be a "transitory state superimposed on comparatively stable dispositions that may or may not be consistent with them"; (4) the level of hostility directed at a member or members of an affiliated group is mild. According to Zillmann, "respondents to disparagement exercise moral judgment in relating the circumstances that produce antipathy to the severity of the disparagement. . . . Debasing treatments that are too severe . . . seem to perturb intuitive justice and, hence, impair mirthful reaction."[26]

As a subgenre of cruel humor, killing jokes move beyond the typical stereotype materials of group-targeting jokes (for instance, images or examples of stupidity or ugliness) to brutal depictions of physical assault. How many Jews or African Americans would find jokes like these directed at their group amusing? What would such amusement suggest about the amused person's level of affiliation with his supposed group? By way of illustration, consider a joke Simon Wiesenthal recounts in *The Sunflower*, his 1970 Holocaust memoir. During an outing as part of a concentration camp work group, Wiesenthal was led past a square in Lemberg in which three Jews had been executed on a public gallows. Two details stand out in his account: that "a witty fellow . . . fastened to each body a piece of paper bearing the words 'kosher meat'" and that citizens on the streets of Lemburg for days after smiled and laughed at passing concentration camp workers because they remembered the joke and saw the passing Jews as so much kosher meat walking by. Though he appreciated humor that provided comfort to the victims of Nazi brutality, Wiesenthal saw nothing to laugh about in this kosher meat joke. Indeed, we can expect that a Jew who finds this joke amusing would have serious affiliation/disaffiliation issues about his Jewishness, just as the appreciation of killing jokes directed not against subgroups but against representative human figures highlights a similar concern or tension about being human in our time.[27]

By providing experiences of revulsion and detachment from human identification, killing jokes appear to operate in the world of globalized risk and ontological insecurity described by Anthony Giddens in *The Consequences of Modernity*. According to Giddens, "The baseline for analysis has to be the inevitability of living with dangers which are remote from the control not only of individuals, but also of large organizations, including states; and which are of *high intensity* and *life-threatening* for millions of people and potentially for the whole of humanity." The sense of living out of control on a juggernaut world (can we stop nuclear proliferation and war? has the environment already been damaged beyond repair?), Giddens argues, generates feelings of species doom, a collective gallows sentence. And, just as gallows humor allows threatened individuals to have brief out-of-ego experiences, killing jokes can transport audiences away from a human race that can seem, at least at times, to be rolling toward destruction. Indeed, these jokes appear to operate as expressions of cynical pragmatism, one of the four "adaptive reactions" to the human predicament described by Giddens that also include pragmatic acceptance, sustained optimism, and radical engagement. As Giddens notes, "Cynicism is a mode of dampening the emotional impact of anxieties through either a humorous or a world-weary response to them. It lends itself to parody, as in . . . many forms of 'black humor.'. . . Cynicism takes the edge off pessimism, because of its emotionally neutralizing nature and because of its potential for humor."[28]

Because they fall somewhere between homicide and suicide, Freddy's dark, cynical and comedic assaults most perfectly illustrate the connection between killing jokes and the yearning Giddens describes. In customizing deaths for individual people, Freddy exploits the psychic patterns and concerns of the troubled teens whose dreams he inhabits, attacking through personal motifs and interests, through much-loved objects—beds, trucks, food, comic book characters, popular films—and people—parents, teachers, doctors. Through his unique control of the sensory field (images and sounds) and through killing jokes, Freddy forces his victims not only to be seen by him (as the object of his gaze) but also to share his perceptions (by moving through the landscape he both creates and controls). By imposing his predatory vision, Freddy literalizes and intensifies the cinematic tradition of the omnipotent male gazer who, as Laura Mulvey says, "controls the film fantasy and emerges as the representative of power." The very notion of a death dream posits a self-shredding mind at war with itself. A mind in this state—ready to consent to its own termination, active in the embrace of death—is further along in a process of disaffiliation than is a mind that can enjoy the occasional self-effacing joke, but the shared sense of detachment is an important similarity. Because they undermine the victim/predator distinction, killing jokes can shock us by revealing that it's not, "One two, Freddy's coming for you," but, "One, two, here's the Freddy in you." According to Edmundson, this sense of universal corruption, of identification with or internalization of the villain, is central to our version of the gothic.[29]

By joining with inhuman predators in moments of shared amusement, killing joke audiences can relate to humanity as an out-group, and this unusual relation allows us to understand the experience in terms of Christie Davies's value-conflict approach to ethnic jokes. According to Davies, ethnic jokes reveal more about the conflicting values than about the hostilities of the groups that tell them. Jokes that appear to revile particular ethnic groups as stupid or unclean, for instance, are based less on contempt for these groups than on the "confused coexistence" of values related to adapting to and thriving within dynamic modern societies. In this way, jokes are told about peoples stereotyped as working too hard (Scots, Jews, Sindis) and about other groups stereotyped as lazy (Irish, Ukranians, Sansui) because the joke-telling groups are ambivalent and anxious about the competing demands of labor and recreation. As "ethnic" humor directed against an entire species—glorying in images of the destruction of representative people—killing jokes can, then, be seen as massaging the tensions that come with human identity today.[30]

The shift these jokes encourage away from both self- and species-identification locates them within a larger project in popular culture: the imagining of transhuman life forms. Such fantasies evoke a range of moods from nostalgia and grief over lost humanity (Phil Kaufman's 1978 remake of *Invasion of the Body Snatchers* and the *Alien* films) to delight in the acquisition of new power (Spiderman and Lestat). More often, like killing jokes, these fictions arrive at an uneasy ambivalence. For instance, Marvel Comics' Hulk and Thing—horribly disfigured by exposure to exotic forms of radiation—have for decades agonized over whether they want to return to their human shapes—an odd question given their deformity and isolation. Similarly, in the 1984 film *Toxic Avenger* a nerdy janitor who mutates grotesquely after he is dropped into toxic waste, manages to be more appealing than his human enemies. Like any number of other mutants, monsters, cyborgs, androids, and aliens—these characters literalize what may well be the central question of our time: Do we still want to be human? It is no coincidence that, as this sense of species ambivalence intensified in the 1980s and 1990s, killing jokes proliferated.

As the examples above suggest, many of these transhuman creatures have come to life in recent horror films—an observation that would not surprise Andrew Tudor. In his 1989 historical and sociological analysis of the genre, Tudor follows the movement of horror films away from reassuring-because-successful conflicts with external threats toward terrifying encounters with threats that reveal the instability and unreliability of authority figures, the family, and the self. Tudor notes the emergence and dominance in the 1970s and 1980s of a strain of paranoid horror films that feature losing battles against "escalating, unstoppable disorder." The hopelessness of the physical and affective landscapes depicted in these films would seem to cry out for the detachment and relief available in killing jokes. Indeed, while the role of Freddy as monster/joker highlights the connection between contemporary American horror and humor, Tudor's work suggests that the forces that have had an impact on horror films over the past twenty-five years (and Tudor sounds like Anthony Giddens when he describes these forces as the "post-sixties erosion of the foundations of social legitimacy") have also fueled the development of killing jokes in the past decade.[31]

The rise of sadism and nihilistic violence in horror films has been attributed to larger social and political trends of the post–Vietnam War period, as the following passage from a collection of essays on the modern American horror film demonstrates:

The horror film has engaged in a sort of extended dramatization and response to the major public events and newsworthy topics in America since 1968: fluctuations in "key economic indicators" and attempts to redirect domestic and foreign policy; Watergate and the slow withdrawal from Vietnam; the Moral Majority; and the continuing debate over abortion, military spending, and woman's rights. Further, contemporary horror can and has been interpreted as an index to and commentary on what have often been identified as the more general cultural conditions of our age: its "crisis of bourgeois patriarchy," to borrow Sobchak's phrase; its narcissism, postmodernism, and sense of the apocalyptic; and its attitude toward technology, death, and childhood.

Tudor's study arrives at a similar sense of "apocalyptic despair" enacted in "a battle which . . . must always be lost. . . . Paranoid horror is paranoid both in its inbuilt prognosis of the likely outcome and in its assumption that the roots of disorder are to be found within ourselves and our institutions. It is not just doubt that is ubiquitous in this world; it is self-doubt."[32]

   In the face of such doubt, while these jokes offended and continue to offend many viewers, they are neither deviant nor abnormal, but the appropriate product of a civilization only half aware of its self-destructive tendencies: powered by hydrocarbons, "defended" by radioactive isotopes, hyperactive in the creation of toxins. What is, perhaps, most surprising about this humor—coming at the close of an almost unceasingly genocidal century—is that it seems to have drawn on new sources of vulnerability and guilt that filtered into consciousness in the 1980s. Throughout the decade—from Bhopal to Rocky Flats, from Chernobyl to Valdez, in almost daily stories of toxic leaks, acid rain, ozone depletion, and global warming—a sense of gradual but inevitable ecological ruin spread. Like the charred and sulfuric scenes Freddy frequently conjures up to torment his victims/butts, the contemporary world (Giddens's juggernaut) can seem distressingly post-Darwinian: a world in which human beings are their own worst enemies and in which the most fit species (that is, the one most likely to triumph in competition with other species) may well not survive. Added to earlier fears of an instantaneous nuclear holocaust, the insidious presence of toxic substances within our bodies and throughout ecosystems bubbled up in popular culture in mutant comics, in superheroes and monsters created by exposure to toxins, in horror films, and in killing jokes.

Noting the appearance of environmental themes in recent gothic work, Edmundson highlights the defeatist way they are treated: "when discourses of environmentalism . . . make the Gothic turn, and stay on that road—when they become formulaic horror stories—the result is passivity and fear. Motives for political action or for scientific research can disappear beneath waves of Gothic paranoia." And, it would be appropriate to add, both empathy and humanity vanish beneath waves of laughter, since gothic nihilism seems most apparent in moments of irresistibly cruel humor directed at attractive and generally worthy butts.[33]

Killing Jokes: Theme and Variations in *Interview with the Vampire, Heathers,* and *Carrie*

My point is not that American culture in a uniform or monolithic way became suicidal over the past decades but that, in a range of moods and forms that included killing jokes, it produced fantasies of suicide and humanicide, postapocalyptic scenarios of transhuman life related to a sense that problems were becoming both global and unsolvable. While I have argued that killing jokes appeal to this shift in consciousness, I want to complicate the point by observing that this appeal to the transhuman is at most an underlying force or theme present in different ways and to varying extents in specific jokes and for particular members of any audience. Even if the need for this corrective were not explicit in humor theory—which suggests that different people both find different kinds of jokes amusing and find the same joke amusing for different reasons—it is a salutary prescription of *No Respect,* Andrew Ross's 1989 study of the ways popular works and genres have often been subjected to the controlling judgments of intellectual elites. Cautioning against reductive views of the "affective world of popular taste," Ross insists that individual consumers of popular culture respond autonomously—that is, individually, not mechanically—even to pornographic and violent works. Insisting that it has been all too easy for critics to revile such works for their "bad values" (sexism, militarism), Ross calls for a "more popular, less guilt-ridden cultural politics" and points to the radical appeal such works/genres can make to a liberating power based on "disrespect for the lessons of educated elites." Like such apparently visceral genres as pornographic magazines and slasher films, then, the killing jokes described here and the works in which they appear have undoubtedly inspired a wide range of responses—from revulsion to amusement—and served diverse psychological functions for viewers and readers—including entertainment, the venting of hostile impulses, the licensing of such impulses, and a nihilistic rejection of norms and values. Still, it is possible to see the broad area within which these jokes operate. Just as pornography provides sexual fantasies and slasher films provide fantasies of aggression—so killing jokes mingle humor with horror, providing transhuman fantasies of surrender to and/or transcendence of death and defeat.[34]

Within the context of this broad fantasy, particular killing jokes may well have particular concerns and analytic force, as they expose specific values, people, and institutions to violent ridicule. Works containing a number of these jokes are, moreover, likely to develop a view or views— celebratory, critical, relativist—of this humor. The *NES* films, for instance, allow for ambiguous responses to their own jokes, as even the most jaded of Freddy's fans appreciate his kidding because it is not only amusing but also outrageous, immoral, distasteful, and terrifying: in a word, gross. As a comedian, the killing joker invites us to laugh at images of our own annihilation; as a monster, he can remind us that we have someone worth fighting, someone we should still want to destroy. In both Anne Rice's 1976 novel *Interview with the Vampire* and Michael Lehmann's 1988 film *Heathers,* the tension and ambivalence surrounding the reception of killing jokes is an explicit theme. In the former, Louis recoils from the predatory humor Lestat directs at human victims; in the latter, the heroine Veronica Sawyer is attracted to killing joker J.D. but then pulls away from his increasingly violent behavior. In their responses to killing jokes, characters like these move through processes of disaffiliation from and reaffiliation with (their own) humanity. Moving in the opposite direction, desperate to belong, to fit in, to laugh with and not be laughed at by her peers, Stephen King's Carrie endures a childhood of constant ridicule that culminates in a practical joke that turns her into a killing joker.[35]

In *Interview with the Vampire,* the first of the Lestat novels, Louis is torn between a dying affiliation with humanity and the struggle to understand what it means to be and feel like a vampire, a struggle seen perhaps most clearly in his relation to killing jokes. Early in the novel Louis is neither entertained by Lestat's spectacularly theatrical murders nor amused by Lestat's cruel humor. When Lestat serves up versions of famous Shakespearean lines—saying "Good night, sweet prince" to one victim after drinking his life blood, and "Put out the light, and then put out the light" as he attacks another—Louis feels "weary" or "angry." Accusing Louis of hanging onto his human sensibility, Lestat argues that "vampires are killers. . . . Predators. Whose all-seeing eyes were meant to give them detachment." And for Lestat this detachment manifests itself in "the ability to see a human life in its entirety, not with any mawkish sorrow but with a thrilling satisfaction in being the end of that life." But resisting Lestat's plea to live as "an immortal" who has God's power to take life, Louis clings to his old identity, responding in horror and disgust to killing jokes, refusing to join in what he calls "the hollow vampire laughter which is like tinsel or silver bells."[36]

This tension in Louis's development becomes particularly intense after he escapes from Lestat, travels to Europe, and watches others of his kind at the Théâtre des Vampires in Paris. Alternately entranced and revolted, Louis sits above "the all-too human" audience and watches as a "Trickster" figure, carrying a scythe and played by a vampire, refuses to kill an old woman who begs comically for death. In response to this early sequence, "laughter erupt[s] uncertainly from the human audience" and then becomes louder and more unrestrained. Perhaps because it reminds him of his ironic position as neither human nor vampire, Louis finds this laughter unpleasant. The main drama concerns a scantily clad young woman who is forced on stage and begs for her life as the "demon trickster" urges her to give into death. As the "helpless mortal girl" stares "blindly toward the laughter," and gradually stops resisting, Louis is suspended between sympathy and vampiric lust, between what he calls the "jaded audience" and the "community of vampires," between two species, unable to laugh with either. Claudia, the child vampire who is Louis's companion and daughter, provides a contrast by continuing to laugh even while the young woman begs the vampire for her life and the audience for help.[37]

It is worth noting that the Lestat we see in this first novel is at a low emotional ebb; the far larger frame of Rice's vampire saga focuses on Lestat's own struggle to be both vampire and human: indeed, in this larger context, his relationship with Louis reminds Lestat of the importance of the human perspective to a vampire who wants to preserve emotional vitality. Though he never becomes a killing joker, Louis—who represents human consciousness not only to Lestat but to *Interview*'s other ancient vampire, Armand—suffers enough in this first novel to sink into emotional numbness. Lestat, in contrast, rises both literally and emotionally from this nadir, bringing an entirely different sense of humor first to *The Vampire Lestat* (1985) and then to later novels in the series.

Like Rice's vampire heroes, in Lehmann's cult classic *Heathers,* the protagonist Veronica Sawyer undergoes a painful and dangerous crisis of affiliation. Rendered representative by the association of her name with quintessentially American teenagers (the brunette from Archie Comics and Mark Twain's all-American boy)—Veronica, played by Winona Ryder, is at the start of the film torn between an empowered trio of malicious girls named Heather and the other students (including jocks, geeks, bloats, and former uncool friends) in her high school. She is also attracted to the seemingly cool new guy in town, Jason Dean (J.D.), played with increasingly savage humor by Christian Slater. Like Veronica, J.D. finds the elitism and condescension of the Heathers and jocks unappealing, so unappealing that he draws his new girlfriend into unwittingly helping him stage a series of suicides that disguise his inventive and funny acts of criminal violence.

When Heather Chandler, the first leader of the claque, dies from drinking poison presented to her by J.D. as a hangover remedy, Veronica is both stunned and amused; the rest of the town is perfectly willing to chalk it up to another teen suicide. In his next lethal but also practical joke, J.D. makes his murder of Kurt and Ram, two football stars, look like the dual suicide of socially scorned gay teens. Telling Veronica that they will be shot with non-lethal tranquilizer bullets, he gets her to forge the following suicide note: "Ram and I died the day we realized we could never reveal our forbidden love to an uncaring and unundersanding world. The joy we shared in each other's arms was better than any touchdown, yet we were forced to live the lie of sexist, beer-guzzling jock assholes." To J.D. this note provides the "perfect punch line" for the trick; to Veronica it serves as a sign that her life has taken a dreadful turn. Burning her hand with a cigarette lighter, she screams out that she did not want the jocks to die. Nor is she amused when J.D. tries to reach her by saying, "Football season is over. Kurt and Ram had nothing to offer the school but date rape and AIDS jokes." At Kurt's funeral (*Heathers* is understandably punctuated by funerals), Veronica starts to laugh at the absurd spectacle presented when Kurt's father stands over the open casket and proclaims that he loves his "gay, dead son," but she stops abruptly when she sees the tears on the face of Kurt's younger sister. Nor does Veronica find the attempted suicide of a fat girl cruelly referred to as "Martha Dumptruck" amusing. When J.D. says that Martha "dialed suicide hotlines in her diapers," Veronica replies, "You're not funny."

Set in Sherwood, Ohio—a name that alludes directly to Freddy's Springwood, just as J.D. reprises and interrogates Freddy's relation to teen consciousness and high school cultures—*Heathers* follows Veronica's struggle to find a way, as she says, to make her school "a nice place." In the end this requires literally blowing off killing joker J.D. before he can set off bombs in the school basement. But it also requires her to step away from cruel humor and embrace the very kids (starting with her old friend,

Fat Martha) who are its most frequent butts. As a response to teen suicide, *Heathers* highlights the role of intense ridicule by showing both its allure (J.D. is by far the cutest, perhaps the only attractive guy in the movie) and its potential for extreme inhumanity.

The opposite movement defines Stephen King's treatment of cruel humor in his 1974 coming of age novel *Carrie*. Both the novel and 1976 film adaptation by Brian De Palma provide an analysis of the way the teasing and mocking of children can have disastrous consequences. Raised by a monstrously repressed born-again mother, Carrie is enough of an outsider and geek to serve as the target of ridicule throughout her childhood:

There had been all those years, all those years of let's short-sheet Carrie's bed at Christian Youth Camp and I found this letter from Carrie to Flash Bobby Pickett let's copy it and pass it around and hide her underpants somewhere and put this snake in her shoe and duck her *again,* duck her *again;* Carrie tagging along stubbornly on biking trips, known one year as pudd'n and the next year as truckface . . . Billy Preston putting peanut butter in her hair that time she fell asleep in study hall, the pinches, the legs outstretched in school aisles to trip her up.

As a result of this, Carrie comes to expect to be ridiculed and she plots revenge, dreaming that Jesus will come not with a "shepherd's crook" but "with a boulder in each hand to crush the laughers." But up to the tragic climax she also yearns to fit in, to belong, not to be laughed at, not even to laugh at others but to join with them in shared amusement and normal teen pleasure. But this is not to be. Drawing on her mutant power of telekinesis, Carrie responds to one final comic assault by destroying her high school and much of the rest of her hometown during senior prom. The assault is planned by the novel's most loathsome couple, Chris Hargensen and her greaser boyfriend Billy Nolan. Together they scheme to get Carrie and her date elected prom queen and king and then, at the height of the celebration, to drop pig blood on Carrie. When their plan succeeds and Carrie stands on the podium drenched in blood, the promgoers burst into laughter. As one of the few who survives the event recalls, "It was either laugh or cry, and who could bring himself to cry over Carrie after all those years?"[38]

In a spasm of self-loathing and rage, Carrie decides to use her power against the laughers. Giggling "hysterically," she slams the gym doors shut, trapping students and faculty, bursts water pipes loose, and snaps high-voltage electrical wires through the air. As a musician starts writhing in shock, she laughs and thinks, "by Christ then let them all look funny."

In this plot, King provides a plausible, if heartbreaking, psychological history for a killing joker, the antecedent story or prequel. An irony that arose in responses to the Columbine shootings concerned a tendency to blame everything goth or gothic (including King) for the tragedy. Though *Carrie* and real school massacres follow similar patterns, the novel weighs in as a diagnosis and prevention guide to, not a cause of, teen violence.[39]

Joking Criminals and Criminal Joking: Killers and Copycats in *Beavis and Butt-Head, Bumfights,* and *Jackass*

One notices two trends as horror films play out in multiple sequels: they tend to become both more explanatory and more self-conscious. Illustrative of the former is the way *NES 4* and *5* explore Freddy's origin, probing events that the earlier films left shrouded in mystery. Illustrative of the latter is the way films like *Bride of Chucky* adopt a self-referential irony that has Chucky talking about events in the earlier films as though he knows that he is now in a sequel. Each of these conventions in rather different ways seeks to bridge the gap between the implausibility of horror/mystery genres and something like a real-world perspective. *Wes Craven's New Nightmare* (1994), the sixth film in the *NES* series, literalizes this move by bringing Freddy back not to Elm Street but to the Los Angeles populated by Craven and the actors who created the earlier *NES* films. In this way, Heather Langenkamp, who played Nancy, one of Freddy's victim/opponents in *NES* and *NES 3*, is troubled by nightmarish intrusions into her life, Robert Englund finds himself producing oddly dark paintings, and Craven's dreams are troubled. His sequels finished, Freddy is trying to find a new life in our world, to break through.

The varied cultural significance of killing jokes becomes apparent if we follow them, like Freddy in this film, beyond the realms of fictive/dramatic production into actual use, noting that several of the more infamous crimes of recent decades were flavored with wit:

★ James Oliver Huberty—who armed himself to the teeth, prior to entering a San Diego McDonald's in the summer of 1984, killing twenty-one people and wounding nineteen—indulged in a Kreugeresque quip. "I'm going to hunt humans," he told his wife.
★ Robert Chambers—who strangled eighteen-year-old Jennifer Levin in the summer of 1986 in what became known as the "preppy murder case"—was probably kidding when he told police that the much smaller Levin had molested *him* in the park. According to Paul Slansky, a home videotape of Chambers taken before his trial shows the killer "cavorting around with several lingerie-clad teenage

girls . . . [and] amusing himself by pretending to strangle a doll. 'Oops [he says], I think I killed it.'"[40]

★ The teenagers who were convicted of going on a wilding rampage—attacking various people and raping a young woman—through New York City's Central Park on April 20, 1989. Their supposed crime spree became a megastory overnight because of the boys' alleged lack of motivation. Although the convictions were overturned in 2002, at the time people following the case were both appalled and fascinated when Elizabeth Lederer, a prosecutor, reported the youths showed no remorse when they were first brought in, that one of them told the police he had "whipped the woman with a lead pipe about the head because 'it was fun.'"[41]

★ The March 1991 beating of Rodney King by members of the Los Angeles Police Department, who joked about their victim.

★ The attack on trucker Reginald Denny, beaten during the 1992 Los Angeles riots by attackers who seemed to take gleeful delight in the seemingly random assault.

★ George Hennard who killed twenty-two people and injured twenty more before killing himself in Luby's Cafeteria in Killeen, Texas, in October 1991. Four months before the killing started, Hennard wrote as follows to a cousin: "Please give me the satisfaction of laughing in the faces of all the treacherous female vipers . . . who tried to destroy me."

★ Henry L. Meinholz, who was convicted in November of 1991 in Plymouth, Massachussetts, of the kidnapping, rape, and murder of his neighbor, thirteen-year-old Melissa Benoit. Throughout his lurid testimony, Meinholz smiled at the jury—a sign, his lawyer argued, of the killer's insane sense of humor.

★ Two assaults by fire: the January 1993 case of an African American tourist set on fire by three white men in Tampa, Florida. One of the alleged perpetrators was wearing a shirt that had a picture of a gun over the words, "I don't dial 911"; and the February 1993 case of a sleeping man set on fire by a group of teenage boys on a New York subway. "Look, look," one of the attackers said to the others, "he's still sleeping."

★ On March 6, 1999, six weeks before Dylan Klebold and Eric Harris went on a rampage in Columbine [Colorado] High School, they produced a video of themselves walking through a local woods, carrying and shooting guns at bowling pins and trees, and joking about what it would be like if people were their targets.

★ During the debate in the fall and winter of 2005 about whether Stanley (Tookie) Williams, the former Crips Gang leader then awaiting execution in San Quentin, should have had his sentence reduced to life in prison, opponents of leniency pointed to the role of humor in demonstrating the particularly "cold-blooded" nature of his crimes. According to Robert Martin, a prosecutor in the case, on February 28, 1979, during a robbery at a 7-Eleven in Pomona, California, Williams forced Wayne Owens, a clerk, "into a back room at gunpoint, shot out a security monitor, then ordered, 'Get down on your knees, (expletive),' and shot him twice in the back." And, Martin continued, "Williams later laughed about it as he was eating his hamburger."[42]

The point I want to make about these crimes or the jokes told by perpetrators of violent crime is not that they were inspired by similar moments in pop culture but that they are similar enough to raise questions about the potential role of humor in criminal assaults. To the extent that joking about violent conduct helps relax criminals (by inhibiting conscience and empathy or lightening mood) during their crimes or after they are committed, it is obviously harmful. The testimony of a Los Angeles police officer in the second Rodney King trial in March of 1993 drives this observation home. By her own account, Melanie Singer, a member of the California Highway Patrol at the scene, decided not to give medical assistance to the wounded and bleeding Rodney King after hearing other officers "joking around" about his suffering.

Few works more forcefully dragged killing jokes across the line between fantasy and reality than Mike Judge's *Beavis and Butt-Head,* the MTV cartoon series that introduced viewers to its eponymous characters: two music-video-watching, mindlessly destructive, and constantly laughing teens. Early episodes, broadcast in March 1993, and then from May through October 1993, had the lads exploding lizards, tormenting pets, sniffing paint thinner, setting fires, and chanting "breakin' the law." When on October 6, 1993, Austin Messner, a five-year-old boy in Moraine, Ohio, started a fire that killed his two-year-old sister Jessica, both his mother and the local fire chief blamed the show. As Chief Harold Sigler put it, "When you take a child in the formative years and you get these cartoon characters saying it's fun to play with fire, this is going to stick in that kid's mind." Almost immediately, MTV and Judge reconsidered both the show's content and airtime, moving it from its regular 7 P.M. slot to 11 P.M. and removing all fire-based plots. Still, even in reissued DVDs in *The Best of Beavis and Butt-Head* series, the boys are reckless and cruel. As a matter of routine, they destroy property (*Cleaning House*), trick fast food customers into eating fried rats (*Work Sucks*), and misdirect traffic during a blackout in ways that cause serious accidents and injuries (*Blackout*).[43]

During the first season, when the program drew both a large youth audience and a chorus of indignant critics, Judge admitted that his characters were strikingly foolish but denied that they were "really cruel or vicious. They're just out to have a good time," he told a *Washington Post* reporter. "They're not bullies. They don't have a lot of hatred. Most of the time, they're in a pretty good mood." But their mindless pursuit of entertainment (things that are cool) and avoidance of boredom (things that suck) leaves ruin in its wake. Unrestrained by teen anxieties about being smart and attractive enough to connect with other people (for instance, teachers, bosses, or other teens of both sexes) and meet performance standards, uninhibited by norms of politeness, empathy, and common sense, they provide fantasies of a life lived without rules in a moment-to-moment pursuit of amusement. If we assume that their teenage fans, like Veronica in *Heathers,* were suspended between the competing appeal of cynicism and conformity, then Beavis and Butt-Head's utter inability or refusal to perceive this or any other dilemma of teen life serves as a break from normal teen stress. As Beavis's even more libidinous and verbally challenged alter ego, Cornholio, suggests, the boys are too stupid to learn anything in school or life and untroubled by this or by their innumerable failures to comprehend and connect.[44]

As an intervention in a cultural landscape crowded with competing messages—be yourself, be thin; abstain from sex, be sexy; try pot, this is your brain on drugs—and with images of success and failure, *Beavis and Butt-Head* provided not just comic relief but a laugh track for fantasy escapes from nuance, reflection, subtlety, and, perhaps most of all, empathy. In their astounding stupidity, they connect to other models of mindlessness (for instance, Homer Simpson, Bill and Ted, Lloyd and Harry in the *Dumb and Dumber* series); in their unattractiveness, they connect to such repulsively appealing antiheroes as Urkel (in *Family Matters*), the eponymous characters in the *Revenge of the Nerds* series, the Oblongs, *Freaks and Geeks,* and Napoleon Dynamite. But because everything is a joke for them, because they always laugh when they speak (the famous heh-heh-heh and huh-huh-huh that children imitated much to the dismay of parents), and because they frequently hurt people and property (both deliberately and inadvertently)—their amusement brings them into the world of the killing joker. As Judge suggests, the sadism of their humor flows not so much from a Freddy-like vindictiveness as from an amoral disregard for the consequences of their acts. They are not only less cruel but far, far less imaginative than Freddy. But when they laugh while victimizing others, they draw their audience into (and perhaps also discredit) states of detachment from suffering familiar to Freddy's fans.

By moving from cartoon fantasy to live-action drama, the stunts in both the *Bumfights* videos and the MTV *Jackass* TV show and movie intensified Beavis and Butt-Head's practice of laughing while they inflict pain on themselves and others. Though no one died in the making of either of these works, in *Jackass the Movie,* called "the funniest film of 2002" by e! online, one has the sense that real pain is being inflicted on

Johnny Knoxville and the others when they ride downhill in an oversized shopping cart while rocks are hurled at them, crash a rented car into other smashed up vehicles, apply electric shock to their pecks and crotches, allow an alligator to bite their nipples, walk across a floor festooned with mousetraps, get shot with nonlethal projectiles, eat urine snow cones, get beaten up by boxers and kick boxers, snort wasabi, swim with hungry whale sharks, jump up into ceiling fans, and vomit repeatedly. In several of the stunts, many of which were filmed in Japan, onlookers are startled, appalled, at times sympathetic. But their concern is wasted, indeed ludicrous, in this *Twilight Zone* of mindless suffering.

Like *Beavis and Butt-Head, Jackass* inspired copycat stunts, one of which led to the death of Adam Ports, eighteen, of Wooster, Ohio, who fell from the back of a pickup truck after his "friends" set him on fire, filming all the while. Though both the TV show and movie come with disclaimers that insist that the stunts are performed by professionals and should not be imitated by "you or any of your dumb little buddies," critics have drawn their own conclusions about influence. Seneca County Sheriff Brian Hescht was far from alone when he noted in his report about the death of Ports that the victim and his friends "were trying to create some type of stunt like they have on the TV show *Jackass*."

In the spring of 2003, Ryan McPherson, Daniel Tanner, Zachary Bubeck, and Michael Slyman, the young men who created the *Bumfights* video, were convicted of conspiracy to stage an illegal fight, fined, and sentenced to perform 280 hours of community service. Controversial from the outset, their crudely made movie shows homeless people performing stunts, injuring themselves, allowing themselves to have the word "Bumfights" permanently tattooed on their knuckles or forehead, and, of course, fighting each other. Promoted on the Bumfights Web page as "the most hilariously shocking video you've ever seen," at $20 a pop the video was widely reported to have sold in excess of 300,000 copies. In November 2003, having watched *Bumfights,* four Australian teens shot a video of their own in which they taunted a homeless man and set his bedding on fire, an act that led to his death. In October 2004, five high school students in Toms River, New Jersey, attacked Larry Radomski, a sleeping homeless man, with baseball bats, a hockey stick, and a steel pipe, cracking six of his ribs, breaking his left arm, and puncturing a lung. Both crimes were associated with the perpetrators' familiarity with the *Bumfights* video.[45]

The creators of *Bumfights* showed no remorse after their sentencing in 2003: McPherson, Tanner, and Bubeck "smirked, giggled and wisecracked in front of a small clutch of news cameras seeking their reaction" (Slyman was tried separately); in February of 2005 Bubeck and McPherson, having failed to perform the required community service, were sentenced to spend time in jail. But others drawn into the project or affected by it have recoiled from their initial responses, reconnecting to a sense of human dignity. Rufus Hannah, the homeless Vietnam veteran called "Rufus, the Stunt Bum" in the video, subsequently gave up drinking, got a job, and looked back at his encounter with the *Bumfights* boys as a low point in his life—especially his willingness to fight and injure Donald Brennan. "If there's one day I wish never happened, it's that one," Hannah told a reporter, "He's my friend." The Australian copycats were convicted not of murder but of gross negligence for throwing a small piece of burning carpet into their victim's camp and then going off to watch the footage they had shot of their assault. The judge in their case sentenced them to five years in prison and noted that the "odious" *Bumfights* film "was the genesis of the crime."[46]

The extent to which artworks—however violent or suggestive, however lacking in subtlety or depth—can cause copycat crimes is a point of contemporary sociological debate and research, as is the general rise in violent crime that seems to accompany the introduction of television into previously unconnected societies. Of greater interest here is the potential role of violent ridicule in relaxing moral inhibition. To the extent that empathy is based on fellow feeling, attacks accompanied by humor can make it easier to achieve distance from victims by providing a gleeful alternative mood. In fantasy experiences (watching a video, reading a comic book), this mood can resonate differently, often harmlessly. But actual assaults and murders in which killers operate in comic mode remind us that what we laugh at can be a matter of life and death.

Conclusion

There was a boy up on stage by Tommy, gesturing wildly and shouting something. As she watched, he climbed down and ran toward the rock band's equipment. He caught hold of one of the microphone stands and was transfixed. Carrie watched, amazed, as his body went through a nearly motionless dance of electricity. His feet shuffled in the water, his hair stood up in spikes, and his mouth jerked open, like the mouth of a fish. He looked funny. She began to laugh.

(by Christ then let them all look funny)

STEPHEN KING, *Carrie*

At its close, James Cameron's movie *Terminator 2: Judgment Day* (1991) follows the death agonies of an evil cyborg made out of a futuristic liquid metal that can assume any shape. This monster has, after a long battle, been forced into a cauldron of molten steel that finally terminates him. But in his dying moments he rises repeatedly from the fire, briefly assuming the human shapes of his past victims. Between descents into the rolling boil, his desperate effort to be (or at least appear to be) human is an appropriate image of the mindset that seeks but also dreads the uneasy pleasure of killing jokes.

By allowing us to shift from impotence to power, from victim to predator, killing jokes can provide distance from both vulnerability and guilt. By bringing audiences to the moment of danger and then adopting a playful attitude, they assume a willingness to reject or repudiate humanity. The multiplication of this humor, the resonance of these jokes through the past decades, suggests that they are performing what Frederic Jameson describes as "transformational work" on social anxieties and what Philip Fisher has called "cultural work," that is, they are contributing to changes of consciousness by "massing small patterns of feelings in an entirely new direction."[47]

If popular jokes can reveal widely shared anxieties, then the diagnostic value of humor analysis should help us identify both social problems and appropriate countermeasures. Seen as gallows humor for a poisoned planet, killing jokes are an understandable response to the human—indeed, the planetary—predicament two millennia after Christ. In *Despair and Personal Power in the Nuclear Age* (1983), West Coast therapist and deep ecologist Joanna Macy approached the same emotional cluster in a more redemptive spirit. Noting that "the present condition and future prospects of our world engender . . . widespread feelings of distress, . . . [but that] these feelings are largely repressed" because of "fear of pain [and] social taboos against expressions of despair," Macy developed therapeutic techniques to help people move through an acknowledgment of fear to a sense of power based on renewed feelings of common humanity. Macy's analysis, like Giddens's, suggests that the enjoyment of killing jokes may be based on the respite they offer from both fear and repression. Like more conventional forms of gallows humor, killing jokes provide moments of detachment from threatening conditions. They can allow us—as they allow Freddy or the Joker, Lecter or Lestat—to stand above human beings, laughing at *their* woe. By suggesting that we are both moribund and self-destructive, killing jokes affect consciousness. Not just kidding, they are disturbing, even arresting, because they move between the killing joker and his victim, between humor and fear, exposing our ambivalence about the end of human life.[48]

2 | Red Noses at the Ready!

THE POSITIVE HUMOR MOVEMENT

We've all heard the saying "Laughter is the best medicine," but now it's scientifically proven!

DAVID GRANIRER, MA, North America's Psychotherapist/Stand-up Comic

Surround yourself with pictures and other items that keep reminding you of your goal. My bulletin board, for example, is filled with cutouts of laughing lips, smile buttons, and clown cards. These little reminders are like road maps constantly showing me which direction I want to travel toward.

ALLEN KLEIN, *The Healing Power of Humor*

I have adhered a small "clown nose" to the picture on my driver's license and wait[ed] for someone to say as I write a check, "I'll need to see your driver's license." I hand it over and while they are glancing down to see what the heck is stuck to the photo, ... I place a clown nose on my face and wait for the reaction when they look up!

Reply posted on November 5, 1999, to the following question on the Humor Project Web site: What did you do to tickle someone else's funny bone this week?

If only the victims of Freddy's cruel wit, the teenagers whose doubts and fears are used against them in comic scenarios that discard their humanity along with their lives, had known about the Big Tee-Hee: an exercise developed by laughter therapist Annette Goodheart to chortle problems away. If only, in addition to biology and English, they had studied New Age self-healing, dabbled with crystals, spent at least one spring break at a spa in Sedona or Mill Valley, they could have laughed in Freddy's face.

Apprised of the healing force of laughter, they would have known, as humor consultant and self-described "jollyologist" Allen Klein put it, that "humor has the power to turn any situation around." For the price of a pop psychology book, audio cassette, or retreat seminar, help was available. Yes, for on the other side of Freddy's nightmare, across a cultural divide separating fear from hope, self-destruction from self-cultivation, entropy from liberation—a different spirit possessed and still possesses the upbeat world of healing laughter. As Freddy approached, clicking his razor claws and cracking jokes about their overweight bodies or sexual naïveté, they could have put on a clown's red nose, whipped out a wind-up toy mouse, and laughed him into nothingness.[1]

To put this in a less dramatic way, it would be fair to say that every cruel joke discussed in the last chapter is anathema to advocates of positive humor, so much so that, in addition to warning practitioners and people in general to avoid hurtful humor, they sometimes want to argue that mean jokes aren't (or shouldn't be) amusing at all. As Joel Goodman, the director of the Humor Project based in Saratoga Springs, New York, and the most successful humor consultant in the United States, put it in an e-mail edition of his magazine sent out in October 2004:

Laughing with others builds confidence, brings people together, and pokes fun at our common dilemmas. Laughing at others destroys confidence, ruptures teamwork, and singles out individuals or groups as the "butt." This is captured so well by a fifth grade teacher who attended a humor graduate course I was teaching in Ohio in 1979. She started each school year by writing these words on her blackboard: "You don't have to blow out my candle to make yours glow brighter." Her students "got it"—humor is laughter made from pain, not pain inflicted by laughter. I subscribe to Susan RoAne's AT&T Test—is the humor Appropriate, Timely, and Tasteful? If so, you can reach out and touch people positively with humor.

When Goodman says that "humor *is* laughter made from pain" (my emphasis), he probably means something a bit less comprehensive and more tautological, such as laughter that comes from sharing with, not ridiculing, others is more likely to be beneficial. Similarly, though Klein encourages us to look for humor everywhere, he also warns against telling potentially offensive jokes and offers practical strategies for minimizing "your humor risk." Humor, Klein observes, is a potent medicine; to use it effectively one "must read the label and follow the guidelines . . . to get the benefits and avoid the risks." In *Laughter Therapy: How to Laugh about Everything in Your Life That Isn't Really Funny*, Goodheart goes further by repudiating jokes as oppressive and joke telling as a control mechanism:

Because I am fairly well known in my home town, people often approach me in public with "Aren't you the laugh lady?" When I respond they pounce on me with "Want to hear a funny joke?"

My face lights up and I respond with a delightful "NO!"

They always laugh. They then inquire, "Why not?"

"Because I don't listen to jokes," I say.

"Well, what do you laugh about then?"

"Everything! What's not to laugh about?"

In general, advocates of positive humor and/or laughter caution against cruel joking (or joking altogether) because their intentions are very different from the writers, directors, characters, and people associated with killing jokes: they are not trying to terrify through taboo violation but to comfort and nurture; not trying to provide imaginary experiences of transhuman detachment but to affirm a common humanity based on shared amusement; and not trying to model humor as a weapon but as an effective strategy in teaching, therapy, self-help, ministry, medicine, and business. There is, nonetheless, one interesting similarity: like the purveyors of killing jokes, humor consultants are out to make a buck.[2]

By providing empirical evidence for and critiques of the often excessive claims of these practitioners, academic humor researchers (who have been known to refer to their field, perhaps regrettably, as humorology) exist in an uneasy relation to the commercial world of humor promotion. When researchers in a number of fields—including psychology, linguistics, biology, medicine, psychiatry, sociology, anthropology, literature, history, and philosophy—began to sponsor interdisciplinary conferences in 1976, created the International Society for Humor Studies (ISHS), and went on to produce *Humor: International Journal of Humor Research* (1988–present), they were not kidding at all but seriously dedicated to the study of humor as "an important and universal human activity." In the first article that reviewed research to date, "The Biology of Humor," published in 1994 in *Humor,* William F. Fry provided an upbeat, if qualified, summary of the state of what was then known about the physiological and psychological effects of laughter and humor. Noting that, while humor is a "genetic, biologic characteristic of human life," Fry concluded that every individual develops a distinctive sense of humor. The physiological, metabolic impact of humor, Fry observed, persists during laughter: "Heart rate goes up; blood pressure rises; blood circulation increases; pulmonary ventilation increases; skeletal muscles are exercised; the brain experiences electrochemical activity which is typically found with greater degrees of alertness; pain perception is decreased; skin temperature rises;

hormone production is stimulated; and circulating immune substance effectiveness is enhanced." The benefits of this period of stimulation and the period of relaxation that typically follows, Fry noted, include cardiac exercise, immune system stimulation, alertness, animation, and sociability. According to Fry, how enduring these benefits are and whether they are (or which ones in particular are) derived from humor (comic amusement that can but often doesn't lead to laughter) or from laughter alone remained unclear, a matter for future research. Indeed, when Fry conceded that "all of the well documented health values of aerobic exercise are recognizable in . . . mirth muscle activity," he implied that most if not all of the physiological benefits suggested by research might be derived not from humor as a cognitive and/or emotional experience but from laughter. While generally approving of the still-young positive humor movement, Fry was careful to note that "there is little . . . scientific evidence" that supports its claims. Laughter and humor seemed to Fry to have positive, if perhaps, transitory benefits; whether attending a seminar, lecture, workshop, or retreat could impart and/or extend these benefits over longer periods of time was, Fry observed, a matter not yet established by research.[3]

If Fry's article suggested that the evidence for the healing power of humor was weak in 1994, subsequent studies—by Rod A. Martin in 2001 and 2004; Leslie R. Martin et al. in 2002; Gillian Kirsh and Nicholas A. Kuiper in 2003; and Nicholas A. Kuiper et al. in 2004—have demonstrated that this is still the case. After evaluating all of the published research on the "effects of humor and laughter on physical health" extant in 2001, Rod A. Martin, a professor of clinical psychology at the University of Western Ontario, concluded that "more carefully conducted and theoretically informed research is needed before one can have any confidence that humor or laughter impact physical health in a positive way." Three years later, Martin offered the following update: "Despite the popular belief in health benefits of humor and laughter, and the proliferation of therapeutic interventions based on these ideas, the empirical evidence for these claims to date is actually quite weak, inconsistent, and inconclusive." Contrary to widely held, perhaps universal, conviction, Martin showed that there was little empirical evidence to support claims about the role of humor and/or laughter in boosting immune system responses, decreasing self-reported illness symptoms, or increasing longevity. On the contrary, while some experiments suggest that humor or laughter can reduce stress and pain, studies of humor and longevity in 1,178 people followed since 1921 in the Terman Life-Cycle Study (and reviewed by Friedman et al. in 1993 and L. R. Martin et al. in 2002) found an inverse correlation between cheerfulness and/or sense of humor (as reported by parents and teachers of twelve-year-olds) and how long subjects lived. In other words, though it seems counterintuitive, the best evidence we have suggests that being cheerful and laughing more frequently might cut your life short. Both the Friedman and Leslie. R. Martin teams considered the possibility that cheerful and easily amused people may "have poorer health behaviors . . . because they are less concerned about things that could go wrong with their bodies" than people who worry more and expect the worst. If "cheerful children grow up to be more careless about their health," as the Martin team hypothesizes, you've got to wonder about the healing power of anxiety.[4]

Shifting from physical to psychological health, an article called "Humor Is Not Always the Best Medicine," published in *Humor* by Kuiper et al., undermines the validity of the widely shared view that humor boosts well-being by promoting a positive outlook, social connectedness, and self-esteem, while reducing anxiety and depression. Following Rod A. Martin's work, this group began by noting the mixed evidence produced by previous research, which showed that "greater humor does not always lead to higher levels of intimacy in interpersonal relationships . . . nor does it always relate to higher levels of optimism, self-acceptance, or environmental mastery. When considering negative elements of psychological well-being, some research has failed to find a decrease in depression and anxiety levels for those with a greater sense of humor." To understand these contradictory data, the Kuiper team worked on two related tasks: complicating what we mean by the term sense of humor, by distinguishing between three dimensions and four styles of humor, and then testing to see how each of these can be studied in relation to components of mental health. Shifting from a single concept of beneficial humor, they distinguish between people who are skilled in the social use of humor (able to "elicit laughter from others and use humor to maintain and bolster relationships") and those who use humor in rude or ineffectively boorish ways. While they conclude that all generalizations about the benefits of "humor" conceived as a "unitary construct" are "untenable," they offer preliminary evidence suggesting that people who are able to use humor effectively are likely to feel better, while people who use humor to attack others or in failing efforts to promote themselves are likely to feel worse. But at this point, they insist, only correlations, not causal patterns, have been demonstrated. Whether feeling depressed makes one more likely to misuse humor or vice versa is not known. And the same is true for people skilled in the social use of humor: whether their use of humor enables them to be effective, more optimistic, less anxious, and so on or vice versa is not yet known. The practical implication for the positive humor movement is profound if also not much noted: at this point we can't be sure whether we need workshops on optimism and anxiety reduction as a way of enhancing positive humor use or workshops on using humor designed to promote general well-being. We do, however, know this: because humor is a multidimensional concept, simple assertions about what it is and how it functions are necessarily flawed.[5]

In spite of the mixed results and still-immature state of empirical research, humor practitioners have felt licensed by anecdotal evidence (supplied by Norman Cousins, Patch Adams, other practitioners, and/or their own practice) and the zeitgeist to hawk their wares with abandon. Whether they are calling for more humor in workplaces, homes, hospitals, churches, or schools, they often begin by insisting, for instance, that research has demonstrated that humor is "strong," "the best," or at least "the jest" medicine. Leaving caution behind, practitioners fill their Web sites with articles, interviews, and promotional prose suggesting that humor can "empower people to greater health & happiness" (Dan Gascon); strengthen both our physical and psychological immune systems (Stephen M. Sultanoff); and deliver "therapeutic belly laughs" (Larry Wilde). Promoted in these ways and in press accounts of the latest, perhaps, flawed or inconclusive study, the myth of healing laughter is abroad in the land, one of the reassuring pieties of New Age medicine and spirituality. And yet, to locate your inner skeptic, consider this: if you had to get sick, would you rather have a disease with a known and effective cure or one for which you have to rely on the healing power of humor? Not laughing now, are you?[6]

By surfing the Web, the patient Googler can get a sense of the size and diversity of the positive humor movement. At http://www.humorproject.com/, one finds that Joel Goodman founded the Humor Project in 1977, that it is devoted to helping people get "more smileage out of life" through annual conferences and programs, and that it has been featured or discussed on or in "over 3,000 television and radio shows, newspapers, and magazines." At http://aath.org/, one finds that the Association for Applied and Therapeutic Humor (AATH) was established in 1988 as "both a personable *network* and a *resource* of humor and laughter authorities and enthusiasts [designed to assist members] representing fields ranging from healthcare and education to business and faith communities." At http://www.laughteryoga.org/, one learns that the Dr. Madan Kataria of Mumbai, India, has inspired followers to participate in over 2,000 Yoga Laughter Clubs in the United States, the United Kingdom, Canada, Australia, Germany, France, Italy, Belgium, Switzerland, Singapore, Malaysia, Hong Kong, and Dubai. At http://www.worldlaughtertour.com/, one learns that, "as of February 2004, more than 1,000 people [had] completed the training designed by psychologist and self-proclaimed 'Joyologist' Steve Wilson to qualify for the designation of Certified Laughter Leader." At http://www .jesuslaughing.com/, the Jesus Laughing homepage, one can order prints, T-shirts, buttons, sweatshirts, and postcards of Christ with his head dropping back and his mouth opened wide in mirth. These products commercialize the theology of Christian humor, an outlook both embraced and harshly criticized on-line.

On a smaller, more local scale, and typical of the grassroots level of enterprise this movement has inspired around the United States, at http:// members.aol.com/LinnyandMo/laughter.html, you can meet "caring clowns" based at Rex Hospital in Raleigh, North Carolina: "She's Nola Nurse, RN! In case you don't know what RN stands for, in her case it means really nutty. . . . He's Dr. I. Fixem's. Whatever you've got wrong he'll fix it. If you have something that needs to be removed, he's the one to do it. . . . He usually has a few spare parts left over when he finishes a job. You may never be the same again!" At www.FUNsulting.com, we are introduced to Ron Culbertson who, "as Director of Everything! at FUNsulting," offers his services as a professional public speaker to healthcare organizations and businesses "that want their people to lighten up by using humor to minimize stress and maximize effectiveness." At http:// teachers.net/mentors/humor/posts.html, you can browse a humor chat board hosted by teachers.net, containing "a free exchange of classroom humor and amusing stories related to teaching." At http://www .kushnergroup.com/, you'll encounter Malcolm Kushner, "an internationally acclaimed expert on humor and communication," who, since 1982, "has trained thousands of managers, executives and professionals [in] how to gain a competitive edge with humor" by way of keynote addresses that include "Jest for Success" and "Public Speaking for Dummies." And at http://www.larrywilde.com/programs.htm, "America's Good Humor Man," Larry Wilde offers three specific programs on humor, health, and success as well as programs that are "customized" to the needs of clients. In a presentation called "Humor: A Tool for Success in the Workplace," available as either a forty-five-minute keynote or a one- to three-hour seminar or workshop, Wilde explains his "Five-Step Formula," which will help listeners learn "how [humor] can lubricate the wheels of communication; reduce tension; promote health and vitality; and enrich the quality of life."

For several reasons, which full disclosure obliges me to be upfront about, I approached this merry band of humor- and self-promoters with a mixture of fascination and skepticism that has already, no doubt, begun to color this chapter. First, their mission—to help people appreciate humor—can strike me as less than crucial, since most people already value experiences that bring pleasure and delight, like good food, good sex, and good humor. Second, I value doubt more than faith and am inclined to question assumptions many people seem eager to adopt about such things as ghosts, alien invaders, and the virgin birth of Jesus. (In fact, I've watched enough episodes of *The X-Files* to wonder if the virgin birth of Jesus was somehow caused by alien ghosts!) Third, I prefer spontaneous (that is, unplanned and unforced) amusement for its own sake to strategies for laughing more and looking for humor in everything as a source of other benefits (health, stress reduction, etc.). Fourth, far from repudiating all hostile, critical, or targeted jokes, I treasure the role of humor, satire, and derision in mocking and assailing appropriate targets: people, policies, and ideas. The use of this kind of humor requires an ethical filter, but this should not eliminate it as a weapon that can be wielded against injustice and folly. And, finally, I have never, not even as a young child, found clowns either entertaining or funny. Quite the contrary, in yearly excursions to the Ringling Brothers Barnum and Bailey Circus, I appreciated the multiple rings mostly because I could look away from the clown acts at flying acrobats and stair-climbing dogs. Some of the clown's physical comedy made me smile, but their stunts seemed repetitive and, therefore, predictable, and there was something off-putting about the way they seemed to take the audience's amusement for granted, as if just looking funny in the conventional clown way was enough to earn belly laughs. Stair-climbing dogs? Now they're funny! So the appearance of an uninvited clown in my hospital room or of a supervisor or teacher who puts on a red nose to get me laughing would probably produce the opposite effect. Such mechanical humor stimuli make me feel mildly slighted, as though the humor deployer feels that I'm not worth the effort to be clever or witty, that he can whip a humor-causing device out of his toolkit or say the first potentially comic thing he thinks of, however lame, and get me laughing. I'm just not that easy, Mr. Baggy-Pants Smiley-Face!

This aesthetic distance applies to many of the verbal flourishes of the positive humor movement. Though *Laughing Matters,* the quarterly minimagazine Goodman's Humor Project published between 1987 and 1998, included interesting brief interviews with comedians, comedy writers, and humor practitioners as well as some sensible advice sent in by readers, its tendency toward obvious puns could be grating. Regular features included "Readers' Di-Jest," "Grin and Share It," "Funformation," "Fun-Liners—Jest for You," and "Happy Adversity." And articles, mostly written by Goodman himself, fell back on strained expressions like "funderful," "ho-ho-holistic," "rhyme and punishment," "playing with a fool deck," "glutton for funishment," "the Information Super Ha-Ha Way," and "seeing is beeleeheeheehing." The no doubt intended but nonetheless unfortunately infectious result of all this straining for laughter is apparent in reader comments:

I enjoy adding levity to faculty meetings by contributing "lay" perspectives on educational jargon—e.g., "We need to interface with the community"—"You want me to do what? I only do that with my husband!"

I pun on a daily basis at work and at home. Word play fascinates me, and there's lots of ways to use it in the health field—e.g., when a patient doesn't need a cane anymore, you can say "there was a cane mutiny."

Read enough of this and you can find that, perversely enough, it's nurturing your inner Malvolio or, worse, your inner Freddy: either driving you away from laughter or stirring up the very impulse to laugh at others that it seeks to repress.[7]

Getting inside the world of killing jokes required only that I live through the 1980s and 1990s with one eye on the expanding body of sadistic movies, comics, joke books, and horror fiction. Getting inside this alternate universe of workplace kidding and cancer-ward clowns required that I read around in its literature, talk with consultants, and observe them at two of their national meetings during the winter and spring of 2005. And it required opening my skeptical mind up to the possibility that these speakers, therapists, managers, nurses, teachers, and ministers were not entirely driven by financial self-interest but also by the desire to improve the quality of life for the people with and for whom they work. With this ambivalence, I plunged into their world feeling a bit like Christopher Guest, the director of such films as *Waiting for Guffman* (1997), *Best in Show* (2000), and *A Mighty Wind* (2004): aware of the potential for geek eruptions but respectful of the conviction and humanity of the people I would meet and open to the possibility that they would at the very least be funny.

Positive Humor: Articles, Books, and Web Sites

When Norman Cousins (fig. 8) took control of his own treatment for what had been diagnosed as degenerative collagen disease and cured himself by moving out of the hospital, watching comic films, laughing heartily, and taking large doses of vitamin C, he probably had no idea how his experience would resonate through the culture. Though his experiences left him with an agnostic's curiosity and a respect for the mystery of

FIGURE EIGHT. Norman Cousins, AP/WorldwidePhotos

the placebo effect, his followers have found ways to convert the mystery into a small industry, laughing, as it were, all the way to the bank. His best-selling book *Anatomy of an Illness* (1979) has certainly provided quotable claims, including his assertion that "ten minutes of belly laughter had an anesthetic effect and would give me at least two hours of pain-free sleep." But his use of humor was part of a complex strategy based on moving from negative emotions (including anxiety and sadness) to positive ones, including hope and joy. Toward the end of the book, he presents an exchange he had years after his illness with a young woman he calls Carole who was suffering from the same condition:

> Carole said she was curious about the laughter. Was it really as important in my recovery as the article had indicated?
> What was significant about the laughter, I said, was not just the fact that it provides internal exercise for a person flat on his or her back—a form of jogging for the innards—but that it creates a mood in which the other positive emotions can be put to work, too. In short, it helps make it possible for good things to happen.[8]

Situating what had been widely reduced to a laughter prescription in press accounts of his work in the wider contexts of humane medical care—

Head First: The Biology of Hope and the Healing Power of the Human Spirit (1989), the second book Cousins wrote to follow up on *Anatomy of an Illness*—encourages doctors and patients to cultivate "the full range of positive emotions ... love, hope, faith, will to live, festivity, purpose, determination." "Obviously," he wrote, "patients must not be deceived into thinking nothing more is required to combat a serious disease than a strong will and a good laugh." Still, even as he offered what would become the standard caveat of the movement he inspired, in his eagerness to support and report empirical research that confirmed his convictions about humor and healing, Cousins was quick to accept evidence provided in preliminary and flawed studies. For instance, contrast Cousin's personal, upbeat and vague account of the 1988 work of Dr. Lee S. Berk et al. on laughter and the immune system with Martin's later, more critical analysis:

I shared some of the research funds available to me with Dr. Lee S. Berk of the Loma Linda Medical Center in California, to help support his studies of the way laughter might enhance the immune system. He and his colleagues measured changes in several "stress" hormones in ten healthy male subjects after they viewed a sixty-minute humorous film. Dr. Berk hypothesized that laughter has beneficial effects on the immune system. Indeed, in a subsequent study, he found a significant increase in spontaneous blastogenesis (immune cell proliferation) accompanied by a marked decrease in cortisol, a hormone that has immune-suppressing capability. (Cousins, *Head First*)

Although some promising results were obtained in this study, there are a number of methodological limitations that cast doubt on the findings. Besides the very small sample size of males only, the participants were informed several days beforehand which condition [watching a comedian or sitting quietly in a room for sixty minutes] they would be in, resulting in evident differences in their mood states on arrival and significant baseline differences in two of the physiological variables. ... It is not reported whether the participants were randomly assigned to groups, and there was an age difference between the two groups ($p < .10$). In addition, the no-videotape control group did not adequately control for a number of factors, such as diversion of watching a videotape or general emotional arousal, that might account for the findings. Manipulation checks were not included, and laughter was not monitored. ... Thus, although these findings seem encouraging, they do not provide conclusive evidence of immuno-enhancing effects of laughter. (Martin, "Humor, Laughter")

Cousins's credulous, uncritical assessment of this experiment provides a perfect example of the way biomedical research results can be and all too frequently are taken at face value. In recent years we've been subjected to press accounts of experiments that "find" that X is inversely correlated with Y, and when the X is something delightful, like humor, chocolate, or being overweight, and the Y is something frightening, like heart disease, cancer, or decreased lifespan, news of the finding circulates rapidly. But, as Martin's analysis demonstrates, all studies are not created equal, all "findings" are not equally significant. Indeed, though Cousins embodied the ideal of the public intellectual before the term became popular, and though it will seem heretical in some circles to say it, the invidious contrast above suggests that his career shift from editor to medical ethicist in 1978 when he retired from the *Saturday Review* and joined the faculty of the University of California at Los Angeles School of Medicine may well be an example of the Peter Principle: a promotion away from what ones does best. For, although *Anatomy of an Illness, The Healing Heart: Antidotes to Panic and Helplessness* (1983), and *Head First* spearheaded the reform of medical care, they also licensed the at times excessive marketing and deployment of humor by consultants and practitioners working with and for a range of clients, patients, students, and parishioners in corporate, therapeutic, educational, medical, and religious settings.[9]

Second only to Cousins, perhaps, Patch Adams (fig. 9)—reformer, activist, healer, and clown—has provided source material for the positive humor movement, especially in its medical application. Though capable of making hyperbolic statements—of claiming, for instance, that "humor is an antidote to all ills"—Adams developed a wide and deeply humane alternative approach to medical care. Perhaps because he frequently dresses as a clown or perhaps because in the eponymous 1998 movie he was played by Robin Williams, one of the great comic performers of our time, it is easy to miss the breadth of Adams's critique of contemporary medicine and the humane depth of his prescription for curing the problems. For, in addition to bringing humor into hospital wards, exam rooms, and death watches, Adams is committed both to the range of up-to-date conventional treatment options and to a comprehensive affirmation of the humanity of both patients and healers. And this humanity includes not only kidding and fun but art, nature, imagination, community, family, nutrition, exercise, intellect, in short, as he puts it expansively, to living HUGE! Typically, when Adams proposes that terminally ill patients be encouraged to talk about how they want to die in an effort to come up with a "fun death," he is not trivializing their sorrow or the grief of soon-to-be-bereft loved ones. Nor does he assume that their idea of fun will be telling jokes or clowning around. On the contrary, he says: "most patients I've spoken with want only to be home with their loved ones and in familiar surroundings, perhaps with some music, messages, prayers, and memories added."[10]

FIGURE NINE. Patch Adams, AP/WorldwidePhotos

While it is certainly true that most medical relations and interactions, especially between caregivers and patients, still take place without much humor, a remarkable feature of the positive humor movement is its assumption that Americans in general are unable or unwilling to laugh as much as they should. Considering that even the Puritan settlers had a sharp sense of wit, as anyone who has read Edward Taylor or Anne Bradstreet can attest, and that Colonial New England also hosted wags like Thomas Morton, famous, among other things, for carousing with Native Americans and calling Miles Standish "Captain Shrimp," this would seem not to take our long-standing interest in laughing into account. Given the cascade of joke cycles over the past five decades, the rise of sitcoms in the 1950s and of stand-up during the 1980s, the continuing popularity of Hollywood comedies, nightly TV monologues, and the recent development of comedy networks for cable TV, as well as joke, comedy, and satire Web pages and blogs galore on the Internet—given all this, one wonders about the claim that we are too serious, too fear-driven, or too stressed out to laugh. Can it really be true, as Patty Wooten, RN, a.k.a. Curly the Clown, self-styled "Queen of Jest," suggests on her Web page that "all of us have a pent-up need to laugh"?[11]

The positive humor movement works at many levels. At the top, according to John Morreall, an academic humor researcher who doubles as a humor consultant, the most successful speakers/motivators can earn up to $5,000 for presentations, keynote speeches, and/or workshops. On the receiving end of these effort are professionals—doctors, nurses, orderlies, therapists, teachers, managers, and employees—as well as individuals and family members who are encouraged, nudged, and tickled into "using humor" in their daily lives as a way of coping with disease, pain, anxiety, and stress: the thousand "upsets" to which flesh and psyche are heir.

Because professional credentialing in this area is somewhat haphazard, the two essential requirements for humor consulting are a book and a Web site that expound the consultant's unique and entertaining philosophy of and practical ideas for promoting humor. By the time Klein published his book, *The Healing Power of Humor: Techniques for Getting through Loss, Setbacks, Upsets, Disappointments, Difficulties, Trials, Tribulations, and All That Not-So-Funny Stuff* in 1989, he was able to list, in addition to academic studies of humor, eleven books that had risen from this corner of the zeitgeist, including Raymond Moody Jr.'s 1978 *Laugh After Laugh*, Herb True and Anna Mang's 1980 *Humor Power: How to Get It, Give It, and Gain*, Laurence J. Peter and Bill Dana's 1982 *The Laughter Prescription*, E. T. Eberhart's 1983 *In the Presence of Humor: A Guide to the Humorous Life*, Dan Keller's 1984 *Humor as Therapy*, Bob Basso and Judi Kloesk's 1986 *Lighten Up, Corporate America*, Esther Blumenfeld and Lyne Alpern's 1986 *The Smile Connection*, and Tal D. Bonham's 1988 *Humor: God's Gift*. As the titles suggest, these books seek to provide the benefits of humor to readers and potential workshop participants. Associated with several features of the post-1960s American Dream—health, power, wealth, sanity, redemption, and intimacy—humor had become an "it" not only to be enjoyed ("Get It") but also deployed ("Give It") in an effort to enrich oneself, the responses of others, and the world at large ("Gain").

Just as beginning singer-songwriters these days need a dozen songs and a self-produced CD to set out on their careers, so humor consultants need to publish to do well on the circuit of corporate and institutional presentations. Although there are various areas of private and personal life that can serve as their focus, whether they address teachers, medical personnel, or the general public, their books and articles tend to include such common elements as (1) an account of the underlying biomedical and social science research that "proves" that specific physical and psychological benefits can be gained from being amused, adopting a lighter attitude, and/or laughing; (2) an explanation of why people in general or in specific situations (business, medicine, etc.) need the services of a humor consultant who can help bring these benefits to those who hear his or her program; (3) philosophic, religious, and cultural underpinnings of adopting a comic, or ironic, or detached approach to pain, stress, and death; (4) quotations from famous people extolling the benefits of humor; (5) disclaimers and caveats about not suggesting that humor is a panacea; (6) warnings about avoiding harmful humor or jokes in general; (7) heartwarming examples of people who used humor and/or laughter to cope with or triumph over adversity, pain, and/or disease; and (8) specific exercises and practices designed to enhance one's sense of humor. To develop contexts for a more detailed consideration of the work of a few humor consultants and my observation of the two national meetings, a discussion of each of these rhetorical strategies follows.

Scientific Foundations

Overviews of research relating to the benefits of humor tend to be brief, especially in books directed toward the general reader. The curative and medicinal efficacy of humor has become so widely accepted in the United States that little evidence is required to support particular or general claims. Perhaps this is why many practitioners assert that humor offers benefits while citing few specific studies and implying that Norman Cousins's personal (and therefore anecdotal) experience has scientific bearing. Typical of this approach, in *The Learning Power of Laughter,* published in 2004, Jackie Silberg cites the work of Berk and Tan from the late 1980s, without saying when it was done, to support the general assertion that "Increasingly, studies are demonstrating that laughter and humor boost immunity, diminish pain" and "enhance the treatment of many illnesses and diseases" through the release of endorphins; on his Web page David Granirer cites only three studies in support of the claim that the potency of laughter as medicine has been "scientifically proven"; and in *Laughter Therapy,* published by the Less Stress (and, perhaps, less-interested-in-fact-checking) Press, Goodheart glides over empirical research, preferring to observe that laughter "re-balances" "chemicals" and "leaves our internal organs invigorated, juicy, plumped-up, and alert." But the truly plumped-up and alert reader has reason to wonder about such claims.[12]

In 2001, Martin noted that while "humor and laughter may induce physiological changes that affect the sensory components of pain . . . [no] studies have examined correlations between laughter frequency and pain tolerance to determine whether laughter is the important ingredient in the effects." Since "negative emotions such as sadness, disgust, and horror" seem to have the same minor analgesic effects as humor, Martin noted, the pain-reducing function of humor may be due to "general emotional arousal" and not to amusement specifically. Yet, none of these cautionary comments has constrained "Giggling Guru" Madan Kataria from offering the following less qualified and more anecdotal statements on his Web page:

Natural Pain Killer: Laughter increases the levels of endorphins in our bodies, which are natural pain killers. Norman Cousins, an American journalist who was suffering from an incurable disease of the spine, was benefited by laughter therapy when no painkiller could help him. Endorphins released as a result of laughter may help in reducing the intensity of pain in those suffering from arthritis, spondylitis and muscular spasms of the body. Many women have reported a reduced frequency of migraine headaches.

Although Martin concluded in 2001 that "further studies are needed . . . before firm conclusions may be drawn about the immunological effects of humor and laughter" and although he confirmed this in 2004— the Holistic Online Web site represents a large number of similar humor boosters when it says:

Research results indicate that, after exposure to humor, there is a general increase in activity within the immune system, including:

- ★ An increase in the number and activity level of natural killer cells that attack viral infected cells and some types of cancer and tumor cells. An increase in activated T cells (T lymphocytes). There are many T cells that await activation. Laughter appears to tell the immune system to "turn it up a notch."
- ★ An increase in the antibody IgA (immunoglobulin A), which fights upper respiratory tract insults and infections.
- ★ An increase in gamma interferon, which tells various components of the immune system to "turn on."
- ★ An increase in IgB, the immunoglobulin produced in the greatest quantity in body, as well as an increase in Complement 3, which helps antibodies to pierce dysfunctional or infected cells. The increase in both substances was not only present while subjects watched a humor video; there also was a lingering effect that continued to show increased levels the next day.[13]

Why the World Needs Humor Programs

Early in the development of the movement, Patch Adams observed that "most individuals in our society are unhappy about their lives and need a huge amount of psychological and spiritual nourishment." Even if this is true, by honing in on humor, these practitioners are selling experiences normal people desire: not castor oil, condoms, or swiss chard but amusement, detachment, relaxation, and, well, pleasure. Klein observed that humor is "rarely acknowledged as an important coping tool." Even if this was true in the late 1980s, following eighteen years of humor advocacy, can this still be the case? And even if we acknowledge (as who would not?) that humor is not only pleasant but essential to sanity and wisdom, can we be sure that so fundamental an aspect of personality or temperament can be modified by exposure to a humor practitioner's program, seminar, or presentation? The authority offered by the AATH in support of an affirmative answer to this question does not quite establish the point: "Can one increase one's sense of humor? According to the comedian Steve Allen, we can indeed increase our sense of humor."[14]

Philosophic, Religious, and Cultural Underpinnings

These tend toward a New Age rainbow of Native American–Zen-Buddhist-Yogic-Jewish-Irish-African upbeat spirituality and wisdom. Goodheart contrasts our overly serious Puritanism with more emotionally alive, authentic, and dynamic "Native American and Eastern cultures." In a chapter called "To Die Laughing: Lessons from Religious Traditions and Other Cultures," Klein discusses the Zen notion that understanding leads to laughter, a Jewish joke about the death of a famous actor during a performance, and a Chinese story in which a king learns to laugh at his own mortality.[15]

Famous Quotations

Read enough of these books and you'll realize that just about everyone you've ever heard of is on record with a platitude about humor. Not just wags like Voltaire ("The art of medicine consists of amusing the patient while nature cures the disease"); James Thurber ("Humor is a serious thing. I like to think of it as one of our greatest earliest natural resources, which must be preserved at all cost."); Milton Berle ("Laughter is an instant vacation"); and Mel Brooks ("Life literally abounds in comedy, if you just look around you")—but deep thinkers like Winston Churchill ("The greatest lesson in life is to know that even fools are right sometimes"), Abraham Lincoln ("If I did not laugh I should die"), and, well, God. God, that is, or whoever is responsible for writing that "there's a time to laugh" in Ecclesiastes 3:4 and "a merry heart doeth good like a medicine" in Proverbs 17:22—both quoted everywhere in this literature.

Disclaimers and Caveats

Eager to avoid the appearance (if not always the reality) of overpromising, prudent consultants set limits to claims they make about the efficacy of humor. Though they sometimes slip in assertions like, "humor can turn around *any* disagreeable situation, diffuse an attack, and disarm the attacker," they are also likely to cover themselves partially by admitting that not all situations are appropriate for humor, that not all people are open to laughing, and that laughter cannot always affect the material conditions (or facts) of a hard situation. In this spirit they concede that laughter, though physiologically beneficial, can't prevent death; that sorrow and its expressive markers (crying, moaning, grim ideation) are also important parts of life; and that we may not yet understand the full effects of humor. Some disclaimers are straightforward; some are dodges. In 2002, Dr. Merry McBryde-Foster, an assistant professor at Baylor University's Louise Herrington School of Nursing and a practicing hospital clown, qualified her general claim that humor "aids in healing" as follows: "Last fall, I took a hard look at the research and critiques of the research out there and the findings are not well-documented. They have been able to document some of the physical changes in the body when someone laughs, though." But when a consultant says that "humor is the jest medicine," as Joel Goodman and his many followers do, it's fair to wonder what precisely the pun is intended to insinuate. That humor is as effective as prescription drugs? If so, would this be true in the case of diseases with known and effective treatment (for instance, pink eye) or just for diseases for which no effective treatments have been found (ALS)? Was it true for, say, multiple sclerosis five years ago and likely not to be true five years from now? True, that is, only when there is no effective medical or surgical treatment for the illness?[16]

Harmful Humor Warning

As though they were distributing weapons of mass destruction, consultants always emphasize the importance of avoiding harmful humor. Common advice includes admonitions always to laugh with and not at people, to avoid offending others, to make sure your jokes are appropriate, timely, and tasteful. David M. Jacobson—MSW, LCSW, and director of Humor Horizons of Tucson, Arizona—offers a typical version of this admonition: "The basic rule here is that any humor that is exclusive, separates people, puts someone down or ridicules others, destroys self-esteem, uses stereotypes of groups, encourages a negative atmosphere, offends others or lacks awareness of others' feelings is inappropriate."[17]

Heartwarming Humor Stories

These abound in the literature and include both autobiographical and biographical exemplars. Like the obligatory discussion of Cousins's experience, consultants are eager to explain how they personally discovered the power of humor in dealing with their life crises (illness, divorce, the death of a loved one) and to recount comic successes from their practice. Goodheart offers the following story about a client named Jerry:

He had a tumor on his thymus gland that had been medically diagnosed, and he thought that laughter therapy might have an affect [*sic*] on it. He wanted to try many alternative methods before he opted for surgery. When Jerry laughed, his face did not go up . . . [because] the muscles on the side of his face opposite from the tumor no longer functioned. His eyelid and his mouth drooped considerably. It was so strange to watch him laugh without his face going up, that I suggested he prop his face up when he laughed . . . [and] continue his laughter exercises at home, which he did. . . . Jerry's tumor began to shrink, and I always suspected that I had unknowingly interrupted a cycle of physical deterioration by helping him exercise his facial muscles.[18]

Specific Exercises and Practices

The invention and promotion of these, as adapted to different situations—including the classroom, office, pulpit, hospital ward, and therapeutic couch—is the creative and practical thrust of the movement. It's why the many afflicted, stressed-out, and humor-impaired Americans need consultants in the first place. So whether you make funny faces, play games, wear red noses, read, watch or hear comic materials, frolic with animals, carry a teddy bear, or skip all stimuli and just make yourself laugh, your goal is to seek humor and/or laughter everywhere or at least more frequently—in happy and sad moments, in the surprising and the expected, the foolish and the worrying—to strive consciously at first and then habitually for more laughter. How much more? Well, "international business speaker, humorist, trainer and author" Mike Kerr attempts to quantify his message by promoting workshops during which participants receive a handout that offers "130 Ways to Put Humor to Work" while learning not only "Why Laughter Is the Best Medicine" but also "The Three R's of Humor and Stress Management" and "Six Guiding Lights to Put Humor to Work With." Over at the Discover Fun Web site, we are introduced to five hundred ways to, you guessed it, "discover fun," and are admonished not to let our "'Fun Well' run dry." In case we wonder about where this metaphor will take us, the text continues: "Make sure you always have a brimming bucket of humor to turn to whenever you need a laugh." Among the five hundred "ways" these folk have found are:

* Build a fort with pillows from the couch
* Collect all bad news from newspapers and make a ritual campfire to burn them
* Go to a waterslide
* Go to the playground
* Hang a bird feeder
* Have a bonfire and roast marshmallows
* Have a lemonade sale
* Play Twister
* Water balloon fight

As this list suggests, much of the advice offered here assumes a level of severe impairment of both sense of humor and common sense. It is, similarly, frightening to think of a person witless enough to benefit from "international speaker on humor and stress management" Mike Moore's "Five Ways to Sharpen Your Sense of Humor and Improve Your Relationships" if way no. 2 is "if you don't laugh as much as you used to and want to correct the situation, start associating with humorous, fun loving people and avoid the downers." Meanwhile, who could require "The Twelve Affirmations of Positive Humor" offered as part of Dr. Christian Hagaseth III's on-line course for the Learnwell Institute if they include:

1. I am determined to use my humor for positive, playful, uplifting, healing and loving purposes.
4. I will express my humor physically, using my whole face and (when so moved) with my entire body.
9. If I offend another by my use of humor, I will make amends.
10. I will be eternally vigilant for the jokes and absurdities of the universe, and I will share my observations with my companions in life.
12. On the day of my death I will look back and know that I laughed lovingly, fully and well.

And who could suspend disbelief long enough to laugh with, rather than at, the image conjured up in the visualization offered by psychotherapist David Granirer in "Laughter: The Best Medicine": "So here's a tip for the next time you feel stressed and need a wellness break. It's called the Smile Time-Out. Take a deep breath, smile, exhale, and say 'Aaah' while visualizing all your muscles and cells smiling."[19]

As the countless lists, checklists, and plans being promoted suggest, one or two tricks are far too few; you'll need, in Joel Goodman's view, "1,001 ways to add humor to your life and work," including: "What is the first step you need to take to have humor enter your life today? Every now and then have fun with your fellow workers by giving out a PMS Award (Positively Motivating Smile)" and "How can you turn groans into laughs today? On the way to work, listen for the worst joke on morning radio; during the day share it with fellow employees." In a similarly jocular spirit, psychologist Ed Dunkleblau encourages listeners to develop "mindfoolness" and uses stuffed bears and finger traps to lighten up therapy sessions, while Yvonne Francine Conte's *Guide Book to a Happier, Healthier, More Productive Life* insists that "there is fun in dysFUNctional." These expressions and techniques highlight the potential downside of the movement: that it encourages the humor impaired to try anything, however desperate or dumb, to amuse. In the presence of the resulting bad jokes, joy buzzers, pratfalls, and cheesy puns, one can find oneself sharing the spirit of the *New Yorker* cartoon (fig. 10) below.[20]

"Put the punster in with the mime."

FIGURE TEN. "Punster, Mime," © The New Yorker Collection 20904 Pat Byrnes from cartoonbank.com. All Rights Reserved.

As you can no doubt tell from the divided tone of the above overview, immersion in the literature of positive humor left me with my ambivalence undisturbed, feeling a bit like Gollum, the double-voiced villain in J. R. R. Tolkien's *Hobbitt* and *Lord of the Ring* trilogy. On the one hand, like Gollum's more human alter ego Sméagol, I could see that the movement is devoted to improving the felt experience and health of as many people as it can influence and, by extension, of American society broadly imagined. If people would only laugh more, there would be less disease and less hostility. We'd live longer and fight fewer wars. So said one part of my mind after making its way through Goodman's 1,001 strategies for adding humor to your life. But then my Gollum side—no doubt embittered and shriveled after decades in which I had laughed selectively only when an idea or image struck me as funny (that is, from the point of view of these humor promoters, nowhere near enough)—my Gollum side noticed that Goodman calls these 1,001 strategies "laffirmations," presenting them by way of an obvious pun. "Hissssing," then, as it recoiled, my inner Gollum stopped laughing long enough to frame questions that I would bring to discussions I would have with humor consultants and to the pro-laughter conferences I would attend in February and April of 2005:

Q: What balance of hucksterism and altruism, of snake oil and wisdom defines this movement?

Q: Though laughter and humor may have a place in many aspects of life, do most of us need to work consciously on cultivating these experiences? Can the conscious effort to increase our "humor IQ" come at the cost of lowering aesthetic standards and spontaneity? When serious or frustrated old school teachers tell giggling, disruptive children to wipe the smiles off their faces, don't they have a point? Or is everything is a joke?

Q: Is our culture humor deprived? Do we value laughter too little?

Q: Granting that humor promotes creative thinking and that laughter has at least short-lived physiological benefits, what evidence is there for the efficacy of humor consultancy? Do presentations, seminars, workshops, and self-help plans significantly change the behavior of individuals and groups?

Q: In the broad context of a U.S. pop culture large and diverse enough to contain contradictory impulses, how should we understand the relation between the positive humor movement and the killing jokes rife in the land? While humor practitioners abhor cruel wit, they do not seem to appreciate its potency and standing. According to Edmundson, serious New Age spirituality has done little to resist or refute the dominant gothic nihilism that plays an empowered

Mr. Hyde to its enfeebled Dr. Jekyll. Does this assessment accurately describe the limits of positive humor? In a one-on-one contest does Freddy cut up Norman or does Norman laugh Freddy away? And how do these seemingly opposite strains of humor play out in wider cultural frames of politics, religion, morality, and taste?

In advance of traveling to the AATH and Humor Project meetings, with these and other questions under serious internal debate, I contacted two figures in the movement: Paul E. McGhee (formerly a psychology professor at Texas Technical University and the author of several books and edited collections, more recently the founder and director of the Laughter Remedy) and John Morreall, who describes himself as "a philosophy professor turned business consultant" and the director of Humor Works. I was acquainted with McGhee and Morreall from time spent together at academic conferences back in the 1980s when I was trying out ideas for a book on literary humor. Restrained by their familiarity with empirical work on humor and by the highbrow aesthetic preferences shared by many academics, their promotional materials and guide books for the humor impaired tend not to exaggerate the known benefits of humor and/or laughter, are more likely to attend to the nuances of joking or clowning around, and far more likely to stay away from the kind of easy puns that are the unappealing default mode of so many other motivational humor speakers.

Indeed, once past the title of McGhee's book *Health, Healing and the Amuse System* and the conditions he intends to treat (Terminal Seriousness [TS] and Acquired Amusement Deficiency Syndrome [AADS]), one can rest comfortably in the expectation that, although puns will be recommended as starting points for humor creation, they will not be deployed as a primary stylistic device. On the contrary, McGhee (fig. 11) makes his case for his eight-step program for humor enhancement by emphasizing the value of humor in coping with stress without over selling the physical benefits. Conceding that no one has shown an "endorphin-humor connection," that there is no evidence that humor helps "the body battle AIDS," and that it is possible to laugh and kid around too much, losing the ability to "get serious about anything"—McGhee returns repeatedly to the value of taking stressors lightly. Citing the cases of Gilda Radner, the *Saturday Night Live* comedian, and Michael Landon, *Bonanza*'s Little Joe, both of whom faced fatal illnesses with good humor, McGhee notes that, while humor may not add years to your life, it can "help you live every day fully." And this is consistent with the most honest appraisal of what has been proven about humor so far. As Rod Martin noted in a late-2004

FIGURE ELEVEN. Paul E. McGhee of *The Laughter Remedy,* with permission

e-mail, "there is much better evidence for the potential benefits of humor for psychological (rather than physical) health." And, Martin continued, "there is fairly good research evidence for humor as a way of coping with stress." Because McGhee's laughter remedy concentrates on humor as a coping mechanism, it seems more focused in its claims and, therefore, potentially more useful than the over-the-top presentations of many of his competitors.[21]

This utility is augmented by McGhee's system, an eight-step process that moves from easy tasks (Step 1: Surround Yourself with Humor You Enjoy; Step 3: Laugh More Often and More Heartily) to more demanding ones (Step 5: Find Humor in Everyday Life; Step 7: Find Humor in the Midst of Stress). Along the way, he has come up with both humor log writing that seeks to make conscious one's past and present practices and individual and group exercises that hone specific humor creating and appreciating skills. Though individual readers or workshop participants will find different instructions more or less palatable, the plan thoughtfully addresses a concern raised for me by reviewing the work of other consultants: that they may encourage listeners to desire more or better humor, laughter, or wit but leave them short on ways to achieve meaningful changes in personality and temperament. Particularly valuable is McGhee's sense of tact as an important feature of humor. Rather than ruling in all laughter or ruling out all hostile joking, he looks for balance and perspective:

If humor comes from something you've just witnessed, always remember to put yourself in the place of the person being laughed at. Keep in mind whether your laughter would be offensive or embarrassing to him/her. When in doubt, go ahead and enjoy the funniness of the situation in your own mind; just hold off laughing until later. But funny is funny! So don't worry about whether humor itself is appropriate. Your sense of humor is just as valid as the next person's. But no one likes being laughed at, so wait until the proper moment to let your laughter loose.

McGhee recommends similar sensitivity in all social situations, noting the importance of knowing "when to stop joking and be serious." And yet, having said all this about the thoughtfulness, subtlety, and usefulness of McGhee's "remedy," I brought questions as well as compliments to our discussion. When he made the move from professor to practitioner between 1988 when he left the academy and 1991 when he started to earn money as a consultant, wasn't he concerned about developing a conflict of interest? No longer the objective social scientist, he would now be trying to profit from promoting humor's benefits. Though more restrained than most, when he suggests that completing his program can promote health, success, sanity, and happiness, doesn't he worry that he and his product can start to sound like snake oil? Cultivating my inner Gollum led me to wonder: if it looks like ssssnake oil and walks like ssssnake oil and quacks like ssssnake oil, isn't it probably ssssnake oil? What evidence, for instance, does he have for the assertion, ubiquitous in this literature, that many Americans lack or need humor, are, in his own phrase, terminally serious? And doesn't he worry that by encouraging humor-deprived folk to access their joking potential in hundreds of ways—including laughing louder and more, writing down jokes they like in a notebook, and wearing rubber animal noses—doesn't he worry that this will unleash a tide of geek humor previously held in check by taste and modesty? Does even the best of humor boosters risk turning our living rooms and work spaces into joke-sharing karaoke lounges in which everyone thinks he's Robin Williams or Whoopie Goldberg? In which case, I'm sorry dear but not tonight; I've got a headache.[22]

Though I hadn't spoken with him for fifteen years, when I reached Paul McGhee, he was eager to discuss his work. Skeptical of the overselling of humor by speakers unqualified or disinclined to evaluate research studies, McGhee acknowledged that, with hundreds of humor consultants active, many were "fast and loose" in their approach to the benefits of humor. The need to be not only informative but also amusing came home to McGhee in his early performances and in discussions with stand-up comics who were trying to develop this work as a sideline even though they were better at being funny than at understanding humor. His own view is that the field has "been ahead of the data" from the outset, but that many of its assumptions about humor and health, especially in the area of immune-system response, will eventually be demonstrated. He was, he said, comfortable about his own approach to the subject, confident about having avoided conflicts of interest of the sort that his former colleagues in the academy worry about.[23]

Suggesting that top consultants can earn as much as $7,500–$10,000 for a presentation, he guessed that a fee of $2,500–$3,500 plus expenses is more typical and that a reasonably successful consultant could hope to average between five and six gigs a month—with most bookings coming in the spring and fall, few in the summer and midwinter. The challenge of this work, McGhee suggested, comes from the limited time one has for keynote speeches. Considering the need to be witty and to promote the value of humor and playfulness in the specific work context one is addressing, there is little time to "get into the details" of humor research. Even the distinction proposed by Kuipers et al. between socially skillful and self-destructive humor, McGhee observed, might be more nuanced than one can achieve in the forty-five to sixty minutes generally allotted to keynoters. In his own presentations, aimed largely at corporate and medical audiences, he insists that we need to stop repressing and start cultivating appropriate humor. To get beyond habitual seriousness and to counter the stress and anxiety that can undermine the ability of individuals and teams to work at their highest, most creative, and productive level, McGhee argues, we need to license and access our ability to find humor in difficult times. "People often say that one's ability to find humor in stressful situations is a matter of innate temperament, but I don't accept that. Most children kid around and laugh readily, but by middle school they are in the process of becoming serious. Though most people will never become brilliant humorists, they can get to the point where their sense of humor will not abandon them in tough situations."

When I e-mailed John Morreall in the winter of 2005, he was wearing at least three hats: professor of religion at William and Mary College; president of the International Society for Humor Studies, and humor consultant. Like Paul McGhee, Morreall has used his academic credential to validate his work for corporate clients. Like McGhee, he believes in the importance of humor especially in the workplace. Interestingly, Morreall puts less emphasis on specific strategies for improving humor appreciation, suggesting at one point that "all [people] need to unlock their sense of humor is to stop suppressing their playfulness."[24]

With a career-long interest in the philosophy of humor and several books on the subject on his résumé, Morreall is an effective, persuasive, and witty public speaker, well known on the corporate lecture circuit. The previous summer, during the run-up to the presidential election, I had heard him make the keynote speech at an international humor conference. Concerned as many progressives then were about the rise of religious fundamentalism in the United States, Morreall offered humor as contrasting force. Fundamentalism, he argued, is rigid, literal, purposive, and serious, while humor is flexible, creative, imaginative, and playful. Because it seemed to me that this overstated the intrinsic virtues of humor, I spent some time over dinner with him drawing out the dark side: the use of humor as a tool of denigration, attack, and, with the Abu Ghraib photographs fresh in mind, even torture. At some point during the meal, I started a sentence that Morreall, very much the philosophy teacher eager to tease out all arguments and ideas, helped me finish. "If humor is an ideal weapon and instrument of torture," I began and he interjected, "how can we say that it's intrinsically beneficial"?

In interviewing Morreall several months later, I took him back to this discussion by way of ideas he developed in *Humor Works,* the book he wrote to support his move into humor consulting. In the book, he emphasizes the varied positive functions of humor, noting that (1) it brings people together; (2) reduces negative emotions and enhances critical thinking; and (3) has persuasive power:

(1) Why do we laugh together easily? Several scientists have suggested that laughter developed in early humans as a way of establishing, strengthening, and smoothing out social relationships. As a species, we are dependent on one another, but at the same time we tend to get in each others' way and even threaten each other. Humor and laughter bring us together and reduce the natural friction between us.

(2) With a sense of humor we view problems from a distance—in the big picture instead of with the incapacitating tunnel vision of fear and anger. We keep our cool and see beyond the here and now, and so we can think more objectively and clearly. We are not denying the problem, but we see it with enough perspective to realize that it is not the end of the world. And remaining in control, we can act rather than react.

(3) We pay attention to people who make us laugh, and we tend to like them. Funny people make us follow their train of thought, and their agenda. That's why humor is used so much in persuasion, especially advertising.

I wanted Morreall not only to comment on the work of other humor consultants and the movement in general but also to respond to alternative views of humor function. For instance, while it is true that humor can build bridges between individuals and solidify in-group affiliation, are these bonds necessarily beneficial? Once bonded and enjoying shared laughter, some groups set out to do rather wicked things in this world, right? And, more profoundly, do we need to consider that in-group bonds come at some cost to a broader sense of affiliation with our ultimate in-group, humanity or, even more, life broadly conceived? While humor certainly can reduce fear and anxiety, is this always desirable? Especially in the areas of persuasion, doesn't humor frequently operate as a delightful fallacy, persuading by distraction and cleverness, not fact and logic? If humor can laugh us out of well-founded fears, persuade us to purchase harmful or unnecessary products and to vote for politicians whose scripted witticisms create an aura of likeableness, is it, in the words Morreall found for me, reasonable to say that it is intrinsically beneficial?[25]

Noting, as McGhee had, that the brevity and purpose of a keynote speech provide no time for nuanced assessments of humor as a multidimensional concept, Morreall suggested that corporate clients care about one thing only: Did the presentation entertain their audience? Were listeners engaged and amused? While he was perfectly willing to concede that humor can be destructive in personal interactions, politics, and advertising, and, while, like most consultants, he routinely alludes to the distinction between kidding and sarcasm in his presentations, at its bottom line, the requirements of the business have little to do with an intellectually balanced or nuanced presentation of the subject.

This isn't academia, [he said]. In fact, your motives are quite the opposite. On the speaker's circuit, much of what we value in academia—the willingness to backtrack, the willingness to withdraw a claim, the willingness to consider a critical question—stopping and thinking, what you do in the classroom is not what you do on the speaker's platform. And there's nobody looking over your shoulder. In academia you've got to publish. In this field you can publish with a pop press, a trade paperback that can be complete fluff. Motivational speakers—all they have to be is entertaining.

If this is the highest standard a knowledgeable and responsible speaker can aspire to, it's no wonder that Morreall expressed "not much admiration" for most other consultants, including the Humor Project's Joel Goodman, who "claims to have addressed two million people over the past few decades." Goodman's annual conference, Morreall noted, is "actually a set of invited non-academic seminars built around a bookstore and

FIGURE TWELVE. Hospital clowns Deb Price and Joyce Friedman, with permission

designed to raise as much as $500,000." Developing his critique, Morreall went on to say that "Goodman has no theory of humor of his own and, therefore, mostly retails other people's anecdotes." A typical "seminar" at a Humor Project meeting, Morreall recalled from the time he spent at a past conference, "featured a Texas state government official showing (and telling) how she gets humor into the office by opening a big basket and pulling out whoopee cushions, red noses and other props." The far smaller AATH conference, Morreall said, is less a marketing scheme and more of a professional gathering, though both it and the Humor Project provide settings in which humor consultants can present their ideas to audiences of local practitioners: managers, educators, and health and mental health care providers sent by their employers to learn more about positive humor.

Having spent this time talking with consultants, I began to think that I needed to see the field from the ground up. Aware of the restraints placed on high-powered keynoters and seminar leaders—the pressure to sell humor and, above all, be funny—I began to suspect that this movement might be at its best at the community, rather than the national, level and in the hands of unpaid volunteers rather than well-paid consultants. These folk, I began to suspect, would have stories that would represent this work at its best. So, starting at the most local level, I spent some time speaking with Joyce Friedman (fig. 12): a musician and stay-at-home mom, who for the past five years had been traveling from her hometown of Newton,

Massachusetts, into Boston twice a month to engage patients on the two pediatric floors at Massachusetts General Hospital as a member of the Jeannie Lindheim Hospital Clown Troupe. Trained originally over three intensive weekends, members of the troupe attend ongoing training sessions four times a year and work in teams of two. In addition to their bimonthly commitment, the seventeen clowns in the troupe perform at Cancer Kids events and Y-Me parties around the holidays, also at Dana Farber summer picnics.

I was particularly interested in the experience of working with sick children. Friedman stressed the importance of following set procedures that include staying out of designated rooms, asking patients for permission prior to entering their rooms, doing everything possible to avoid spreading infection or disease, and treating each child not as an audience member but an active participant in the clowning. "I have a bag of tricks," Friedman noted, "but I rarely rely on objects or set gags. Instead, we connect with the individual child, drawing him or her into the clown world where nothing makes sense, everything is up for grabs, and everything is crazy and stupid. Clowns know absolutely nothing, we get everything wrong, we never know how to fix things, so it's up to the kids to inform, correct, instruct, and control us. This way we help them out of a space where they have few or no choices into a position of empowerment."[26]

A typical example was a three-year-old boy who had a Spiderman costume at the foot of his bed. Instantly, Friedman's male partner adopted the identity of Spiderclown and started to mime wall climbing all around the room and on the ceiling. When Friedman gave one end of a long rope to the boy and the other to Spiderclown, much hilarity was generated by a game of letting Spiderclown move away and then, at the boy's discretion, pulling Spiderclown back toward the bed. "He was controlling Spiderclown, with a comic burst of power." In another room, they might find a teenage girl and invite her into a game based on *American Idol,* with the clowns performing as absurdly unqualified contestants and the girl serving as all three of the famous judges. In yet another room, they might give a kid a baton and let him conduct a musical performance or give him a magic box that makes it rain inside when it's opened and stop raining when it's closed. As the patient opens and closes the box, the clowns mime responding to torrential downpours and sudden dry spells, and the kid calls out warnings and just laughs and laughs. In every instance, they are trying intuitively to guess what the particular patient would enjoy and then work with it.

Friedman recounted a particularly satisfying recent intervention to illustrate how she becomes her clown self from the minute she gets out of her car in the hospital parking lot. Arriving at the pediatric ward and step-ping off the elevator, she was suddenly drawn into a scene in which a men-tally disabled teenage patient was lying on the floor surrounded by ten staff members who were unable to move her back to her room.

She had obviously escaped from her room, was lying in a fetal position, and no one knew what to do. Physically moving her was against policy. So there I was, you know, as a clown I started to reach her. I got on the floor with her and tried many dif-ferent angles until finally the animal angle worked. I asked, "Do you have a dog at home? Will you be a dog with me," and I started to mime walking around on my hands and feet, and she sort of woke up. She was moving, I was moving—both like dogs with some smiling. And once she was up off the floor, the staff could get her back into her room.

Although her training included overviews of the healing power of humor and though she is convinced that humor stimulates endorphins and boosts immune system responses, matters far from proved, Friedman has a mod-est sense of the value of her work. Content to have an immediate impact on mood, to provide delightful experiences of clowning empowerment, she feels that her work, while not religious, is deeply spiritual, an outreach or ministry. In clowning, she "feels connected to the fool tradition, the Tarot card fool in particular, who juggles everything in the air, existing in a space of nonattachment. Present in the moment. If I can draw children into this space for five or ten minutes and be fully present with them, that's all I can do, all I'm after."

What struck me as wonderful in this account of hospital clowning is its avoidance of shtick. Rather than relying on set tricks or, even worse, jokes, Friedman and her partners first receive permission and then enable kids who may be in pain, tired, depressed, or just out of it to relax into ab-surd and amusing games. Rather than take control, the besetting sin of many joke tellers and comedic performers, they surrender it in the service of bringing pleasure where it is most needed, perhaps most welcome. As I prepared to attend the AATH meeting, I was particularly interested in see-ing whether this generous approach to humor intervention is typical: Is this the way most deliberately funny nurses, teachers, therapists, and con-sultants operate? Or do their comic personas strut and pose, belaboring gags and jokes, and assuming, perhaps with little justification, that when they smile the whole world is smiling with them?

To put this another way, I was eager to gauge the extent to which pro-fessional humor advocates and practitioners had absorbed the clear mes-sage they have been receiving from academic humor researchers. Were they aware of, and willing to accommodate, a multidimensional conception of humor that includes destructive and counterproductive impulses? Aware of their general prohibition of ridicule and cruel wit, I wondered whether they were as sensitive to the presence of belabored humor in their work: aware of the possibility that in trying too hard to amuse they may do more harm than good. In general, were they willing to see, as Kirsh and Kuiper propose, that "any further implementations of humor in the classroom, workplace, or therapy should first be validated by research which more clearly elucidates the exact nature of humor as a construct; and does so by considering more fully both its positive and negative attributes"? Above all, had they interrogated their own approach to amusing others— the advice and model they provide—in terms of key distinctions between adaptive and harmful humor?[27]

Humor Associations: They Meet, They Eat, They Let Their Fun Flags Fly

We are now in the Twenty First Century. The Association for Applied and Therapeutic Humor has evidence that humor reduces stress, boosts immunity, relieves pain, decreases anxiety, stabilizes mood, enhances communication, inspires creativity, and bolsters morale. . . . Humor is a vastly underutilized resource and yet it's all around us.

FOREST WHEELER, *Using the Power of Humor to Improve Your Life*[28]

As I made my way from Tampa International to the Safety Harbor Spa and Resort where the 2005 AATH Conference was getting underway, I found myself expecting a certain level of pink hilarity, both because I was (against most natural yearnings) in the pinkest of states, Florida, and because preconference mailings and postings had made ample use of the flamingo motif. So I wasn't entirely surprised to find three-foot-high flamingo balloons hovering overhead in the lobby, receptionists using flamingo pens and wearing flamingo deely boppers, and assorted attendees, their faces seemingly fixed in broad smiles (like early victims of the Joker?), lounging on sofas wearing red hats and pink boas. When one fellow in a multicolored fool's cap greeted two of the conference planners by chanting "Jolly, jolly, ho-ho-ho" without a trace of self-consciousness or irony, I knew that I had arrived, praise Norman!

Acclimating myself as best I could, I walked through the temporary conference shop, checking out the assortment of humor props and toys on sale, including: smiley-faced whoopee cushions, rings, and noise makers; clown noses; film holders labeled "STOOL SAMPLE" that contained tiny three-legged wooden stools; invisible purses; no. 2 pens that look quite

FIGURE THIRTEEN. Humor products. Photographer: Stephen E. Vedder, Media Technology Services, Boston College.

realistically like molded poop; rattlesnake eggs; rubber chickens and funny glasses with big noses and bushy eyebrows (fig. 13). The book tables, like the talks I heard over the next two days, followed the major subdivisions of the movement: humor in the workplace, in medicine and therapy, in education, and in everyday life. Prominently displayed among the latter was the self-published minibook quoted at this section head. Had its author, Forest Wheeler, bothered to write *Using the Power of Humor to Improve Your Life* for a regular publisher, one with silly old editors and those pesky fact checkers, he might have been spared the embarrassment of assuming that biomedical research is best accessed through the Web pages of advocacy organizations like the AATH and that one need only allude to the existence of evidence out there somewhere to prove a point: as if all evidence is created equal, and once one "has" some, one can live in its glow without bothering to consider how it should be valued.

The next morning, eager to participate in a Laughter Club workout, I joined a sunrise-saluting group led by the cofounder of the World Laughter Tour, Steve Wilson, at 7 A.M. out on the hotel lawn. Forming a circle with about twenty other seekers, I was guided through breathing and vocalizing exercises that had us repeatedly reach forward to pick an imaginary flower, bring it to our noses in exaggerated mime movements, inhale as though we were smelling it, saying "ahhh," and exhale, saying "haaa." In another exercise, we moved around in inner and outer circles, with big smiles on our faces and smiling eyes, making eye contact with and pretending to tickle the people we passed, while chanting "hee, hee, hee, hee, hee." After each exercise, the group reformed as one large circle and chanted "ha, ha, ho, ho, ho!" As a fairly disciplined jogger, I was unimpressed with the cardio effects of this start-and-stop workout, but I was glad I got up early to do this because it allowed me to feel the humor-laughter distinction in a way I never quite had. As Wilson explained at the outset, laughter clubs are not about jokes or humor; they are about laughing as a physical workout. After ten minutes of these exercises, however, Wilson broke form for just a moment and said something funny about what would happen later in the day to people who held back breath on their exhalations. In the nanosecond it took to get this joke and laugh at it, I was fleetingly but palpably aware of the cognitive and emotional process of humor-enjoyment, felt it like a switch being gently shifted in my brain. Experiencing pure laughter for a time made it possible to experience humor as something new and unexpected, actually unfamiliar and, therefore, fascinating.

If providing such experiences—a very minor workout and occasions for gathering with like-minded others—were the only goals of the Laughter Club movement, then one would be hard-pressed to object to its sense of mission. But Dr. Kataria has broader ambitions based on his sense that, since laughter is universal, it will bring people together and have a positive impact on human history. As an e-mail preparing for World Laughter Day on May 1, 2004, put it: "I would like to remind the whole world that human beings are the only species blessed by the Almighty with the Gift of LAUGHTER. Laughter is a universal language which has the potential to unite the entire humanity. The way Laughter Clubs movement is spreading across the world, it leaves me with no doubt that the laughter is a common link among all the nations. If we consider the entire world as an extended family and develop the network of Laughter Clubs worldwide, it will build up global consciousness of brotherhood and friendship." In this spirit, the message sought to organize laughing peace marches through major cities with participants "carrying banners and placards [saying] World Peace through Laughter, The Whole World is An Extended Family, Laugh for Life, Love & Laughter, Laughter has No Language, HO, HO, HA, HA, HA, Laugh & Make Others Laugh, Laughter, A Positive Energy, Join Laughter Club—It's FREE and I Love to Laugh." The assumption behind all this, that laughing undermines warlike acts and thoughts, is belied by the laughter inspired by hostile, angry, and hateful jokes about the "enemy" generated on all sides of conflicts; by the fact that both concentration camp prisoners and guards can enjoy laughter; and by the implausible notion that periods of practiced laughter shifted out of its normal connection to humor are universal.

Most of the AATH keynoters were professional speakers, and most of their presentations were comic routines promoting humor. Corporate entertainer Brad Montgomery put it succinctly when he said, "Sunrises, flowers, rubber noses, minivans—life is fun. How cool is that?" To avoid becoming a "psychic vampire, someone who sucks the life out of others," Montgomery suggested that we should "dare to be dorks." And by this he meant that we should play practical jokes on total strangers. An example he offered concerned a time when he went with his baby into a post office and pretended that she wasn't his. "Whose kid is this," he asked loudly. "Who left her? Does anyone know her? Quick, someone, give her a stamp." Once this went on for a few minutes, Montgomery said "she's mine" and noticed that "no one else laughed," but that he "felt great." His handout included the following ideas in a list of "FUNNY THINGS TO DO IN ELEVATORS":

While the doors are opening, hurriedly whisper, "Hide it . . . quick!" then whistle innocently.

When at least 8 people have boarded, moan from the back, "Oh, not now . . . motion sickness!"

In a similar vein, Tim Gard, introduced as a "nationally recognized humorist and authority on stress reduction through humor who has taught thousands to unlock their comic vision," began by noting that good and bad things happen to everyone. The trick, he said, was to turn bummers into woo-hoos. By way of illustration, he offered the following story: when a college-aged waitress serving him seemed bored, he urged her to take pride in her job by telling her that it was important, not a bummer but a potential woo-hoo! "If you can be a good waitress," he told her, "you can do any job on this planet well." A few minutes later he heard her voice coming from the kitchen saying, "I'm a waitress" in an upbeat tone and then another voice chimed in, "Well, then, I'm a cook." Standing below a screen with the words "HAVE FUN! HAVE FUN!" in large letters, Gard urged listeners to "let the stress go," find their "mental magic," "learn from their inner child," and "use humor to refresh and renew yourself." Despite his tendency to reduce the tragic to the level of transformable irritation, Gard deserves credit for a rare moment of candor for asking the audience whether "humor is the best medicine" and, after a general shout of "yes" resounded through the hall, saying "Well, actually, no it isn't." To make his point, he then told a story about having endured the agony of a ruptured appendix and finding relief in morphine. "Laughter is not the best medicine," he concluded, "maybe the fifteenth best or the tenth, but not the best."

Between keynote and breakout sessions, I spent time talking with other attendees, including Deborah (Deb) Price (fig. 12), a nurse who now works as a writer and editor in the Office of Communication at the National Cancer Institute and who volunteers every two or three weeks as a caring clown on both children and adult wards at the National Institute of Health Hospital in Bethesda, Maryland. When I asked for her response to Tim Gard's account of the value of morphine during his appendix crisis, she agreed that "an acute surgical abdomen requires narcotic pain relief" but disagreed with Gard's premise: "Bringing a patient in the ER or ICU gentle humor is as essential as bringing them morphine. I absolutely believe that emotions are contagious, that anger, fear and tension breed more of the same. Smiles and laughter generate more smiles and laughter too."

Price acquired this view over the course of her career and confirmed it during the eighteen months she had been performing at the bedsides of cancer patients enduring the protocols of phase 2 or 3 treatment studies. After securing the permission of unit staff to visit particular patients, she and her partner (decked out as Hugs and Klutzy) knock on doors and ask whether the occupants are ready for Clown Rounds. Trying to pick up clues about individual patients from their personal articles, the clowns use jokes or riddles to get them talking about their life outside the hospital: "Sometimes we joke about the hospital routine, the dinner trays, which leads to talking about fine dining and restaurants and travel. And sometimes our caring clowning is as simple as sitting by the bedside, holding or stroking a patient's hand and smiling, helping them to relax and sleep or speak." If patients are depressed or disappointed, clowning does not always change their mood, Price notes, but when it goes well, they distract them from brooding about their diseases. Sometimes Price uses props, including a sponge foam dog named Frank shaped like a hotdog with a yellow mustard stripe "walking" at the end of a stiff leash. And often she relies on puns. About Frank she'll say, "He's a champion: the Hebrew National Champion." Or, "In his last race he fell behind and I shouted out, 'Hey, Frank, ketchup!'" Sometimes, especially with children, she relies on visual comedy and puppets. "Most nights," she says, "are terrific. We leave jazzed."

Other keynote speeches and breakout panels focused on humor in the workplace. Leslie Ann Yerkes, corporate consultant and author of *Fun Works: Creating Places Where People Love to Work* and *301 Ways to Have Fun at Work,* emphasized her combination of take-charge efficiency and light-hearted fun by asking listeners to think of her as Sergeant Mary Poppins. Her objective is to "transform workplaces into temples where the whole selves of workers can show up." Reminding listeners that we have known about the utility of humor in the workplace for a very long time—that this knowledge is implicit in sayings like, "All work and no play make Jack a dull boy" and "Time flies when you're having fun"—Yerkes went on to speculate about when in human history we lost sight of this and created the stressed-out, humorless workplace. During earlier periods, through the Renaissance, Yerkes opined, workers were probably more playful, so the Industrial Revolution, which required hierarchal business structures, may have occasioned this loss of fun. This, I fear, is the level of historical analysis one expects from Mel Brooks's 2000 Year Old Man, not from a responsible public speaker. Or, to put it another way: if only Marx and Engels or Joe Hill had known about the restorative power of humor in the workplace, the Western world could have skipped its pointless flirtation with trade unionism and economic reform and gone straight to clowning around. Workers of the world unite, you have nothing to lose but your frowns!

Working the same corner of this project but eschewing the effort at historical analysis, Ann Fry, an Austin-based consultant who describes herself as "the CEO and Dean of Humor University," insisted that "there's no evidence that life is serious" and guided her audience through a list of ways in which adding fun to offices promotes positive outcomes in such areas as employee retention, absenteeism, stress reduction, team building, problem solving and creativity. In this and the other business presentations, the speaker seems to posit an office setting in which each individual is expected to contribute innovative strategies and ideas, on the model of a software startup where people wear comfortable clothes, suck lollypops, and daydream or think-outside-the-box their way toward seven-figure salaries and increasingly valuable stock options. How applicable these up-with-fun approaches are to more severe and, perhaps, more common workplaces is an intriguing question. No doubt telling jokes might help the time pass standing over a meat-processing conveyor-belt line, but do workers have the time for mirth as animal parts fly by and sharp knives flash around their hands, and does their corporate employer care about their creativity or loyalty when new replacement workers are in the system on their way up from Central America? While there is little reason to question the importance of humor for work-related stress reduction, wouldn't it be better to tackle the causes of workplace stress—including poor benefits and salaries, inadequate job security, the promotion of products and services of dubious value, a profit-above-people orientation, indeed all of the abuses of a competitive and globalizing market system rushing to the bottom? Rather than urging workers to lighten up and make the best of all this, perhaps they need help in finding the inner outrage and solidarity that will help them demand fundamental change. In many of our workplaces, whether they are high-efficiency factories or service centers, all work and no play will not only make Jack dull, it will leave him with massive credit card debt, chronic lower back pain, an inability to put his kids through college, and the prospect of having to work at a Wal-Mart in his seventies. HA-HA-HO-HO-HO!

Like several other presentations, Fry's program lingered over her own life story long enough to provide anecdotal evidence for moving toward humor, opening yourself up. Horribly stressed by a joyless administrative job, Fry found herself crying at night after work, sometimes as soon as she reached the company parking lot. One evening, after her son asked her whether she would always cry at night, she decided to quit her job and devote herself to promoting serious fun in the workplace, functioning as a "productivity therapist" who taught "resiliency and surrender, the ability to bounce back by trusting that things will get better." "Pain," Fry concedes, "is inevitable. Suffering is optional."

Also drawing on a dramatic personal story, Saranne Rothberg, founder of the ComedyCures Foundation, built her AATH keynote address around her direct movement from cancer diagnosis to humor promotion. On the very night after she was diagnosed in 1999 with breast cancer, Rothberg began laughing and hasn't stopped since through multiple operations and an advancing illness. Drawing inspiration from Cousins, she began by renting stand-up comedy videos and deciding to laugh at least a hundred times every day. A single mom, she shared the work of fulfilling this pledge with her daughter, making dates to tell each other jokes, wear funny costumes, and play. As her story spread on local and national TV and print media, Rothberg had no trouble raising funds to support her foundation, which brings laughter programs to public schools and hospitals. A list of ten ways to "Get the Recommended 100 Laughs a Day" distributed by Rothberg includes:

1. Make an appointment to laugh each day with a friend or family member. . . .
3. Keep a joke book (or funny pages) by your bed. . . .
8. Smile at yourself 2x per day in a mirror.

Though her story is compelling, though she tells it with the practiced spontaneity of an accomplished speaker, leaving few dry eyes or unlaughing mouths (as appropriate) in the audience, and though virtually no one doubts the value of a positive attitude in coping with pain and illness, like virtually all of the speakers at the AATH meeting, Rothberg went too far. For starters, her laugh-seeking lists and strategies are so hyperintentional, overwrought, and belabored as to leave one wondering why she doesn't skip the jokes altogether and join a Laughter Club instead. Would you really want to live with or work next to someone who follows Comedy-Cures' suggestions number 9 (laugh from the tips of your toes) and number 10 (look for humor in every situation)? Every situation? Come on, get a grip and remember that this mindset and the incessant nudge-nudge-wink-winking it could motivate would be as likely as "all work and no play" to make Jack a "dull boy."

Feeling every bit the cynic in Ambrose Bierce's sense of "a blackguard whose faulty vision sees things as they are, not as they ought to be," I boarded a plane back to snowy Boston and left the merriment of the AATH—its joke-telling sessions and laughter circles, limbo contests and conga lines, pole dancers and geriatric clowns—behind in Floridian memories flooded with sunlight. If this was the Medina of positive laughter, the much larger and far more lucrative Humor Project gathering just six weeks ahead was surely the Mecca. And, with a fairly clear sense of what to expect, I looked forward to the pilgrimage.

In its promotional literature, the Humor Project promises not to "analyze humor to death" but "provide a goldmine of practical ideas on how to bring humor, hope, and healing to life." The descriptions of introductory talks by Humor Project Director Joel Goodman ("20 Humor Conferences Ha-Ha-Highlights") and comedian Yakov Smirnoff ("I Bet You Never Looked at It That Way: Lessons on Life, Laughter, and the Pursuit of Happiness") suggested that the Humor Project would differ more in size than content and purpose from the AATH meeting: it would proceed from the assumption that a humor-deprived America is in desperate need of comic retooling in the form of (1) how-I-discovered-laughter-in-a-world-of-woe-and/or-stress personal narratives and (2) instruction in "a variety of skills and ideas for developing your own sense of humor."

The balance at the Humor Project Conference tilted more heavily in the direction of comedy than the AATH meeting, that is, its presentations were funnier and, as John Morreall suggested they would be, a bit less professionally oriented. Many of the 500-plus attendees from thirty-five states and several foreign countries seemed to be regular folk searching for humor rather than professionals seeking to hone the use of humor in their work, though a good deal of this was going on as well. A unifying theme was the importance of looking for humor and laughter everywhere. In this way, though keynoter Jeanne Robertson, an award-winning public speaker and past president of the National Speakers Association, insisted that having a sense of humor has nothing to do with one's ability to make other people laugh, almost all of her speech was shtick about her experiences as a tall teenager, beauty pageant contestant, and wife of a left-brained husband. When Robertson shifted briefly away from set jokes, she tended to arrive at familiar pop psychology prescriptions, including, "Accept things you can't change about yourself and other people." Similarly, the Russian expatriate comedian Yakov Smirnoff punctuated the biographical jokes in his keynote address, many of which were based on multiple meanings of English words he was in the process of mastering, with the increasingly apposite and arch refrain, "I bet you never looked at it that way." Though many of the ideas at the conference were familiar and though some were predictably dubious, because the comic material was generally at a rather high level, people who came to laugh had no trouble achieving their goal.

Several attendees seemed ill; a few used a walker or wheelchair. Was this their laughing Lourdes? Were they hoping for the intercession of Saint Norman? Certainly Joel Goodman held out the promise of healing during his featured presentation: "Humor 101: Taking Serious Things Humorously and Humor Seriously." Though he briefly alluded to a press account of a "recent study of humor and cardiac health at the University of Maryland," he neglected to mention critical reviews of older research on the physiological benefits of humor, and, perhaps predictably, dwelt at length on Norman Cousins's almost thirty-year-old story. "If you need evidence of the healing power of humor," Goodman said, "then here it is." But, of course, Goodman knows that his audiences, particularly at Humor Project sessions but more generally as well, require very little in the way of evidence in support of ideas that he has helped guide into the mainstream of unchallenged American truisms. Still, healing power or not, one would be more open to Goodman's version of the nurture-your-sense-of-humor pitch if his prescriptions were less belabored, if, for instance, he refrained from urging listeners to wear funny buttons and play with droopy, sad-looking dolls.

Because it focused on humor and creativity, avoided overpromising, and drew on its presenter's talent for spontaneous invention, Jon Pearson's preconference workshop was a refreshing break from the otherwise repetitive Humor Project message. In the extended five-hour format,

Pearson—an actor, consultant, public speaker, and former cartoonist for the *Oakland Tribune*—urged participants "not to try to be more funny but to be less serious." Pearson encouraged the group to suspend judgment and be more playful, more childlike, to try not to suppress but to follow distractions, random associations, peripheral vision: ideas and feelings that interrupt normal patterns of serious, linear thought. Guiding us through cartoon-drawing exercises that led to some ridiculously silly pictures, he then had us describe what we had created in flowing, stream-of-unchecked-consciousness accounts. "If you observe what you've drawn without judging it, the blues will become bluer, the birds birder [*sic*]." Though he had probably used this line a hundred times, the idea of a "birder bird" not only seemed original, its unconventionality captured his idea about letting random thoughts blossom into wit. Drawing on his expressive body language, modulated voice, and animated expressions, Pearson demonstrated how one can "go through nuts and funny to get to creative." His large point, directed at teachers specifically but also at life growth in general, was that "achievement without enjoyment leads to success without fulfillment."

Was Pearson, an entertaining speaker and humane thinker, full of good ideas about generating humor, or was my resistance weakening, my cheese-ometer drifting toward dysfunctional under the influence of all the unreflective good cheer around me in Saratoga Springs, where many of the retail store windows had signs greeting Humor Project participants and the early spring evenings were awash in beer and country music? It was getting hard to tell, but I had to wonder when I found myself nodding responsively to an exercise Pearson asked us to try during a coffee break: walking up to a total stranger, smiling, pointing a finger at his or her head, and saying, "I hear good things!" One, two—had Norman come for me?

Though Pearson's insights often seemed original and even spontaneous, the rarest commodity in the world of public speaking, and though he provided essential caveats about the importance of authenticity, imagination, and nuance in humor creation, I held back when his presentation veered into at least one blind spot of the positive humor movement. "Put-down humor is not a sign of intelligence," he insisted. "Humor is a species of friendship. It's about making people feel good. If it makes someone feel bad, it's not humor." Alas, who among us would reject this idea but for the fact that, like Hamlet, we have bad dreams? Hearing Pearson say this revived my inner cynic, never all that dormant, with a flood of peripheral images. Resisting the instinct to suppress them, I let the movie in my mind run on. In it, Freddy Krueger walked onto the set of *Saturday Night Live* and morphed into the Church Lady while Pearson's comment played and replayed: "If it makes someone feel bad, it's not humor . . . if it makes someone feel bad, it's not humor . . . if it makes . . ." As the Church Lady/ Freddy strutted and danced, the sound of sharp claws on a blackboard gave way first to demonic laughter and then to the expected rhetorical question: "Isn't that specialll?" One can dislike or reject cruel or sharply targeted jokes, sarcasm, even satire, but one cannot honestly and thought-fully deny utterances or texts of this kind the status of humor or insist that they cannot also be more or less clever.

Before leaving the Humor Project Conference, I spent some time pe-rusing books and joke props in the conference's large retail operation. The many self-published tomes (pamphlets would be a more appropriate noun) reminded me of an old gag from the flip side of the *2000 and One Years with Carl Reiner and Mel Brooks* album. The bit, part of the hilarious routine about a psychiatry convention, concerns Dr. Buck Mitcheson, a self-certified shrink voiced by Brooks in a loopy (because half-Jewish and half-Texan) twang. Like the other shrinks in the sketch, Mitcheson is obviously nuts, phobic about the possibility that people will poke him in the eyes. "Get away from my eyes," he says repeatedly, "Don't touch my eyes!" When Reiner, increasingly skeptical about his legitimacy, asks him where he earned his degree, Brooks says, "Texas." "Oh," Reiner says, "you mean at the University of Texas?" "No," Brooks replies, "the state. Put my hand on a rock, looked up at the sky, and said, 'I am a psy-chi-a-trist!'"

And then there were the toy tables, even more heaped with silly stuff than at the AATH meeting. Here, in addition to a cornucopia of yellow smiley face buttons of all sizes, were flashing smiley face earrings and necklaces. Here were practical jokes such as hand buzzers, phony burgers, hot candy, fake vomit (called Whoops), and no fewer than three variations on the ever-popular theme of fake pet poop called Doggie Doo, Dog Dirt, and Kitty Crap. Looking down I noticed an orange cloth bag. When I picked it up and pressed what seemed to be a button of some kind, it be-gan laughing not, I thought, happily but, rather, in a mechanical tone that seemed a bit more menacing, a bit more like Freddy than Norman, as it continued. Ha-ha-ha-ha-ha-ha-ha! Thirty seconds into the laughter, from a few feet away on the table, one of the fart-sound-producing de-vices cut loose loudly and repeatedly between the cascading laughs. More startled than amused, I laughed and thought not of Freddy but of Bela Lu-gosi whose most memorable line in Tod Browning's *Dracula* comes in re-sponse to the far-off howling of wolves: "Listen to them, Renfield," he says, "children of the night. What music they make." The conference had, clearly done all it could: conditioned to find humor in even the least promising of situations, I was ready to leave.

Conclusion

After all the mirth and merriment, the exercises and admonitions, the practiced laughter and willful amusement, the positive humor movement can be summed up in a familiar joke script: the good and bad news about its practitioners is that they are never just kidding; the worse news is that some of them get as close as humanly possible to always kidding. Life raining on your parade? Take out your comic umbrella. Feeling gloomy? Look at one of the cartoons you've been collecting and enjoy a chuckle break. Having a bad day at work? Find a humor buddy and tell her the worst joke you can remember. Mysteriously ubiquitous, supernaturally malevolent, improbably large white whale bite your leg off? Hey, Captain Ahab, lighten up, whistle a happy tune! There's no need to get angry. What's that you say? Your stump grinds, your groin aches, you've dropped your last cindered apple to the ground? Hey, hey now, take a tip from musical theater: "Take off the gloomy mask of tragedy, / It's not your style. You'll look so good that you'll be glad / that you [badum-CHING] decided to smile."

The irony is that Melville's Ahab might well have lived longer if he could have seen the folly of his quest and the comic absurdity of declaring war on the universe, of stabbing at it with unceasingly enraged determination, and screaming: "Towards thee I roll, thou all-destroying but unconquering whale; to the last I grapple with thee; from hell's heart I stab at thee; for hate's sake I spit my last breath at thee." This, of course, is Ahab's style. But if only Norman Cousins or Patch Adams had shipped aboard the *Pequod* for that fatal voyage, an upbeat *Moby-Dick* with a heartwarming ending might have sold more copies in the 1850s, and the culture might have been treated to a sequel in which Ahab, a wealthy, retired sea captain, bounces his son on his knee back in Nantucket and regales visitors with his tropical adventures. "There was this one time," he might say, "when a ferocious spermaceti chewed me leg off, boys, and it hurt for awhile. But then a tune popped into me head and I just sang it over and over: 'Big Fat Moby, Banana, Fanna, Moby. Fee Fie Moby—DICK!' Then I just laughed myself silly and well."[29]

Okay, that's out of my system. I brought Melville's Ahab into this conclusion because he stands in the middle of the most profound nineteenth-century American treatment of the role of humor in a universe that can seem to be pointless at best and pointlessly cruel at worst. Though neither Norman Cousins nor Patch Adams walks the decks of the *Pequod,* Ahab exists in a spectrum of characters defined in part by what they think is funny. Unlike the grim, isolated Ahab, one of the white whale's other victims, Captain Boomer of the *Samuel Enderby,* an English whaler, recovers from having his arm chewed off by drinking and laughing with his friend, Dr. Bunger. Beginning with the doctor's comment, the exchange below captures the spirit of this treatment:

> "I did all I could; sat up with him nights; was very severe with him in the matter of diet—"
> "Oh, very severe!" chimed in the patient [Captain Boomer] . . . "Drinking hot rum toddies with me every night, till he couldn't see to put on the bandages; and sending me to bed, half seas over, about three o'clock in the morning. Oh, ye stars! he sat up with me indeed, and was very severe in my diet. Oh! a great watcher, and very dietetically severe, is Dr. Bunger. (Bunger, you dog, laugh out! why don't ye? You know you're a precious jolly rascal.) But, heave ahead, boy, I'd rather be killed by you than kept alive by any other man."

For the lower officers aboard the *Pequod,* Stubb in particular, everything is a joke, even the sea monsters they hunt down and kill at great peril to themselves. He sings:

> Oh! jolly is the gale,
> And a joker is the whale,
> A' flourishin' his tail,—
> Such a funny, sporty, gamy, jesty, joky, hoky-poky lad, is the Ocean, oh!
>
> The scud all a flyin',
> That's his flip only foamin';
> When he stirs in the spicin',—
> Such a funny, sporty, gamy, jesty, joky, hoky-poky lad, is the Ocean, oh!

For the practical, middle-class, pious Starbuck, humor has its place and time. For the novel's most deeply comic spirit, the narrator Ishmael, learning to laugh even at death, makes it possible to acknowledge the injustice and absurdity of the human predicament but still see humor in a God who frequently seems cruel:

> There are certain queer times and occasions in this strange mixed affair we call life when a man takes this whole universe for a vast practical joke, though the wit thereof he but dimly discerns, and more than suspects that the joke is at nobody's expense but his own. . . . That odd sort of wayward mood I am speaking of, comes over a man only in some time of extreme tribulation; it comes in the very midst of his earnestness, so that what just before might have seemed to him a thing most momentous,

now seems but a part of the general joke. There is nothing like the perils of whaling to breed this free and easy sort of genial, desperado philosophy; and with it I now regarded this whole voyage of the Pequod, and the great White Whale its object.

Even those of us who are skeptical about the positive humor movement, who find its prescriptions corny and its willful laughter unappealing, can see in Ishmael's desperado philosophy a middle ground. Though Ishmael's suspicions that demonic forces govern the world and that all grand questions turn out to be unanswerable are incompatible with New Age affirmation, they provide an unusual context for positive humor. Perceiving, as Ishmael does, the darkness and meaninglessness of existence— the sense that "though in many of its aspects this visible world seems formed in love, the invisible spheres were formed in fright"—leaves us with two options. Like Ahab, we can eschew all pleasure along with all determination-weakening amusement, the better to hurl ourselves body and spirit against the enemy. Or, like Ishmael, we can settle for "attainable felicity" and take comfort in a life of simple pleasures that will, delightfully enough, include "the heart, the bed, the table, the saddle, the fireside," and, of course, laughter.[30]

3 | Shut Up! No, You Shut Up!

FIGHTING WITH AND ABOUT HUMOR

Freddy and Norman: Degrees of Denial

On one end of post-1980 U.S. humor culture, looming and lurking, stand killing jokers. Flashing their pointy teeth, curling their lips into expressions of contempt, holding their enemies aloft impaled in pain—they deploy ridicule not as an alternative to hostile action but as their chosen sauce or flavor. At the other end—wielding rubber chickens and elephant noses and laughing until their muscles go slack and they fall to the floor, kidding and quipping—kneel the humor deployers bringing mirth where no (or too little) mirth has gone before. Seeking to lighten life up, they urge us to take deep breaths and let it all out with a HA and a HO and a HA-HAHO! How should we understand this apparent contest or contradiction, this battle between Freddy and Norman? Beyond the seemingly different intentions that drive their use of humor, what issues are at stake? Why do we seem to embrace, why do we seem to require, both the razor claws and helping hands of these different jokers?

The distinction might seem to turn on the contrast between laughing at and laughing with. No victim of Freddy's violent joking ever joins in the amusement, while the very idea of an offended butt is repugnant to the gentle laughers meeting in clubs and fanning out across the United States into classrooms, offices, and cancer wards. In different ways, though, each of these impulses gains power from its relation to the other. Freddy and his ilk draw energy from their spectacular nightmare deviations from the accepted Elm Street norms of polite joking—as the Tim Burton Joker reminds us by taunting the mobster he has just murdered with a question about the beneficial power of humor. Just as lumbering zombies in such films as *Dawn of the Dead* (1978; 2004) and *28 Days Later* (2002) both exaggerate and exploit expectations about the kind of danger we're likely to encounter on city streets, serving as the muggers to end all muggers—so killing jokers derive some of their impact from hurling tact, sensitivity, kindness, and empathy aside: acquiring power by going beyond, far, far beyond poor taste. Conversely, Norman and his followers build their case around the need for kindness, nurturing, and good heartedness in joking and laughing, rejecting not just sadism but meanness and pointed criticism as well. Each is what it is in part by not being the other.

And yet, for all the venom on one side and treacle on the other, these apparently opposing impulses have fascinating similarities. For starters, as the situation-based use of humor in both strains became conventional, the expectations that laughter might figure in the depiction of violence in horror genres and that humor could be regarded as therapeutic in hospitals and elsewhere, perhaps everywhere else, were established. Audiences watching the first *Jaws* movie in 1975 were relieved but also surprised, even startled, to find themselves laughing en masse in the moments following shark attacks; no one unfortunate enough to be recovering in a hospital from a grueling round of chemotherapy in the mid-1970s would have imagined that a clown might be clomping and honking his way toward him from the nurses station. Though humor appreciation is subjective, the rising conventionality of the puns, jokes, and gags associated with these movements strips them of the element of surprise, often considered essential to humor in classic definitions of the experience, and leads to a lower level of wit based on the sense that simply being funny in these otherwise nonhumorous contexts is enough to achieve the desired effects. In this way, when Freddy murders a girl named Greta who has been pressured by her mother to diet and become a model in *NES 5,* his ingenious violence is accompanied by predictable jokes. No doubt the special effects of the dinner scene in which he appears as a sadistic waiter who force feeds Greta until she explodes—her expanding rubbery mouth and face, her body floating above the table—add kick to what might otherwise be a sluggish, because belabored, set of gags. "Bon appetite, bitch," Freddy says at the start of an attack that ends with her dead body dropped onto the table and a final, seemingly inescapable, remark: "You are," he says, "what you eat." The same situational imperative attached to stressed-out offices and hospital wards by the followers of Norman licenses any and all gentle joking, however silly, as though the humor practitioner's only guiding principles are make them laugh and do no harm. At its extreme, this leads to a celebration of mere laughter, a witless and mechanical reduction of the potentially complex and richly human experience of being amused.

In addition to the predictability and simplicity of much of this humor, it is worth noting that both the killing joker and the healing laugher bring humor to moments of potential misery, tension, anxiety, danger, or death, seeking to shift moods and provoke emotional responses. Though one operates from hostility and the other from empathy, one attacks and the other defends, both urge us not to take a potentially disturbing or menacing situation seriously. For Freddy's butts, the joking intensifies victimization by showing that they are not only doomed but also pathetic, not tragic but comic figures, in their in-process demises. But viewers can adopt a different angle of perception as they are invited by Freddy to step back from otherwise sympathetic victims and join in cruel laughter at their expense. Freddy's implicit refrain, not just "don't cry for them" but laugh yourself silly at their suffering, uses cruel joking both to intensify and distance the horror by detaching viewers from victims. Similarly, learning to laugh at themselves—at the absurdity of office pressures and terminal illnesses—allows Norman's sufferers to draw back and relax into the Big Tee-Hee. Like the shriveled victims of Disney's Sea Witch in *The Little Mermaid,* they need to resist the inclination to see themselves as "poor, unfortunate souls" by using humor to achieve distance from the stress of a momentary, ongoing, or chronic condition.

If these humor impulses are related as norm and deviation, pleasant dream and nightmare, if their mirroring reflects differences between species disaffiliation and personal detachment, they both operate as variants of gallows humor at a time when this ultimate, if transitory, emotional relief and the denial or distance it serves seem to be much in need. The classic discussion of gallows humor in Freud's 1927 essay sees it, like intoxication, as a strategy of evasion. Faced with danger or doom, a worried person kids around in a giddy act of denial. Freud's famous example concerns a prisoner being led to his execution on a Monday morning who remarks, "Well, the week's beginning nicely." The purpose of this joke, in Freud's view, is to allow the inescapably doomed kidder to avoid feeling pain, fear, or horror by relaxing into amusement: "The grandeur in [humor] clearly lies in the triumph of narcissism, the victorious assertion of the ego's invulnerability. The ego refuses to be distressed by the provocations of reality, to let itself be compelled to suffer. It insists that it cannot be affected by the traumas of the external world; it shows, in fact, that such traumas are no more than occasions for it to gain pleasure." Because it seeks to distract uptight workers, patients, students, indeed people in general, from conditions they are directly coping with, positive humor is obviously akin to what Freud is after here. Norman's followers would insist that their humor is therapeutic and therefore potent in helping people not just to deny but also to step off the gallows. But, as we have seen, existing evidence in support of such claims, especially in the area of physical illness, is inconclusive. And, indeed, the more belabored positive humor gets, the less likely it is to provide benefits of any kind. Regarded as an exchange between a comic attacker and his victim, killing jokes appear to fall outside of the gallows humor category, but since most of this humor occurs in fictive pop-cultural contexts, it seems appropriate to concentrate on audience, rather than on fictive victim, response. And to the extent that viewers and readers enjoy this humor—finding Freddy more entertaining than his witless and often mute peers in other horror series (including Michael Myers in *Halloween,* Leatherface in *The Texas Chainsaw Massacre,* and Jason in *Friday the Thirteenth*) or laughing with Hannibal Lecter or the Joker—they are in the moment of comic amusement allowing themselves to feel little or no empathy for victims and the species affiliation on which empathy is, in part, grounded. To the extent that being human in our time, as Anthony Giddens argues, carries the consciousness of potential or impending catastrophe—a species-wide gallows sentence conceived in both religious (that is, apocalyptic) and natural (that is, environmental, military, biological, or chemical) terms—killing jokes can be seen, by way of an application of Giddens's view of contemporary consciousness to Freud's analysis of gallows humor, as an effort to "evade the compulsion to suffer."[1]

As Freud's famous example demonstrates, the concept of gallows humor has two implications: first, the relief it provides is morally neutral, available to all and, second, unable to alter disagreeable, threatening facts or conditions, this kind of joking cannot change the reality it briefly sets aside. In response to the first point, Freddy's followers might take pleasure in pointing out that Freud's joker is a prisoner, that is, a convicted criminal. There's no reason to assume that he is innocent or that his crime was trivial. Though this observation would no doubt provoke squirming in Saratoga Springs, it invites us to move beyond disapproval as a response to cruel humor to a consideration of its popularity and rhetorical effect that begins with noting potential connections to Mark Edmundson's account of the emergence of nihilistic gothicism in the period and Giddens's view of a culture underpinned by a pervasive sense of doom, yearning for distraction.[2]

Academic humor research has in recent years arrived at insights that bear directly on the two strains of post-1980 intentional humor described here. By demonstrating that humor is not uni- but multidimensional, it has invalidated global assertions about its healing, relaxing, or socially adaptive benefits. Extreme, indeed psychopathic in their hostility, killing jokers would be neither surprised nor disappointed to learn that their sadistic wit does nothing to boost their sense of well-being or social integration. Glorying in cruel domination, contemptuous of others, they are defended against hearing cautionary suggestions about the need for tact and sensitivity. To healing laughers, humor research has other pointers, at least one of which seems to be as welcome as the emphasis on nonaggression would by definition be to Freddy-like comedians. To achieve the effects the children-of-Norman aim for, jokers must not only avoid aggression (which is fine with them) but also resist the temptation to force or belabor their presentations. As Kirsh and Kuiper put it, "A strained and incompetent effort to gain the approval of others" by way of willful and potentially witless humor is likely to backfire, resulting in "negative relatedness," that is, in weaker connections to other people. The desire to spread amusement everywhere can become an occupational hazard for humor practitioners, just as the need to avoid aggression at all costs can lead to a hypersensitivity that strips jokes of their potential impact and reduces humor to what can be accomplished with a whoopee cushion.[3]

With this sense, then, that neither killing jokers nor healing laughers would be all that interested in what humor researchers might want them to know (and, honestly, virtually no one is much interested in this)—this study now moves out into wider circles of recent American culture: to the use of humor in social, environmental, and religious debates (this chapter) and in political contests (chap. 4). From the PC/anti-PC conflicts of the 1980s and 1990s to humor surrounding the presidency of George W. Bush and debates about whether particular jokes, joke cycles, and jokers are beneficial or harmful, relaxing or cruel—the Freddy-Norman distinction has explanatory value. Not because radio talk-show hosts or advertising executives think about Freddy while using humor to promote harmful policies or products. Not because disputants objecting to the latest stereotypical cartoon, or politically incorrect gaffe, or sexual or scatological TV commercial are thinking about Norman. The killing joke/healing laughter distinction highlights what is at stake in our most provocative, controversial joking because it both describes a spectrum of possible intentions and raises questions about how particularly striking—outrageous or soothing—jokes are likely to operate for individuals and groups.

Fundamental to disputes about the use of humor to promote products, politicians, or causes are questions about the appropriateness of the butts—haven't they suffered enough?—and the potential for negative social impact: Can it reinforce stereotypes, advance destructive policies, function as an emotional, and therefore, fallacious appeal? As we make our way across battlefields of recent American humor disputation, focusing on conflicts between jokes and antijokes—I invite you to be alert to two possibilities: first, that seeing Freddy's leer and Norman's scowl behind the lines can highlight the intentional ways some jokes and jokers operate and, second, that seeing the intensity with which these struggles are fought and the conditions disputants seek to change can awaken a sense of the morality of humor—the imperative requiring us to take some humor seriously.

Joking, Persuasion and Comic (In)sensitivity

There are so many reasons not to like a particular joke, not to find it amusing. The person telling it is awkward or unpleasant. Getting it is too easy or hard. You resent having the image or idea it evokes brought to consciousness. You just don't like jokes in a particular form (knock, knock me no knocks) or about the subject at hand (proctologists, prophets, pimples, you name it!). Most of the time not liking a joke is no different from not liking other moments in conversation or entertainment. An unamusing joke teller could just as easily bore you with a serious comment of similar duration. You might find the guest rap star on *Late Night with David Letterman* just as entertaining or lame as Letterman's monologue. The perfect guru may enjoy every lived moment equally, indeed, this may be why we imagine him sitting in a cave and constantly smiling, but for most of us life is a mixed affair, shifting in the flow of thoughts and feelings between engagement, fascination, boredom, and fatigue. So, not liking a joke in general is par for the course.

Still, as the 1980s advanced, as joke cycles proliferated and stand-up comedy became a growth industry, a new intensity of concern animated public debate about the meaning and impact of jokes. Underpinned by opposing assumptions about the function of humor, controversies surrounding the concepts of political correctness and anti–political correctness advanced under the shadows of Norman and Freddy: PC advocates insisting that humor should do no harm, anti-PC objectors insisting that the seemingly benevolent effort to render humor benign was a form of leftist censorship.

As they raged both within and beyond the academy, humor controversies marked moments when arguments about the tastefulness of jokes and joke cycles assumed a broader significance. Within the academy, as seen in debates about rules of conduct that sought to limit what administrators and professors defined as hate speech, advocates of academic freedom quarreled with advocates of civility and community. Was it more or less tolerant to restrict hateful speech and ridicule? Did respect for diversity require the repudiation of seemingly derogatory speech, serious and playful? In the larger world, discussions of the acceptability, meaning, and impact of jokes and joke cycles frequently shifted out of context to support broader political or moral positions.

In thinking about controversial jokes, the distinctions developed by Kuipers et al. between socially adaptive, tactful humor and unwelcome and, therefore, maladaptive humor discussed in chapter 2 provide a set of useful frames. Can certain kinds of humor undermine community and fellow feeling? If so, should it or can it be regulated? Influenced by the PC/anti-PC arguments, the criticism and defense of particular jokes and joke cycles by humor researchers in a number of fields have focused on their subject matter. Historian of humor Joseph Boskin has argued that particular joke cycles should be seen as positions taken or battles fought in public debates or "joke wars" waged between social subgroups, with antisexism jokes waging war against antifeminist jokes, WASP jokes combating minority ethnic jokes, gay rights jokes engaging homophobic jokes, and so on. According to Boskin, "Just as humor has been used as a weapon of insult and intimidation by dominant groups, so it has been employed for resistance and retaliation by minorities." Folklorist and theorist Elliott Oring has challenged this understanding of the social function of humor by arguing both (1) that it is impossible to deduce a particular joke teller's intention from the text of the joke she or he tells and (2) that jokes do not seriously advance specific ideas. On the contrary, Oring argues, because they are playful and ambiguous, because there is more than one way to "get" a joke, jokes cannot in a uniform manner represent and promote the interests of particular groups. Where Boskin sees ethnic-, class-, and gender-based joke cycles as weapons in intergroup contestation, Oring insists that they "are not really about particular groups who are their ostensible targets. These groups serve merely as signifiers that hold together a discourse of certain ideas and values that are of current concern. Polish jokes, Italian jokes, and JAP jokes are less comments about real Poles, Italians or Jewish women than they are about a particular set of values attributed to these groups." Like Christie Davies, Oring suggests that subgroup jokes are motivated by the "concerns" of the joke-telling groups and can, therefore, tell us a good deal about those concerns, while telling us far less about the hostility of the joke tellers.[4]

Whatever the intentions of subgroup jokers may be—whether they are lashing out Freddy-like or seeking to soothe their inner worriers à la Norman—there is reason to wonder about the cumulative effect of focused ridicule over time. How and in what ways is humor persuasive?

How do jokes that target particular subgroups affect tellers and listeners? Can the accumulated effect of a humor cluster within a community—regardless of the ambiguity of particular jokes and the intentions of specific jokers (who may, in the spirit of healing laughter, be all about taking it easy and having a good time)—foster contempt, discrimination, and/or abuse (in ways that would no doubt gratify killing jokers everywhere)?

PC or Not PC? Framing the Question

Questions like these about the effects of disparaging humor on joke tellers, audiences, social subgroups, and society at large animated an online debate among fourteen humor researchers in a number of disciplines that I organized, moderated, and then edited for publication in the mid-1990s at the height of the PC brouhaha. A LexisNexis search conducted at the outset of the project in September 1995, using the words "humor" and "politically correct," produced 245 news and magazine stories related to the topic, suggesting that people were choosing sides. One line of argument was summed up in an op-ed piece in which Joseph P. Khan worried that we were losing our sense of humor, that America was "becoming an increasingly brittle, thin-skinned society, where a joke is seldom funny unless somebody else is the butt of it—and perhaps not even then." The opposing viewpoint was captured in a news story that quoted James McDevitt, associate director of the Center for Applied Social Research at Northeastern University, as follows: "We are facing the most racist and sexist generation of high school kids I've ever seen, spurred by the messages they're receiving in their media—MTV, rap, heavy metal and attack comics like Andrew Dice Clay."[5]

Though we considered a range of potentially offensive jokes and incidents in which particular jokers were criticized, many of the most compelling examples were about gender, focused on relationships, sex, and stereotypes. Early on Larry Mintz, a professor of American studies at the University of Maryland, called the group's attention to a joke about the end of a marriage: "A guy comes home and informs his wife that he has been wiped out in the stock market. He tells her that he will have to sell their house, summer home, cars, her furs and jewels. And what is even worse, she will have to get a job so that they can pay off their debts and eke out a meager existence. She screams in horror and dismay, opens a window of their condominium apartment, and jumps fifteen floors to her death. The man looks out and says, 'Thank you, Paine Webber.'" Mintz made a few points about this joke: that he thought it was funny when he was going through a divorce but not since then and that the joke "ex-press[ed] anger, resentment against a woman, perhaps women" but that there was no evidence that jokes like it caused "direct social harm" by lead-ing to violence against women or leading others "toward a more accept-ing attitude toward gender hostility." After a few responses that generally agreed with Mintz's view that the Paine Webber joke presented an oppor-tunity for a harmless release of hostility, the group moved on to jokes about pederasty and an alligator eating an African American. The debate heated up when Elliott Oring offered the following joke for analysis:

Q: What do you call a Negro with a PhD?
A: Nigger.

Some contributors supported Oring's view that, insofar as jokes "can register diametrically opposed messages," it was possible to find this joke amusing either because it denigrates African Americans or because it offers a "critical comment on a society where Blacks are not allowed to succeed no matter what they do." Without questioning the individuality of humor response, I wondered about the role such jokes could play when they ac-cumulate in a society or subgroup. And, in a response essay appended to the debate, Duke University anthropologist of humor Mahadev L. Apte highlighted issues of power and hegemony in the "generation and dissemi-nation of humor": "Until a public outcry and protest against ethnic, racist, and sexist humor occurred, the targets of such humor ... [were] those without any political and economic power and high social status: African-Americans, women, immigrants, and the members of various ethnic and minority religious groups. Political-correctness ideology focuses on this vilification, on the naked power reflected, not so subtly, in jokes, insults, ribbing, and public humiliation disguised as humor."[6]

Six weeks into the debate news broke about a PC crisis at Cornell Uni-versity where an e-mail message called "75 Reasons Women (Bitches) Should Not Have Freedom of Speech," written by four first-year male students—who gave an all new significance to the word "freshmen" but who called themselves "The Players of Cornell"—got out onto the Web and circulated nationwide. Among the more provocative "reasons" were:

1. She doesn't need to talk to get me a beer. . . .
6. Because PMS is no excuse for whining. . . .
10. When men whistle at them in the street, they should just shut up and obey anyway.

11. If my dick's in her mouth, she can't talk anyway. . . .

14. Because that stupid look on her face should not be accompanied by an equally stupid statement. . . .

21. Don't waste your breath. I won't respect you in the morning. . . .

35. Female drunks are annoying unless they put out (for which they don't need to
talk). . . .

38. If she can't speak, she can't cry rape. . . .

43. Only one set of lips should be moving at a time. . . .

47. Nothing should come out of a woman's mouth. SWALLOW BITCH! . . .

60. N.O.W.? NO. NOW BITCH? YES. . . .

68. Because they're not men. . . .

74. Unless the words are "Doctor, can you make these bigger?" shut the fuck up.

75. Big breasts should speak for themselves.

Although this message was originally sent by the writers to twenty of
their friends, in an early demonstration of the distributive power of the
Internet, it soon got around to other campuses where a growing horde of
angry readers launched a retaliatory e-mail campaign against the four
writers and also sent messages to embarrassed Cornell officials. Within
a very short period—the university's judicial administrator, Barbara
Krause, told the *New York Times*—the writers were charged with sexual
harassment and misuse of computers.[7]

Engaged in the PC humor debate, I was fascinated by the version of the
"75 Reasons" piece that arrived in my e-mail inbox both because it was
grist for our mill and because it came with a long string of responses written by irate women who were circulating what they saw as an insidiously
sexist and not at all funny document. The fact that the authors included all
of their names and e-mail addresses made it possible for on-line readers to
strike back, as you'll see in this sampling of their angry responses:

—Subject: READ THIS!
I think this is something that all women need to read. It is not a joke. I honestly wish
it were because it is even more scary to think that there are people out there that actually think this way. It is being distributed to all women so that they can write back
to these misogynistic morons and set them straight.

—Subject: READ THIS!
This unbelievably misogynistic bullshit written by four men of Cornell is being circulated in the hope that both women and men will become more aware of the sexism
rampant in our society.

—Subject: READ THIS!
I think it's a piece of work that affects all of us.

—Subject: READ THIS!
Just when I'm getting idealistic and thinking that people aren't "really" that sexist and no one would want to do something to intentionally hurt someone, things like this come along. I'm at a loss for what to do. How can you change people who are so proud of their ignorance and blatantly, well, assholes?

—Subject: READ THIS!
Read this, it fucking pissed me off like nothing ever has, send it to men and women alike, write to these bastards. Especially send it to anyone at Cornell. These assholes need to be ostracized. I have never seen anything this offensive in my life.

Although Cornell initiated disciplinary proceedings, in the end they decided that no campus rules about computer use or harassment had been violated. Meanwhile, the four students, overwhelmed by the e-mail response their list provoked and eager to redeem their reputations, volunteered to attend a rape education program and perform community service. According to a story in the *Boston Globe,* a letter they published in the *Cornell Daily Sun* expressed "deep remorse" for their "stupid actions" and provided the following exculpatory explanation for what they claimed was intended to be just a joke among friends: "We have seen almost everything on that list in some kind of TV show, rap song, Internet list, comedian's act or talk show. We are not trying to blame anything on society; we just wish to convey that we never meant any of the things we wrote."[8]

Concerned about the criminalization of speech, members of free speech groups objected to the university's actions. One response by an ad hoc group calling itself the Online Freedom Fighters Anarchist Liberation sent a Thanksgiving Day e-mail to Cornell students and faculty (just what they needed!) in the form of a parodic letter supposedly from Barbara Krause in which the judicial administrator called the offenders the "four little pigs" and regretted that it was impossible to further "humiliate" them. Harvard Law School Professor Harvey Silverglate criticized Cornell for considering disciplinary action, insisting that "the answer to bad speech is good speech," a principle columnist Ellen Goodman put into action when she awarded the authors her first annual "Cybermisogyny Prize."[9]

A now-familiar line in the anti-PC backlash was the observation that reacting negatively to what one perceives as bias (racism, sexism, homophobia) in serious speech and in a joke or joke cycle is a characteristic move in identity politics. This is the position Oring took early in our on-line debate in making the point that political correctness was contributing to a rising "politics of emotion" and victimization, that "groups have discovered that anger politics works." Given the rising temperature of our national politics since the mid-1990s, Oring's point, in retrospect, was not only descriptive but prophetic. For, as the "75 Reasons" controversy illustrates, political anger is not confined to one position. Among the forces that motivated the four Cornell "players," one senses delight in what they must have experienced as their own cleverness in elaborating their (no doubt lame but nonetheless) comic premise, as well as the desire for control that animates joke tellers: "Hey, listen to this one, it's funny, man." But, in the Freddy-like tone and content of their more demanding and violent reasons, one senses anger (at feminism, at women who won't put out, at *not* being players?) as well. The outrage that motivated the responses that the e-mail provoked is clear in the ungentle characterizations of the authors as assholes and misogynists and in the call for retaliatory acts. But the wheel of anger continued to roll when anti-PC voices were raised in self-defining condemnation of what they saw as the anti-free-speech intolerance and humorlessness of the PC forces at Cornell and elsewhere. By way of illustration, the free speech–defending Freedom Fighters included the following rant in their protest: "Our action on Thanksgiving Day was just a warning shot across the bows of the decency armada. Let them understand that if they don't shut up, fuck off, and leave us alone, we will strike again in our own inimitable fashion—and next time, we will hit harder."[10]

It is worth noting that the combination here of humor (in the images of naval combat) and anger (in the fuck-off-or-else attitude) played out, indeed continues to play out, on the larger national stage. In *The Republican Noise Machine: Right-Wing Media and How It Corrupts Democracy,* David Brock demonstrates that deploying the term "political correctness" in anger and ridicule to beat up on the left has been a successful part of conservative assaults against affirmative action and many other progressive programs, personalities, and ideas, labeled PC and dismissed with contempt. For Rush Limbaugh—who is chronically unable to perceive nuance, complexity, or ambiguity in even the most complicated matters— anyone who disagrees with him is not only wrong but some kind of liberal, PC, wacko socialist. Indeed, in 1993 the term "political correctness"—though it was serving as an ideal cudgel in his hand (or should I say mouth?)—struck Limbaugh as "too polite and genteel." "From now on," he urged his followers, "let's call it political cleansing." Of course, he could have called it "political vomit," but that might have been more genteel than associating views contrary to his own with acts of ethnic mass murder. The appropriateness of the political cleansing frame for people who were trying (not to create killing fields but) to make American universities and businesses more welcoming to a diverse range of students and workers would indeed appear to violate not only the constraints of civil discourse but of logic as well—unless, unless, unless Limbaugh was ever so slightly kidding, which he certainly was, since no one has ever accused him of being "too polite and genteel." I will return to Limbaugh, clearly one of the most intentional humorists of these tendentious times, in upcoming discussions of environmental discourse and political joking, but before leaving him here I'll just note that on the radio and in his books he has taken delight in uncovering cases like the Cornell controversy and coming down hard on the politically cleansing PC "thought police" he first exposes and then exposes to ridicule. But, rather than exploring how this contest played out (and continues to play out) on the national stage, let's return to the Cornell disputants who, when we left them, were bound in self- and other-defining positions expressed in a range of angry rhetorics, serious and comic.[11]

Insofar as the Cornell controversy produced a circle of screaming that sounds like something out of a talk-show version of Dante's *Inferno*—"you're a bitch," "yeah, well, then you're an asshole," "no, no you're the asshole"—one yearns for a way to get beyond its recursive, self-sustaining assumptions. At the time of our on-line debate, research on humor and prejudice, as several participants noted, had not yet arrived at answers to questions about the psychological and social impact of disparaging humor that could clarify just who in the "75 Reasons" exchange was, in the less-than-elevated terms of accusation operative in the heat of the episode, the bigger asshole: those who gloried briefly in transgressive humor, those who (over)reacted to it, or those who (over)reacted to the (over)reaction. Interestingly, this has changed in the past few years as empirical research, though still in an early stage, has begun to reveal how disparaging jokes function within social systems.

A review of this work focusing on jokes based on gender and ethnicity brings us back to the contrast between Boskin and Oring described above, specifically to their distinctly different takes on the blond joke cycle that gathered force in the early 1990s. Like the "75 Reasons" e-mail, many blond jokes play around with assumptions about women as sex objects:

Q: What's the difference between a blond and a computer?
A: You only have to punch information into a computer once.

Q : What's the difference between a blond and a rooster?
A : In the morning a rooster says, "Cock'll-doodl-doooo," while a blond says, "Any-cock'll-doooo."

Q : How can you tell who is a blond's boyfriend?
A : He's the one with the belt buckle that matches the impression in her forehead.

Where Boskin, following the position advanced in Susan Faludi's 1991 *Backlash: The Undeclared War against American Women,* saw blond jokes as part of male "retaliation" for feminist advances, Oring insisted that they were not aimed aggressively at blonds or women in general. Rather than seriously asserting that blonds (or women) are stupid or sluttish, Oring argued, blond jokes expressed concerns about the need to render "values associated with traditional images of women" foolish. Such jokes, Oring argued, operate in the context of the movement of women into a wider range of workplace environments that cannot "accommodate stupidity or the disruptive forces of sexuality. In other words, women in the workplace should not in any way suggest that they are reminiscent of the dumb blond. They must be the stereotypical brunet: competent, intelligent, and asexual." Though philosophers and scholars have frequently lined up behind hostility- or social-correction-based approaches to humor function (as Boskin and Oring do here), the Freddy-Norman connection suggests that these are far from incompatible: that blond jokes can serve as both combative antifeminist backlash against and potentially helpful social corrective for women in the workplace.[12]

Fortunately, recent research has moved beyond speculation about how disparaging jokes affect prejudice. One study by Olsen et al. in 1999 found that being exposed to disparaging humor about men and lawyers did not increase the intensity or accessibility of stereotypes (for instance, that men are bull-headed or stubborn; that lawyers are greedy or arrogant). Limitations of this study, as the experimenters concede, however, include the use of privileged, rather than disadvantaged, butts and college-student subjects whose encounter with the humor occurs in the social isolation of a lab. Pending "nonlaboratory research with heterogeneous samples," the findings should be regarded as suggestive but inconclusive. Meanwhile, a growing body of research suggests that telling disparaging jokes (as opposed to being exposed to them by someone else) can increase both the teller's acceptance of stereotypes associated with and discrimination against the targeted groups.[13]

Though hearing disparaging jokes appears not to have negative effects on everyone, according to a series of experiments conducted by Thomas

E. Ford, they seem to relax inhibitions against disapproving of acts directed against members of the disparaged group in listeners who already feel antagonism toward the group. Subjects in Ford's experiment were exposed to sexist humor and then to a sexist event. If they had high ratings for hostile sexism at the outset, the humor seems to have made it easier for them to approve of the sexist behavior. "Collectively," Ford concluded, these "experiments demonstrated that exposure to sexist humor uniquely expanded the bounds of socially acceptable conduct, creating greater tolerance of sex discrimination among people high in hostile sexism." In their elaboration of what they call "prejudice norm theory," Ford and Mark A. Ferguson describe "the processes by which disparagement humor creates a normative climate of tolerance of discrimination—the social conditions that encourage the expression of prejudice—as well as variables that accentuate and attenuate its effects." Rod A. Martin concludes his review of studies in this area as follows: "Although simply telling such jokes is not likely to change other people's feelings about the targets of the jokes, for those who do have such attitudes, this kind of humor can implicitly communicate a level of social tolerance for prejudice which may help to perpetuate discrimination and social inequalities."[14]

One emerges from these empirical studies with the sense that, while more work needs to be done on how disparaging stereotype-based humor affects individuals and groups, the dispersion of it in a community can have negative consequences. This is clearly what Gary Spencer found in his 1989 study of Jewish American Princess (JAP) jokes on college campuses. Focusing on one university as a primary site, Spencer interviewed students, analyzed papers they wrote on JAP jokes, and took note of the treatment of JAPs in "posters and tee shirts, parodies and cartoons in student media, graffiti from various campus locations, and observations or corroborated reports of open taunting and harassment." Spencer noted that once JAP jokes focusing on their target's supposed materialism, narcissism, and lack of enthusiasm about sex were prevalent on the campus, they migrated into student publications in such Freddy-like examples as these:

Cartoon: A JAP-dressed female (oversized sweater, stirrup pants, highly polished nails, lots of jewelry, JAP-clip in hair) is surrounded by injured males in a ski lodge. The female is complaining that she has broken a nail. One male is thinking, "They ski?" Another is punching the female with a beer mug.

Three-paneled cartoon is labeled, "Three Endangered Species and the Reasons Why." The first panel shows a blue whale about to be harpooned. The second panel shows a bald eagle about to be hit by a pellet from a slingshot. The third panel shows a darkened bedroom labeled as the "Myron Hernowitz Family." A voice inside the panel says, "Not tonight. I have a headache."

And Spencer found such aggressive, mocking practices as "JAP alert" chants and JAP-joke-based carnival booths. For example, for a fee at a Prove-She's-Not-a-JAP carnival booth students at a campus fair could throw sponges at the "face of an ugly, open-mouthed JAP." If they made her swallow one, that proved she was "not a JAP." A similar booth allowed students to "SLAP A JAP" by hurling baseballs at "a life-sized, stuffed doll made to look like an obese JAP." The conclusion Spencer reached was that "JAP-baiting humor . . . result[ed] in the proliferation of negative stereo-typing, avoidance behaviors, and open harassment directed primarily at Jewish women." It may be, as Oring and Davies have argued, that such jokes are less about their apparent targets (however imagined: JAPS, Jews, or women in general) than about the joke tellers, but this may not provide much comfort to the harassed women who were taunted with chants of "JAP ALERT" as they made their way to their seats at football games or simply walked across campus. Moreover, even if JAP jokes expose a con-cern about such things as class status (JAPs are portrayed as being affluent) or sexual fulfillment (JAPs are represented as frigid women who do not put out), the demand for sexual servicing (implicit in the implication that women who do not provide oral sex and swallow ejaculated fluids are JAPs) can be overly aggressive (as in "What part of 'Don't Say NO' DON'T YOU UNDERSTAND?").[15]

The Spencer study highlights the potential relation between the as-sumption that disparaging jokes are socially acceptable and a predisposi-tion to think and act seriously, perhaps aggressively, on the stereotypes in such jokes. By way of another illustration in a different context, consider the experience of Police Chief Dave O'Malley of Laramie, Wyoming, who in 1998 supervised the investigation into the murder of Matthew Shepard, the gay University of Wyoming student who was picked up in a bar by two men who pretended to be gay and drove him to a remote area, bound him to a fence, and beat him severely. Five years later, looking back at the case, O'Malley told ABC news reporter Bryan Robinson that the experience made him rethink the humor culture in which he had been raised:

I was conservative. I bought into many of the stereotypes and I told many of the jokes associated with someone who is gay, I was close-minded. It's something I'm really ashamed of today.

"I was raised in a conservative, Irish-Catholic family in Kansas," O'Malley continued. "My father would joke around, saying 'There are no gays in Kansas. And if there are, they sure as hell ain't Irish.' . . . I lost my ignorance [after Shepard's slaying]."[16]

What do the Ford and Spencer studies suggest about the Cornell controversy, about whether offended students who saw the player's piece as misogynistic and administrators who pursued disciplinary action were right to be offended or concerned? Though Rush Limbaugh might bust his gut to hear it and though free speech defenders are right to defend free speech, the "75 Reasons" message especially in its original design as humor being shared with like-minded friends might well, had it passed from computer to computer without adverse reaction, encouraged some of its receivers (those with high levels of hostile sexism) to condone sexist acts. No doubt the avalanche of adverse e-mails the players received was a more constitutionally sound response than the official disciplinary action, but both were grounded in the plausible assumption that, if left unchallenged, sexist jokes told in particular situations can undermine norms that restrain misconduct and harassment.

What got out of hand in this case can be attributed to the intrusion of the Internet (mass e-mail exchanges) and the overwhelming publicity and exposure it brought to what was a college stunt. As a stunt it deserved a more local, less infamous, response. Prejudice norm theory suggests that the worst outcome would have resulted from a private uncritical sharing of the message among male students, some of whose antagonism toward women would have found support in a community of laughers. But the best outcome would also have been local and the result of criticism expressed by some offended fellow students (male and female) at Cornell. At its worst, disparaging humor can undermine norms that discourage discrimination, norms that can be reinforced by serious criticism and satiric rejoinders. A piece called "75 Reasons Why Men Should Stop Thinking with Their Dicks" published in the student newspaper would have been just about perfect.

A final thought about the Cornell controversy. To some extent this was a case of he said—she said: that is, he said "Freddy" and she said "Norman." At first blush, it looks as though almost criminal hostility ("38. If she can't speak, she can't cry rape") from the authors provoked disapproval from responders, whose idea of humor differed dramatically from theirs ("It is not a joke."). But then one notes the vehemence of the unamused feminists, some of whom sent the authors threatening messages, many of whom participated in sending what must have struck the authors as an avalanche of anger. Unlike positive humorists, these recipients of what they saw as an outrageous document were not prepared to laugh off their outrage. And, then, for all their surface hostility, the seventy-five reasons allude to familiar anxieties of male college students, including fear of competitive disadvantage ("9. Affirmative Action"), commitment ("16. I don't want to be made to lie and say 'I love you' after sex"), and unintended parenthood ("31. I could give a shit if you're pregnant"). To the extent that these reasons, the many others that crudely expressed sexual longing, and the laughter that no doubt accompanied the writing and sharing of the piece before all hell broke loose—to the extent that all this relieved the authors' stress and was not intended to be sent to unsympathetic readers—the exercise might almost have been therapeutic or, at least, far better than the worst consequences to which such feelings can lead. Still, the controversy heated up when unintended readers of the list found its barely concealed hostility offensive, almost criminal. By applying a moral frame to a heedless performance, they insisted that in a world in which women are subjected to violence, coercion, and intimidation, the last thing needed was a list of playful and amusing reasons why such treatment is justified. While PC codes went too far in assuming that all jokes about particular subjects are harmful, the opposite position—that humor is inherently too playful to be destructive—is equally misguided.

Speed Bumps on the Road to Ecotopia: Redwood Summer 1990, Rush Limbaugh, and Garry Trudeau

On May 24, 1990, before the radical environmentalist group Earth First! could launch its Redwood Summer season of protests in defense of old-growth forest, the mood darkened and the stakes were raised by the bombing of a car in which activist-folksingers Judi Bari and Darryl Cherney were traveling. Coupled with earlier, perhaps exaggerated, reports and rumors of potentially dangerous tree spiking and other acts of sabotage against logging equipment, the bombing made it clear that this struggle was being taken seriously by both sides. In ways that prefigured more recent conflicts, both Earth First! protesters and timber industry representatives characterized their opponents as terrorists. While protesters accused the timber workers of un-Christian behavior, workers accused members of Earth First! of being antilabor. A *New York Times* story that ran on July 10, 1990, described what it called a "war of nerves" fueled by suspicion and hostility: "In the logging industry, there are reports that environmentalists are over on the coast, about 35 miles west, conducting target practice with Uzi submachine guns." At the same time, environmentalists, "frightened by the explosion that severely injured Bari and demolished her car, point[ed] to stacks of hate mail and death threats that [were arriving] on a regular basis at the Mendocino Environmental Center in Ukiah." With both sides dug in, efforts on the part of environmentalists to bridge the gap by finding common ground with timber industry workers who had an interest in pursuing sustainable foresting practices sputtered. According to Ed Gehrman, who participated in Redwood Summer, "They planned also to organize the loggers who cut the trees and convince them that Earth First!'s call for sustainable logging would be the best long-term plan for the health of the community and the loggers and their families." But this is not how the conflict played out.[17]

Considering the stakes—on the one hand, the vulnerability of remaining West Coast old-growth trees, then down to just 5 percent of the prelogging expanse and shrinking, and, on the other, the loss of jobs—the fact that both sides deployed humor in the struggle is striking. Bumper stickers were a favorite medium for those opposed to what Earth First! was doing. These included "Save a Logger—Eat an Owl"; "I like spotted owls—fried!"; "Do you work for a living or are you an ENVIRONMENTALIST?"; "Earth First!ers, America's Favorite Speed Bumps"; and "Earth First! We'll Log the Other Planets Later." T-shirts worn to mock Earth First! said:

Spotted Owls on a Spit
Barbecue the Little Shit

During the Earth First! "Death March" through Fortuna, a logging town where, as Judi Bari wrote in 1991, "the national anthem is 'I'm a Lumberjack and I'm Okay,'" residents stood by wearing yellow T-shirts that were tauntingly comic variants of Earth First! originals. Some simply reproduced the Earth First! design of a clenched fist with the words "Earth First!" above and "NO!" below; others placed the words "Earth First!" inside a circle with a line drawn across; others showed an Earth First! supporter crucified on a tree with a spotted owl up his rectum.

Looking back at the response to Redwood Summer in a March 1991 article, Bari used memos exchanged between timber industry executives to support her contention that they were enjoying "belly laughs" over accounts of efforts to intimidate and attack environmentalists. In the passage below—included in a pro-industry publication mockingly called *The Sahara Club Newsletter* and discussed in a memo between Pacific Lumber's public relations director David Galitz and President John Campbell that became public as a result of civil litigation—Bari found "a sneering, bullying mentality worthy of any Mississippi good old boy":

The Sahara Club needs about a dozen volunteers to form a special division—The Sahara Clubbers! All Volunteers should weigh at least 200 pounds and have a bad attitude. Big, tall, ugly desert riders preferred. We want to set up a few trucks with Sahara Club stickers in "certain spots" and see who might be tempted to break the law. Naturally, the Clubbers will be expected to honor all laws, but if some Earth First scum resist a citizens [sic] arrest in the process, it may be necessary to "subdue" them prior to turning them over to the authorities. If interested, contact us by mail. All names will be carefully checked via the off-road grapevine. Clubbers will be issued personalized walking sticks about the size of baseball bats.[18]

On the other side, drawing on the earlier protest humor traditions of the Industrial Workers of the World (Wobblies) and Yippies, Earth First! wove humor into its meetings and actions, much of it by way of folk songs. Among these were Cherney's "Earth First! Maid," "They Sure Don't Make Hippies Like They Used To," "You Can't Clear Cut Your Way to Heaven," and, most memorably, "Spike a Tree for Jesus":

Now some say the Romans killed Jesus,
And some say it was the Jews,
And some say that it was King Herod,
And some say it was me and you—

But when I think of the cross he was nailed to
And the tree that was logged for the wood,
I realize 'twas the loggers killed Jesus,
And it's time that we got them back good.

Chorus:
So spike a tree for Jesus, spike a tree for Jesus,
And Jesus will love you you know.
Spike a tree for Jesus, spike a tree for Jesus,
And someday to heaven you'll go.

Now the logger who cut that old tree down
He was just going 'long with the mob.
When asked why he did it he answered
I was only just doing my job,
I don't care what they do with the timber

As long as they pay me my price.
They can go make a frame to hang a picture;
They can go make a cross to hang Christ.

Now as Jesus he hung on that cross there,
It was not some thing that he liked.
And his last words were "Father I would not be here,
If all of the trees had been spiked"!

Sung to the tune of "The Frozen Logger," virtually the anthem of the timber industry, "Spike a Tree for Jesus" taunts workers by associating clear cutting, the destruction of old growth forests, and their rationales for what they do for a living with the moral position of the people who killed Christ. The crass materialism, the amoral view of work and its consequences, and the denunciation put into the mouth of the dying Jesus amused members of Cherney's primary audiences: movement activists and potential recruits, especially on college campuses. But how did songs like this one affect the people they held up to ridicule and judgment?[19]

This was the question I put to Cherney in the winter of 2005, fifteen years after Redwood Summer drew international attention to the plight of virgin forests and three years after the jury in the civil case he and Bari brought against the FBI and Oakland police ruled in their favor and awarded them (Bari posthumously) 4.4 million dollars. When he performed "Spike a Tree for Jesus" during Redwood Summer, what was he hoping to accomplish? Did he think of it as intended for audiences of like-minded listeners or as "monkey-wrench" music that would add fuel to the already raging conflict? Insisting that few loggers ever heard this particular song, Cherney nonetheless defended its capacity for shaking people up, "getting them to think, laugh, and take the issue seriously." "Songwriters listen to their muses," Cherney said, noting that he wrote "Spike a Tree for Jesus" during the Reagan/Watts assault on environmental protection to counter what he saw as a religiously based, indeed apocalyptic, rationale for destroying the planet. In this and other movement songs, Cherney says, he has tried "to show the absurdity of organized religion" and to "write and speak without fear of potential reactions."[20]

How far has Cherney pushed this practice of deploying humorous lyrics to agitate and provoke? Well, in November 1988, a year and a half before Redwood Summer, he performed such ditties as "Right to Life Is Coming to Town," "Songs to Abort Fascism By" and "Will the Fetus Be Aborted?" (sung to the tune of "Will the Circle Be Unbroken?") at a pro-choice demonstration in Ukiah. Verses of the latter run:

Annie's pregnancy would kill her
The doctor's warning gave her strife
Fundamentalists said "Jesus take her"
She said "I want my right to life."

Brigit had two kids already
And an abortion is what she chose
Christians showed her a bloody fetus
She said, "That's fine, I'll have one of those!"

And the chorus:

Oh will the fetus be aborted
By and by Lord, by and by
There's a better home a-waiting
In the sky, lord, in the sky.

Taking "great pleasure in being as far out there as possible," Cherney dressed as a "back-alley abortionist" for the rally and joked at the time about the possibility that an outraged pro-life counterdemonstrator might be photographed beating him up with his own guitar and that photographs of the assault could initiate a pro-choice backlash. Parenthetically, as an illustration of the subjectivity of humor reception, consider this: while Cherney saw "Will the Fetus be Aborted?" as an attempt to heal the body politic, those who think of abortion as murder would undoubtedly see it as a killing joke.

Both sides of the Redwood Summer conflict assumed that political humor can have an impact. When an old photo of Bari wearing an Earth First! T-shirt and holding a machine gun surfaced, Bari's lawyer claimed that it was a joke. Earth First! activists had appeared at demonstrations dressed as spotted owls and other endangered animals, and pro-industry responses offered tit for tat. One in particular that Cherney recalled was a song written and performed by members of the Bandits, a Humboldt County country band that was performing regularly during Redwood Summer. The song, called "It Don't Pay to Be an Earth First!er," includes the following lyrics:

I was out in my logging truck one day
There was a guy in the road sitting right in my way
I said "Hey, buddy, you'd better get yourself out of there"
He said "I ain't gonna let you take those trees"

I said "Man, I've got to get to the mill with these"
He said "Over my dead body"
Whohoo! Pedal to the metal boys.

Chorus:
It don't pay to be an Earth First!er
It will only get you hurt real fast
It don't pay to be an Earth First!er
Cause if you join Earth First! you'll have a blast.

And, remarkably enough, the song goes directly at the postbombing Cherney and Bari, mocking and accusing them of criminal behavior:

Now it seems like Oakland had a little scare
From a well-known guitar totem [*sic*] pair
Yep, two Earth First!ers were packing a bomb
Well the FBI asked them about it
And the Oakland Police asked them about it
But they said, "Hey man we don't know what the hell's going on."

Well they got this thing called redwood summer
And personally I haven't heard of anything dumber
I think their brains have been in the sun too long
If they think they're going to take our jobs
By hanging around in great big mobs
Well let me tell you something folks, them people are dead wrong.

Final chorus:
Cause if you join Earth First! you'll have a blast
Cause if you join Earth First! you'll come in last
Cause if you join Earth First! you'll have a blast.

Looking back at Redwood Summer in 2005, the coauthor of this song, John Dias, insisted that it was meant to be funny but to convey the truth as well, to "make environmentalists look stupid" and show that there was "no excuse for what they did." When they performed it at a country showdown in 1990, "the place went crazy" with applause and hooting, he said.[21]

Cherney's take on these humor exchanges is instructive. In response to a question about whether his seemingly provocative lyrics were meant to open or close a dialogue with industry supporters, he insisted that they were supposed to "piss people off, to serve as acupressure for the earth." Like the 1960s Yippies, he has taken "great pleasure in being as far out there as possible, in making people think, laugh, and most important take [environmental issues] seriously." To his credit, Cherney has nothing but praise for the musical response served up by the Bandits. Though, or perhaps because, it was performed almost immediately after the bombing, he and Bari both felt "flattered" when they heard it. Later they learned and sang it often together. He continued, "Loggers and rednecks can be very physically violent. An expression comes to mind from one who after a brief, uneventful flurry of fists commented, 'Where we come from, we don't call that violence.' I'd apply that to the Bandit's song. Songs about oneself are rare to come by and this one is heartfelt, comes from personal experience, and fits perfectly with the folk tradition."

Because positions on environmental issues in our time have been developed by individuals and groups convinced that what they believe is not only correct but crucial, that so much depends on specific and long-term outcomes, that economic survival on the one hand and the preservation of life itself on the other hang in the balance—that is, because people are dug in and pissed off, threatened and committed—disputes generate a good deal of angry rhetoric. For the same reasons, they generate humor that is as likely to say "Drop dead" as "We all live in a yellow submarine." Or it might express both of these sentiments simultaneously, depending on "what you mean by we." Conflicts over issues like the destruction of habitats, the building of nuclear power plants, and the threat of global climate change are necessarily as much about empathy and identification as they are about science and economics. As the Redwood Summer jokes suggest, positions taken in environmental humor assume and delineate more or less inclusive circles based on assumptions about which living things have value or more value. Is it possible that other species are more (or differently) intelligent than we are? How far should empathy extend? Is meat murder? Conceding that different species can have competing needs, should this competition be managed thoughtfully in ways that serve the long-term health of the natural sphere within which it occurs?

Beyond and above the confines of the struggle to preserve jobs and/or old-growth forests in Humboldt County in which humor may have both intensified hostility and defused (without preventing or eliminating) violence, environmental disputes and ideological warfare about them have carried on in mixed moods and tones: the deadly seriousness of the arguments requiring forays into both nurturing and aggressive comedy. On the national level, representative if also distinctive versions of contending positions on environmental issues can be found in battling humor styles—as seen in the jokes and parodies of Rush Limbaugh and the cartoons of Garry Trudeau. To the extent that Limbaugh has an environmental philosophy, it is based on a Darwinian notion of the place of humanity in a natural, violent sphere in which animals kill and devour each other. In his first book, *The Way Things Ought to Be*, published in 1992 when the events of Redwood Summer were current, he includes an imaginary dialogue about "who is threatening the [spotted] owl" between himself and a "long-haired maggot-infested FM-type environmentalist wacko." In the exchange Rush not only has the better arguments but repeatedly interrupts the conversational flow with comments designed to make sure that every reader will see this. Here's a sample:

"Okay," I said. "Would you then say that the human species is far superior to any other species?" "Well, man, let me think about that." You see, they don't want to admit that, but it's true.

"Would you say the owl has evolved to a superior position over the mouse?" I asked. "Oh, yeah, man, an owl can fly, he sees at night, man."

As the imaginary discussion progresses through an account of an owl hunting, killing, and eating a mouse, Rush describes himself as using "pure logic" to trap the environmentalist in a corner and close in for "the conversational kill": "Well, there you have it, I told him. If the owl can't adapt to the superiority of humans, screw it."[22]

The factual basis of many of Limbaugh's supposedly serious arguments about environmental processes and regulation has been successfully challenged by both the independent media watch group Fairness and Accuracy in Reporting and others who have demonstrated his willful ignorance and refusal to acknowledge his many mistakes. Even as I write these words, that is in May of 2005, long after the scientific community achieved virtual consensus about the gathering menace of global climate change, Limbaugh continues to ridicule this notion as pseudoscience used to perpetrate an environmental hoax. And this is encouraging the Bush administration (not that it needs much encouragement in this area) to continue to drag its feet on international efforts to reduce the production of greenhouse gases. There's no doubt that Limbaugh's claim that it is impossible for the human race to have a potentially catastrophic impact on God's world would require a serious upgrade to reach the level of pseudoscience at a time when thermonuclear weapons (a human product, yes?) have the capacity to exterminate life on a global scale and initiate nuclear winter. This is obvious to objective observers familiar with the underlying science and technology. But Limbaugh has never had to worry much about negative feedback because, so far from relying on "pure logic," he shamelessly exploits every fallacious trick in the book and a few he himself has perfected, including many that depend on hostile humor (argumentum ad Freddy?). In the dialogue above, he stacks the deck first by offering a comic description of his interlocutor and then by having the "maggot-infested" environmentalist fall easy prey to the swooping, razor-clawed Rush. (This is no doubt easy to do when you get to write both sides of the exchange, as easy, say, as screening out critical, intelligent callers from a syndicated radio show.) Rather than advancing a view based on the preservation of habitats in which many species coexist and thrive, the "long-haired" one gropes for ideas and gasps when Rush puts forth the "truth" that since owls kill mice, people shouldn't worry about killing owls. Following Rush's account of an animal TV show his interlocutor has seen in which a "mouse gets eaten by the owl headfirst, with its little legs dangling out," all the environmentalist "can say" is "Oh, God, why am I watching this?" With Rush swooping, the environmentalist sinking and calling on God for relief that will not be forthcoming, we are in Freddy's world where victory goes not to the swift or the deserving but to the cunningly, playfully cruel.[23]

As with Freddy, Rush's attacks work through humor to shift identification and empathy. Though "pure logic" would veer away from insult and mockery, environmentalists, according to Limbaugh, are "kookburgers," "nutso," "dunderheaded alarmists and prophets of doom." Deploying a rhetoric of reversal and incongruity, Limbaugh calls the notion that industrial and postindustrial technologies can be dangerous to life on a planetary scale, that our acts have put Earth in the balance, "humanity vanity"—which is (to him) the obviously unbelievable and ridiculous view that "man can come along, all by himself, and change everything for the worse; that after hundreds of millions of years, the last two generations of human existence are going to destroy the planet." The scientists whose work underpins this worldview are "incredibly arrogant" in assuming that they can unlock "every mystery of the universe." Their approach is "presumptuous," in arriving at conclusions he both resents and "refuses to believe." But refusing to believe something, as the creators of the "theory" of intelligent design have unwittingly demonstrated, is not a valid point in a logical proof. Still, who needs logic when one is a veritable fount of put-downs based on the simple trick of ascribing your own greatest flaws (arrogance, ignorance, presumptuousness, intolerance, and stupidity) to those who have the temerity to challenge your views?[24]

When Limbaugh closes in for the kill and startles his defenseless, cring-ing, mousey opponent, reducing him to the level of the "cow'rin', tim'rous beastie" Robert Burns turned up with his plow, he does so by sug-gesting that when endangered species threaten human jobs, it's all right to kill, that is, "screw" them. The humor here plays against norms of com-passion as seen widely in the culture, for instance, in Dr. Seuss stories and in Disney movies featuring talking animals who have been singing Cin-derelli, Cinderelli and celebrating the "circle of life" for decades. Indeed, you have to be tapping your razor claws loudly to achieve the right tone of antisentimentalism in speaking the way Limbaugh routinely does about animals.

This is exactly the spirit that Limbaugh brings to the environmental updates and commercial parodies played on his radio program and archived on his Web page. A recent "Animal Rights Update" consists of Frank Sinatra's cover of "Born Free" with two added sound tracks, the first of which features the calls, whinnies, and cries of various animals, the second bursts of automatic weapons fire. It is a bit difficult to find or fol-low a plotline through this montage, since both the animal sounds and the gunfire seem to last throughout the song, suggesting, I guess, that we can kill animals at will and still preserve the balance of nature. The "Timber Update," also included in Excellence in Broadcasting public service an-nouncements, starts with the firing up of a chain saw to a strong rock music background and features a gleeful voice repeatedly shouting out "Timber!" as large trees are heard cracking and falling to the ground. Among the Excellence in Broadcasting commercial parodies are the "Chipmunk Cookbook," the perfect Christmas gift for those who enjoy carols about "chipmunks roasting on an open fire"; "The Dolphin Tuna Commercial," which promotes a brand of tuna that is "chocked full of dolphins" because its manufacturer refused to "bend over and drop its pants" for "animal rights activists"; and an ad for "The Road Kill Restau-rant," where customers pick out living animals to eat and end up with both a meal and "a new pair of gloves." Dishes include "racoonaroni" and "chincilli." "Hey Billy," a mother asks, "How's that possum?" "Awe-some," her son replies. And the ad concludes: "Earth Cafeteria: You choose it, we kill it, you wear it home. Next to the Shelter on Highway 92." In addition to these gleeful celebrations of human superiority (not to be confused with "humanity vanity"), Limbaugh regularly attacks smoking-restriction laws as Nazi plots and assails energy efficient tech-nology. In "The Next Generation Washing Machine," he describes an ap-pliance that has a hand-turned crank and uses just a "half of a cup of water" and "fifty pounds of pebbles" to wash clothes. The point of all this hilarity is intended to be clear: humans do and should rule the planet, all other life is subservient to our needs, government environmental regulations are fascistic restraints on free enterprise, and companies that respond to the demands of environmentalists are weak.[25]

At both the other end and in the moderate center of U.S. political discourse, using cartoons to assail Republican environmental policies kicked into high gear during the Reagan administration as a response to the appointment of and then work of such deregulators as James Watt (secretary of the interior) and Ann Gorsuch Buford (Reagan's first Environmental Protection Agency administrator), who oversaw a weakening of strip-mining rules, the opening of national forests to increased logging and extraction, and expansion of off-shore oil drilling. Lines of attack focused on specific regulatory decisions, legislative proposals, and general attitudes, including Watt's habit of seeing the value of protecting the environment in relation to an impending apocalypse. Asked in February 1981 about the importance of preserving resources for future generations, Watt replied positively but went on to say "I do not know how many future generations we can count on before the Lord returns." This is the same secretary of the interior who described environmentalists as "a left-wing cult dedicated to bringing down the type of government I believe in." With material like this, satire writes itself.[26]

Something like this sense of the extremism and absurdity of conservative ideas about environmental protection (and other topics) underpins the approach Garry Trudeau has taken in *Doonesbury,* the widely published strip he has written and drawn since 1969. Frequently, with his readers in mind, he allows the actual words spoken by right-wing politicians or media figures to serve as self-parody. Examples of this include his repeated send-ups of Limbaugh that ask readers to find the seven or ten lies in brief quoted examples of Rush's actual on-air comments (for instance, Trudeau's strips of July 15 and August 21, 1994). Alternatively, Trudeau will exaggerate Limbaugh's habit of exaggeration (not so easy to do) by having him insinuate, for example, that Hillary Clinton was Prince Charles's secret mistress (July 14, 1994) and by mocking Rush's "it coulda happened" defense (December 16–20, 1997).[27]

In addition to James Watt, *Doonesbury* frequently went after Newt Gingrich, Speaker of the House and author of the Contract with America, which helped the Republicans take over the House of Representatives in 1994. Drawn as a round, black bomb with a brightly burning fuse, Newt was pilloried by Trudeau for, among other things, trolling for campaign contributions, advocating nineteenth-century orphanage policies, supporting tobacco companies, espousing family values hypocritically, and undermining conservation law. Opposed in the latter effort by Representative Lacey Davenport, an old-school Republican who believes that protecting resources and national park lands is a conservative value, Newt (as bomb) is shown auctioning off assets and land-use rights in national parks for a pittance. In the January 1, 1996, strip, for instance, the Newt-bomb sells an old-growth tree in the Tongass National Forest for $1.46, exclaiming gleefully about the funds he is raising for the federal treasury, "Now that's deficit reduction!"

In a series of strips that ran in November of 1995 when the Republican Congressional majority was attempting to attach pro-industry riders to the EPA funding bill, Davenport objects and the Newt-bomb scolds her in response. Reading from the legislation, she asks why he has been so "quiet on what's in the bill," such as an "exemption for oil refineries from toxic air standards, . . . [and a] ban on wetlands protection programs." He replies in Limbaughesque terms, "Because they don't need to know. The only people who care about this stuff are eco-terrorists and a few bird-loving nuts." She says, "My husband was a birder, Mr. Speaker." And he says, "So get a new dating service." In this and other strips where, for instance, Newt enters Davenport's office without knocking or expresses contempt for other people's views, Trudeau emphasizes the connection between political extremism and personal rudeness.

Perhaps because Trudeau was pleased to see the Reagan crowd depart, criticism of the first President Bush on environmental grounds was muted in *Doonesbury*. In the April 22, 1990, strip, he has Bush senior calling himself an environmentalist while refusing to pay for necessary cleanups since this would require him to make difficult choices. The final panel shows a polluted and littered ocean shoreline with the president saying that his policy is based on a word "found in nature itself: coast." But no such restraint characterizes Trudeau's treatment of the second Bush's approach to the environment. Assailed for appointing big oil executives to sensitive regulatory positions (July 30, 2000), ignoring global weather science (October 20, 2002), and backpedaling on clean water (April 20, 2001), Bush junior appears as a floating cowboy hat below which lurks an inarticulate and scatterbrained fool. On September 29, 2002, Trudeau devoted a Sunday strip to reviewing recent Bushisms; more often he will work halting and wacky comments into the president's remarks, as he does in the April 18, 2001, column in which Bush defends himself at an Earth Day podium in a national park: "I know some of my adversarials are saying I'm not naturalistic," he says, "But I feel very close to our leading species, our good American species, the best species in the world." When a reporter asks whether he feels close to any species "in particular," Bush replies "Sure! 'Bear-meister'! 'Bunny-boy'! 'Antler Guy'"!

While the *Doonesbury* take on the Republican repudiation of traditionally nonpartisan conservation law has been clear from the start, and while the resignation of Representative Davenport in 1990 offered an early foreshadowing of the hard right turn of the national Republican Party, Trudeau has brought an appreciation for nuance and cultural contradiction to his satire that from a purely political perspective may dilute its impact. While Limbaugh misses no opportunity to lambaste environmentalists, Trudeau agonizes over conflicting values, as in the September 2–7, 2002, strips in which Alex puts fake tickets on parked SUVs and her father, Mike Doonesbury, supports the right of individuals to make their own decisions. In the strip that ran on September 3, 2002, Alex explains that: "At first people think they're getting tickets. Then they realize it's something worse—a stinging rebuke from a fellow citizen for making such a selfish choice in buying a . . . gas-guzzling, rollover-prone menace." When Mike asks "What comes after that," Alex's response reveals a mixed sense of inflated self-importance and an ability to laugh at herself when she says, "insight, guilt, contrition and atonement. At least that's what we shoot for."

This sense of contending values (seen in the contrast between the inflated religious language and the deflation of lower expectations that ends her response) is more fully explored in a series that ran around Earth Day in 1990 in which Mike struggles with Zonker's purist approach to environmental issues. According to Zonker, it should be Earth Month and everyone should adhere to the greenest standards, including waking up at sunrise to conserve electricity (April 16), separating reusable and compostable garbage, boycotting PVCs, investing in durables, sensitizing local officials (April 18), biking to work (April 21), and taking extreme care about what one eats (for instance, avoiding shellfish because they're polluted, tuna because dolphins are killed in catching them, meat and dairy products because "the farms are inhumanely run," and salad unless it has "been rinsed of radioactive dust and pesticides" [April 19]). Trying to take Zonker's advice, Mike orders just water at a restaurant and then buys a hot dog on the street, only to endure pangs of paranoia and guilt as he imagines that other people who see him eating it are saying such things as: "Hope you enjoy your meat!" "There goes another rain forest!" "Look! He's wearing leather shoes, too!" "Assassin!" "Polluter!" And Mike's struggle in the April 18 strip (fig. 14) over how to dispose of a gum wrapper falls somewhere between satire and tragedy. The idea that this tormented (psychologically toxic?) flow of anxiety and uncertainty is an en-

vironmentalist's way of "celebrating," that it is impossible as a citizen in contemporary America not to contribute to pollution, is a familiar part of antienvironmentalist criticism of anguished, perfectionist, hypocritical latte liberals. Trudeau's willingness to laugh about such dilemmas, stepping away from hard-edged advocacy to explore cultural and personal contradictions, suggests that the satirical thrust of *Doonesbury* is tempered, restrained by its creator's curiosity about and empathy for the complexities of contemporary life. Though he may miss opportunities to, in Limbaugh's memorable phrase, "move in for the [rhetorical] kill," he no doubt provides Norman-like moments of detached amusement, self-examination, and relaxation to readers who see themselves in his conflicted characters.

Laughing on the Left, Laughing on the Right: Stand Up, Sit Down, Fight, Fight, Bite!

With no apparent disdain for tautology, mirth advocates and boosters assert that—because it allows us to see all sides of an issue, refrain from taking ourselves (too) seriously, and achieve balance—a good sense of humor is, well, good for us. According to Goodheart, mere laughter (and, of course, there's nothing mere-ish about laughter for the author of a book subtitled *How to Laugh about Everything in Your Life That Isn't Really Funny*) has a transformative impact on how we think and who we are: "Our thoughts, greased for spontaneity by laughter, create a more flexible being. . . . Each time we laugh readily, we reinstate a portion of our authentic selves." Even those movement members who prefer to take their laughter not straight up but with humor, like John Morreall and Paul E. McGhee, emphasize the importance of the experience of being amused to increasing intellectual flexibility. According to Morreall, "Humor gets us to shift our perspective" by allowing us to "avoid mental ruts" and "take advantage of what is new and different in each situation." And McGhee offers a useful sense of how to take political and social dangers seriously without allowing them to become overwhelming:

You may feel that people who are sometimes light and playful are shallow and oblivious to the real problems of the world. After all we have cancer, violent crime, unspeakable atrocities committed in the midst of war, chaos and hopelessness in our inner cities, racism, pollution, and more. You should take these conditions seriously. But if you want to improve the quality of your life, one key is learning to maintain your commitments to change these conditions, while taking yourself less seriously in the process.

Intellectual benefits like these, coupled with large claims about the healing power of humor and an unquantifiable sense that ours is a humor-starved culture, led Allen Klein to assert and many others to imply that "mirthmyopia is perhaps today's greatest disease."[28]

Just as Freddy casts a menacing shadow over upbeat generalizations about humor functions and effects, so engaged, partisan, and pointed joking suggests that, while humor can promote flexibility and detachment, it also works very well in expressing hardened attitudes that can be moderate or extreme, enlightened or depraved. While the "75 Reasons" list was neither violent nor criminal, and while its ideas deserve First Amendment protection, the piece does not develop a balanced range of perspectives on male-female relationships. While Darryl Cherney is right to see the country song "It Don't Pay to Be an Earth First!er"—which celebrated the antienvironmentalist bombing that severely wounded his lover, Judi Bari, and warned others about joining Earth First!'s ranks—as an alternative to violence, the song itself expresses the one-sided, angry, and inflexible views of the pro-logging industry workers who wrote it. Indeed, it may well be not so much that humor in general promotes intellectual and emotional flexibility as that a flexible mindset is more likely to use humor to express the broad range of ideas it entertains. What came first for Rush Limbaugh: intellectual rigidity (or the performance of this) or a wicked sense of humor? What came first for Garry Trudeau: a profound sense of the complex, ironic, even tragic nature of existence or the ability to laugh at himself? Why, in short, did both the chicken and the egg cross the road?

Exchanges between jokes and antijokes call attention to the interaction between humor and commitment: humor as detachment and attachment. Though one finds such events widely dispersed—indeed, wherever a joke is told and someone disapproves of it—a few additional high-profile examples chosen from various areas of U.S. culture will allow us to continue focusing on ethical questions raised by these conflicts as they have bubbled up in recent years. Or, to put this another way: What do Strom Thurmond, Abraham Lincoln, Vermont Teddy Bears, and Jesus Christ have in common? No, not Mel Gibson. And, no, they're not all superstars. Each of these seemingly disparate subjects has figured in the kind of value-revealing humor controversy that flares up in our variously divided culture.

Item: On December 5, 2002, Senator Trent Lott (R-Mississippi and, at the time but not for much longer, majority leader) followed Bob Dole to the podium at the hundredth birthday party for Senator Strom Thurmond and offered comments that would catapult him to the top of the list of embarrassed and self-destructive Republican joke tellers that included Earl Butz and James Watt. Prior to Lott's speech, Bob Dole (well known for both electoral and erectile dysfunction) had been at the mike, kidding around with the hundred-year-old Thurmond about arranging a date for him with Britney Spears. Though such sexual innuendoes (about Thurmond's fondness for the Hooters restaurant chain and for groping young women) were flying from the podium, Lott's comment about the segregationist 1948 Dixiecrat presidential candidate's rejection at the polls turned out to be incendiary: "I want to say this about my state: When Strom Thurmond ran for president, we voted for him. We're proud of it. And if the rest of the country had followed our lead, we wouldn't have had all these problems over all these years, either."

Perhaps because there is nothing joke-like about the text of this comment (except, perhaps, having the audacity to say it in public), or perhaps because the response was a mixture of stunned silence and awkward laughter, it took a news cycle for it to emerge from other comments as a failed-humor gaffe. But when it did Lott had to scramble, issuing increasingly accommodating apologies and insisting that he had only been kidding. Along with the serious condemnation, the senator was soon to realize that in the heated post-9/11, post-2000-presidential-race climate, those to whom humor is done (in this case the body politic) do humor in return. Once the dam burst, the flood of jokes included: "Trent Lott has found himself in a lot of trouble over his comments. . . . Keep in mind Lott only says this kind of stuff once every twenty-two years. We like to think of him as the Halley's Comet of bigotry" (Jon Stewart); "Trent Lott said his remarks were a mistake of the head and not the heart. No, that rabid squirrel hairpiece you wear is a mistake of the head" (David Letterman); and "That's why I think the government has been running such a huge deficit. Trent Lott didn't want it operating in the black" (Jay Leno). Ironically pretending to agree with Lott, Roy Douglas Malonson, writing for the African-American

News and Issues blog, insisted that the senator was wrong to apologize for truthfully saying that a Thurmond presidency would have solved the "problem" "White America" has faced in dealing with "freed slaves": "trying to keep the nation's best and brightest in their place."[29]

Item: Babe Lincoln. Winter 2005 saw the release of a controversial biography: C. A. Tripp's *The Intimate World of Abraham Lincoln.* Tripp's thesis—that Lincoln was attracted to men and slept with at least two of them, including for an eight-month period during his presidency when he repeatedly shared a bed with the captain of his bodyguards, David Derickson—provoked responses that ranged from historical critique to comic representation. Examples of the former include critical reviews by Princeton historian Christine Stansell and Rutgers historian David Greenberg. While Stansell sought to place Lincoln's known behavior in this area in the context of mid-nineteenth-century norms of male friendship, questioning Tripp's inclination to both cherry pick facts and ignore "the distinctions between homosexual acts (which have been around forever) and a full-blown gay identity (which is a relatively recent phenomenon)," Greenberg railed on-line at Slate.com against what he characterized as Tripp's "tendentious, sloppy, and wholly unpersuasive farrago."[30]

The Tripp kerfuffle inspired several cartoons, including Robert Grossman's representation of "Babe Lincoln" in the January 24, 2005, issue of the *Nation* (fig. 15). Of the eight letters about the cartoon that the editors chose to include in the February 14 issue, only one defended the artist from the angry responses that had already appeared on the magazine's Web site. The positive comment, offered by one Jorge Pontual, said that "it's worrisome that a mild, sweetly funny and even affectionate take on Lincoln's alleged gayness should cause such a rabid response." Like most humor-gaffe defenders, Pontual called on critics to lighten up and retract their fangs. But most letter writers railed against what they saw as Grossman's retrograde cartoon for obscuring the distinction "between gender and sexuality" by depicting Lincoln as "a cross-dresser rather than a gay man" (Ira Elliott); perpetuating "the old stereotype of male homosexuality as being all about drag" (Stephen C. Bandy); and associating "'gay' and 'woman in a man's body'" (Larry Gross).[31]

These responses, accompanied by a feeling that the cartoon was "deeply and painfully insulting" (John Berendt), provide evidence for Janet Bing and Dana Heller's analysis of the functions of lesbian humor. According to these authors, jokes about lesbians shared by lesbians (as distinct from jokes told by heterosexuals about them) frequently serve as an affirming "narrative means of self-construction" that "undermines the externally imposed definition of lesbianism." Bing and Heller offer the

FIGURE FIFTEEN. "Babe Lincoln," © Robert Grossman in the *Nation* January 24, 2005, by permission.

following example of a joke that "works to challenge the dominant culture's . . . dehumanizing reduction of the lesbian to sexual actor":

QUESTION: What does a lesbian bring on the second date?
ANSWER: A U-Haul.

"The question that leads into the joke," Bing and Heller suggest, sets up an expectation that the answer will include "sex toys, sexual paraphernalia, or objects that carry sexual reference." But since the answer focuses instead on nonsexual ideas—about how "lesbians tend to disregard bourgeois courtship rituals" and to behave in self-reliant ways (in this case by moving themselves)—the joke resists "dominant cultural definitions."[32]

Stunned by the volume of angry letters, the *Nation* editors apologized, saying that they "deeply regretted having offended anyone," as did the cartoonist who described his creative process in an effort to explain how it bypassed his own progressive filters: "When I read a review in the *New York Times* of C. A. Tripp's [book], the words 'Babe Lincoln' suddenly ran through my mind, rendering me helpless. In the impoverished mental landscape of a cartoonist this is what passes for true inspiration. I knew that gay men were not necessarily effeminate, cross-dressers or bearded ladies but I couldn't let that prevent me from having my laugh. Better a cheap and infantile joke than no joke at all, or so I thought." The level of disappointment expressed by readers of this progressive magazine highlights both the fragmentation and embattled condition of the left. Rather than treating "Babe Lincoln" as nonthreatening and playful in-group humor offered within a community that supports gay rights, offended letter writers took it as a serious statement about what it means to be gay. Some, like Doug Ireland, worried about how the cartoon would be viewed and used in "the political context in which we live": "We've just come through an election the Republicans won, in part, by bashing gay people over the head with odious stereotypes and discriminatory referendums. That makes running this cartoon, which pretends that a man who loves a man really wants to be a woman—the oldest canard in the world—even more insulting." Not all jokes about gays and lesbians are created equal; one expects different approaches from, say, Kate Clinton or Ellen DeGeneres and the lout standing by the water cooler with his mouth fixed in a twisted grin, apparently eager to tell you the one about "these lesbians, see, they go into this bar and walk right up to this guy . . ." Objectors found the cartoon insulting precisely because of where it appeared: in a progressive magazine they read with the expectation that it will offer respite from the rising conservative tide. Because it struck them as providing ammunition to their political foes, indeed as humor only those foes would enjoy, the *Nation* readers were distressed. Expecting Norman, they felt Freddy's ungentle fingers flashing close, and shuddered.[33]

Item: Not so crazy for laughter. Aware of the power of labeling, mental health organizations and individuals have in recent years objected when print and radio ads have played off the multiple meanings of the word "crazy," as in serious mental illness versus unconventional behavior or intense devotion. In April of 1992, the *New York Times* Business Section ran a story about two such controversies. The first involved a radio ad for the New York State Lottery's Crazy 8's game in which "when an announcer asks a man why he plays Crazy 8's, he [the man] says he is 'crazy,' 'cuckoo,' 'nuts,' and 'riding off the rails like a runaway train.'" When listeners objected to the ad, it was pulled off the air. In a print ad for Daffy's, a chain of New Jersey-based clothing stores, that was running around the same time, a picture of a straightjacket appeared above the words "IF YOU'RE PAYING OVER $100 FOR A DRESS SHIRT, MAY WE SUGGEST A JACKET TO GO WITH IT?" Critics quoted in the *Times* article include Jean Arnold of the Alliance for the Mentally Ill of New York State, who said, "People who suffer these illnesses are really damaged by having society treat them in a flippant way. That stigma is the burden they find hardest to deal with," and Katina Zachmanoglou of the Friends and Advocates of the Mentally Ill who said, "that stigma is at the core of why this illness is ignored [and] ads like this shape public thinking, and public thinking shapes policy."[34]

With these earlier controversies as precedent, the Vermont Teddy Bear Company could have expected trouble when, for Valentines Day 2005, it added the Crazy for You Bear to its line of such favorites as the Movin' On Up Bear, the Bride and Groom Bears, the Feel Better Bear, and the Golfer Bear. The bears, in either tan or brown, came dressed (or wrapped) in white straightjackets with bright red hearts at throat level and with "commitment" papers that play around with the association of the word with both romantic engagement and institutionalization. At the company Web site, the on-line promotional text read:

She'll Go Nuts over This Bear
15″ Crazy for You Bear

Dressed in a white straight jacket embroidered with a red heart, this Bear is a great gift for someone you're crazy about. He even comes with a "Commitment Report" stating "Can't Eat, Can't Sleep, My Heart's Racing. Diagnosis—Crazy for You!" Trust us. She'll go nuts over this Bear!

In a letter to the company's CEO, Jerry Goessel, executive director of the Vermont Chapter of the National Alliance for the Mentally Ill, wrote, "I was dismayed this morning to learn of your company's use of involuntary psychiatric treatment to promote the sales of a Valentine's Day product. As advertised on your Web page, the 'Crazy for You Bear' is a tasteless use of marketing that stigmatizes persons with mental illness." As criticism intensified, Elisabeth Robert, CEO of the Vermont Teddy Bear Company, resigned as a member of the Fletcher Allen Health Care board of trustees, saying that the controversy distracted from her "ability to serve effectively." And the company agreed to pull the bear once existing product sold.[35]

The controversy stirred mixed responses on the nearby campus of Middlebury College. As reported in the student newspaper, undergraduate Maggie Higgins (class of 2008) felt that the stuffed animal had "a really cute name, which does not have a negative context, but a not so cute image," while her classmate Richard Daniel said "I think it's funny, but I can see where these groups [such as the National Alliance for the Mentally Ill] are coming from." Weary of what can easily be seen as yet another PC critique of humor, many people who read about the issue no doubt agreed with Marshall Traverse, a Middlebury dorm resident adviser who said "I don't feel it should have caused that much controversy."[36]

And yet—considering that the mascot for our largest fast-food chain is a clown, and that an incredibly cute bull terrier named Spuds Mackenzie, called "The Official Party Animal" was featured in Bud Light commercials in the late 1980s until Mothers Against Drunk Driving complained that the fun-loving "spokesdog" was selling alcohol to underage drinkers—there are uses of humor in advertising that strike a much broader spectrum of U.S. opinion as raising ethical questions. For, along with the artery-clogging Ronald and beer-'n-babe beast Spuds, there was Joe Camel, the multitalented and appealingly anthropomorphized animal who, until halted by litigation, was sent out into the world to promote the carcinogenic products of the R. J. Reynolds Company.

With Joe's eroticized nose and mouth, one did not need to probe for subliminal imagery to find sex appeal, but the humor in the campaign was less obvious. With its overlapping of human and animal scripts, Joe's depiction as a man-beast often seen living the good life playing tennis or riding in motor boats with attractive women could be amusing. Beyond this, Joe was featured as a member of the rock band Hard Pack, the members of which wore Blues Brothers suits and sunglasses and were said to have recorded such "classics" as "Song for an Old Flame" and "Empty Lighter Blues," while the Camel Cash program ran on a set of matchbooks (fig. 16) that included comic pieces of "Joe's Smooth Philosophy"—such as "The early bird usually falls asleep before the party starts" and "ON SMOKE RINGS: once you've mastered the art, try making squares." This may seem amusing until you realize that at the height of the campaign American kids were more familiar with the death-bringing camel than with Mickey Mouse and that they associated him with cigarettes. As evidence mounted during the early 1990s that Joe was effectively marketing tobacco to children—the company terminated him, bringing the career of America's most lethal killing joker to an abrupt end. Wesleyan psychology professor Scott Plous's oppositional campaign, built around the antijoke character Joe Chemo (fig. 17), offered a "not so funny" alternative to the industry's dromedary of doom.[37]

FIGURE SIXTEEN. Joe Camel matchbooks. Photographer: Stephen E. Vedder, Media Technology Services, Boston College.

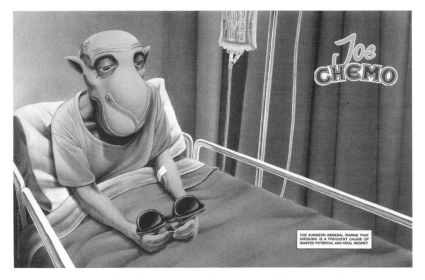

FIGURE SEVENTEEN. "Joe Chemo" © Scott Plous at www.adbusters.com, by permission

When Plous noted that "although Joe Chemo may seem like a joke, there's nothing funny about chemotherapy," he meant not to minimize the efforts of cancer ward clowns (the Norman side of chemotherapy humor) but to assail the use of humor in persuading children to smoke (the Freddy side). When we consider that a 1991 study in the *Journal of the American Medical Association* found that "Camel's share of the illegal children's cigarette market segment . . . increased from 0.5% to 32.8% [during the first three years of the ad campaign], representing sales estimated at $476 million per year, [and concluded that the] Old Joe Camel cartoon advertisements [were] far more successful at marketing Camel cigarettes to children than to adults"—it's hard not to conjure the image of the Reynolds board of directors listening to quarterly reports, morphing into Freddies, and laughing all the way to the bank.[38]

Conclusion

On any given day in America, people tell jokes that others find distasteful or offensive. Casting our minds back over the past twenty-five years, it's appropriate to ask: Have you heard the ones about Ethiopian famine sufferers, dead babies, bleeding nuns, and hundreds of lawyers (or therapists, gays, feminists, African Americans or terrorists) at the bottom of a river? About the exploding or burning up space shuttle? About the victims of 9/11, the African genocide, Pacific tsunami, or New Orleans hurricane? Disagreements about jokes like these, about ad campaigns intended to be amusing but objected to on grounds of taste and social impact, and about jokes told by individuals that provoke angry outcries, as well as the self-congratulatory posturing of the supposedly deeply offended, have all become familiar parts of an American culture not just divided but fragmented along lines highlighted by contests between humor appreciation and its opposite. Indeed, one legacy of the PC/anti-PC struggles of the 1980s and 1990s is a default mode of antagonism to jokes that strike a nerve, seem indifferent or hypersensitive to suffering, and/or evoke unwelcome images. Everyone scorns political correctness until his or her own ox is gored.

These contests between the impulses to seek and to resist humor occur along the outward moving edges of acceptable transgression and have become conventional and, therefore, expected, even predictable, in the way they (re)stage familiar conflicts. Objecting to a particular joke by recounting a serious antijoke in refutation (for instance, dead-baby jokes versus photographs of aborted fetuses) can be purely an expression of personal preference, a way of saying "I didn't think that was amusing and here's why, you jerk!" But it can also be based on concern about how the joke and others like it operate in wider social or political contexts. At any moment a shared joke, witticism, wisecrack, or put-down can present a dilemma to ethical listeners. It's true that we instinctively seek the pleasure, camaraderie, and relaxation of shared humor. Beyond this, if we are in pain or anxious, we may crave distraction. And yet between the stimulus and our response, humor and amusement, questions can rise: What if joining in laughter about the evoked images and ideas would be tactless or cruel? What if the distraction, pain, or anxiety-reduction on offer could be hurtful to others?

Torn between your inner Freddy and inner Norman, between cutting humor and blessed laughter, perhaps prayer can be of assistance. But, then, to which deity, demigod, prophet, spirit guide, or saint should you pray? (Readers familiar with *The Daily Show* are encouraged to think of the rest of this paragraph as a version of its regular feature "The Week in God.") Would it be appropriate to consult (beep) taboo-violating Hopi clowns, or (beep) Shakespeare's comic bungler Puck, or (beep) wine-soaked Bacchus, or (beep) the smiling Buddha, or (beep) the half-elephant and half-human Hindu deity Ganesha, or (beep) the Old Testament God who laughs often at tribal enemies of the Jews, or (beep, beep, beep and here we'll stop at) Jesus? And yet, if you prayerfully bring your conflicted sense of humor response into New Testament frames, will you find clarity there or yet another humor controversy? Which Jesus will you consult? The laughing Jesus of upbeat New Age veneration or the anguished and stern Jesus of the crucifixion and Armageddon?

Books like *Laughing Together: The Value of Humor in Everyday Life* by Dotsey Welliver, *The Joyful Christ: The Healing Power of Humor* by Cal Samra, and *The Humor of Christ* by Elton Trueblood recommend a religious faith informed by laughter. Once criticized for laughing in church, Welliver insists that "God pronounced all the things he had made good . . . [including] the mechanism he built into the human being for laughter." Arguing that "we focus too much on the sorrowful Jesus," Samra concedes that, though there are no accounts of Jesus laughing in the Gospels, he did, on the eve of the crucifixion, admonish his disciples, saying: "These things I have spoken to you, that my joy may be in you, and that your joy be full" (John 15:11). And Samra provides several visual representations of Jesus with his head arched back and his mouth open wide with laughter: an early presentation of images that have since proliferated on-line at Web sites offering a full range of laughing-Jesus consumer products including not only framed art prints and posters but also T-shirts,

FIGURE EIGHTEEN. "Joy to the World," by Stephen S. Sawyer, www.art4god.com, used with permission

sweatshirts, buttons, and postcards. Typical of this work is Stephen S. Sawyer's painting *Joy to the World* (fig. 18), the chief attraction of his art4god Web store, which also sells Christian lapel pins, puzzles, and tattoos. For Trueblood, Jesus' "obvious wit and humor" have been obscured "by the great stress upon the tragedy of the crucifixion and the events immediately preceding it," a view confirmed by the grim and tortured depiction of Jesus in Mel Gibson's 2004 film *The Passion of the Christ,* which attracted both a huge audience of deeply moved viewers and howls of protest from Christians who prefer more calm wisdom and less flying flesh from their savior.[39]

Conflicts over divine laughter in contemporary Christian teaching and practice can be seen in responses to the work of Rodney Howard Browne—the "laughing evangelist" associated with the Toronto Blessing of 1994 and the "Laughing Revival" that followed—and Charles and Frances Hunter, "the Happy Hunters" and authors, according to the Hunter Ministries Web site, of "53 very powerful and best selling books," including *Healing through Humor* (2003). Both Browne and Frances Hunter's work as evangelists was shaped by conversion experiences that included hysterical laughter. On his Revival Ministries International Web site, Browne includes "testimony" from a couple (Dan and Susie K.) who attended his 1999 Madison Square Garden "Soul-Winning Crusade" to show that laughter is not only redemptive but also contagious:

My wife and I met a man on a park bench in Central Park. His brain was so fried on drugs and alcohol that all he could tell us was his name. Other than that, he could not talk. As I began to share about the love of God, tears began to flow from his eyes. I began to lead him in the sinner's prayer. He began to laugh then cry. My wife began to cry and she bought him a hot dog. When we left he was laughing and shouting and weeping for joy.[40]

Not everyone, however, is amused. On the Biblical Discernment Ministries homepage, Albert James Dager argues that the "holy laughter" movement serves as part of (and he is not even remotely thinking of Dana Carvey when he says) Satan's effort "to meld humanity into a one-world religion." Ominously, Dager warns, "it is not merely coincidental that holy laughter has found its place among the mystically inclined whose beliefs lean toward New Age philosophy." Similarly, at the MM Outreach/MacGregor Ministries Web site, an article called "Laughter in the Bible" argues that, while God (as opposed to Jesus) occasionally laughed, it was not in joyful celebration but "in derision at the puny, futile efforts of His enemies":

Never in joy, never during worship, never in mirth, never to be amused, only in derision against His enemies. He is not frivolous in his laughter, nor is He out of control. He laughs in judgment. Typical of this humor is God's comment in Proverbs 1:23–26: "Turn to my reproof, behold I will pour out my spirit on you; I will make my words known to you; Because I called and you refused, I stretched out my hand, and no one paid attention; And you neglected all my counsel, and did not want my reproof; I will even laugh at your calamity; I will mock when your dread comes."

Call me a benighted agnostic if you must, but it seems to me that if your God sounds like Freddy Krueger ("I will mock when your dread comes"), prayer may not be the most efficacious way for you to resolve your humor-reception issues.[41]

In the kind of religion-based jokes I heard and told as a kid, Jesus, Moses, and Saint Peter are in heaven playing golf. One of them, let's say Moses, behaves in a way that breaks the rules of the game, taking unfair advantage. After hitting into a pond, he uses miraculous powers to induce a carp to push the ball out of the water, a fox to carry the ball to the green, a team of chipmunks to roll it to within inches of the hole, and a swarm of bees to nudge it into the hole. The punch line delivered by one of his competitors is, "Hey, do ya wanna fuck around or do you wanna play golf?" Depending on who tells it and who hears it, this kind of joke might seem more or less edgy. At the very least, it humanizes or trivializes saintly religious figures; at the most it could be seen as an attack that libels religion by associating revered figures with profanity, mortal recreation, and cheating. Philosophically considered, the joke can be seen as challenging the very notion of fair play in a universe controlled by powers that can choose whether they wish to obey natural law. That said, for the most part most jokes like this come and go without eliciting much reflection.

At a higher level of tendentiousness are the jokes about the Catholic clergy many of my humor course students collected back in the late 1980s around campus in completing an assignment. Asked to bring in a list of at least ten jokes on any subjects currently circulating at Boston College, a Jesuit and Catholic university, they invariably brought in several that dealt with the sexual transgressions of priests who were attracted to each other, having sex with nuns, and, of course, screwing choirboys. When the jokes were shared, everyone in the room knew before the punch lines what to expect, hence the "of course" in the last sentence. A typical choirboy joke runs:

CHOIRBOY 1: Hi! I have to go to confession today, and I'm a bit worried. You've known this priest a long time already. What would he give for committing sodomy?
CHOIRBOY 2: That's two chocolate bars.

Years later, when the sex scandal broke in the Boston Archdiocese, one had to wonder about these jokes. While this particular example turns on the double meaning of the verb "give" (first as penance for a confessed sin and then as reward for service rendered), it plays with the idea that choirboys are routinely sodomized by priests. If years earlier, the idea of the pedophile priest was so familiar among American Catholics that just mentioning a priest and a choirboy at the start of a joke brought knowing smiles all around, how were the jokes functioning? Did they undermine the authority of priests in ways that would eventually encourage victims to come forward? Or did they normalize and in this way decriminalize brutal behavior rife in the community, making it easier for church leaders to protect offenders and enable their infamous careers? Did the jokes make it easier for crimes to hide in plain sight? At the very least, Ford and Ferguson's prejudice norm theory suggests that these jokes may well have contributed to the creation of a "climate of tolerance" in which criminally deviant violence seemed normal enough to be laughed off.

A pedophile priest joke that made the rounds on the Internet in 2000 as the scandal played out provides a contrast to the seek-and-hide jokes my students found back in the late 1980s:

One fine sunny morning, the priest took a walk in the local forest. He had been walking by the small stream when he noticed a sad, sad looking frog sitting on a toadstool.

"What's wrong with you?" said the priest.

"Well," said the frog, "the reason I am so sad on this fine day is because I wasn't always a frog."

"Really!" said the priest. "Can you explain?"

"Once upon a time I was an eleven-year-old choirboy at the local church. I too was walking through this forest when I was confronted by the wicked witch of the forest. 'Let me pass!' I yelled, but to no avail. She called me a cheeky little boy and with a flash of her wand, turned me into this frog you see before you."

"That's an incredible story" said the priest. "Is there no way of reversing this spell that the witch has cast upon you?"

"Yes" said the frog, "It is said, that if a nice kind person would pick me up, take me home, give me food and warmth and that, well, with this and a good night's sleep I would wake up a boy once again."

"Today's your lucky day!" said the priest, and picked up the frog and took him home. The priest gave the frog lots of food, placed him by the fire and at bedtime put the frog on the pillow beside him. When the priest awoke, he saw the eleven-year-old choirboy beside him in bed.

"And that my lord is the case for the Defense."

Anyone, even a former victim, could find this ingenious joke amusing. By contriving the most far-fetched and yet theoretically possible theory of the crime, it ridicules the notion of the innocent or falsely accused priest. Its appropriateness and resonance at the time of court cases and public exposure is clear in the way it arrives via indirection at the wrenching image at the tragic center of the story: a defenseless and violated child in a position of vulnerability. This image and the jokes surrounding it—like the other pointed and provocative, constructive and destructive examples considered throughout this chapter—remind us that dangers can be denied, concealed, and/or revealed in humor and that this can matter at times as much as life itself.

4 | Ridicule to Rule

THE STRANGE CASE OF GEORGE W. BUSH

Will a day come when the race will detect the funniness of these juvenilities and laugh at them—and by laughing at them destroy them? For your race, in its poverty, has unquestionably one really effective weapon—laughter. Power, money, persuasion, supplication, persecution—these can lift at a colossal humbug,—push it a little——weaken it a little, century by century: but only laughter can blow it to rags and atoms at a blast. Against the assault of laughter nothing can stand.

MARK TWAIN, *The Mysterious Stranger*

Q: At what point in the Iraq war did you start joking about Bush again?

JAY LENO: I think it really started with Bush saying "Mission Accomplished" and landing on the aircraft carrier. That was probably the point where it's obvious to the audience this is turning into a political tool. When it's obvious to the audience what's happening, then it works. Look, you don't change anybody's mind with comedy. You just reinforce what they already believe.

LA Weekly, September 17–23, 2004

Political and Apolitical Political Humor: Leno, Stewart, and Nast

Those who, like Mark Twain's Satan in the frequently quoted passage above, celebrate the liberating power of laughter emphasize its ability to assail "colossal humbugs," that is, to explode fraudulent, corrupt, and hypocritical ideas, individuals, and institutions "to rags and atoms." This positive force is what eighteenth-century English poet Charles Churchill had in mind in saying that "satire is always virtue's friend." Another view regards satire as a form of power that can itself be corrupted to biased or base ends. In this way, while Jonathan Swift observed that "Satyr is a sort of Glass, wherein Beholders do generally discover every body's Face but their Own," Ambrose Bierce defined satire as a "kind of literary composition in which the vices and follies of the author's enemies [are] expounded with imperfect tenderness." And the view that satire has little or no effect in undermining powerful targets also has a long history, as the following lines from William Cowper's 1785 poem "The Task" suggest:

Yet what can satire, whether grave or gay?
It may correct a foible, may chastise
The freaks of fashion, regulate the dress,
Retrench a sword-blade, or displace a patch;
But where are its sublimer trophies found?
What vice has it subdued? whose heart reclaim'd
By rigour, or whom laugh'd into reform?
Alas! Leviathan is not so tamed.
Laugh'd at, he laughs again; and, stricken hard,
Turns to the stroke his adamantine scales,
That fear no discipline of human hands.[1]

This debate—as old as satire, if not ridicule, itself—has particular relevance to the current and recent state of U.S. political discourse. In a time of multiple and different trends—including the increasingly calculated (that is, deliberate and intentional) use of humorous (and serious) calumny, the professionalization of campaign humor, and the proliferation and distribution of satirical scripts, cartoons, and songs on the Internet—understanding how satire has been both used and abused is essential to following political trends. Whether snarling or snuggling, intentional uses of humor in recent years have created the expectation that political advocacy on offense and defense will often show a smiling face.

The strategic deployment of humor as a political weapon is, perhaps, most clearly seen in the strange case of George W. Bush, strange not because he has both joked and been joked about but because his status as butt-in-chief has undergone extraordinary fluctuations. Though Ronald Reagan, whose presidency in many ways foreshadowed Bush's, was mocked on both policy and personal grounds as a mentally challenged rightwing extremist, his sense of humor was generally applauded by partisans on all sides. Both Jerry Ford and George Herbert Walker Bush maintained their comic standing as clumsy (think Chevy Chase) or inarticulate (think Dana

Carvey) men. And even Bill Clinton, butt of a zillion Lewinsky cigar and stain jokes, was ridiculed from the start of the 1992 campaign as a loose-living hedonist, the image that followed him through the scandal and impeachment trial and has stayed with him ever since on late-night TV where familiar joke tropes are infinitely recycled. George W. Bush stands out in this group of recent presidential joker-butts, men who could laugh at themselves when necessary and who were regularly pilloried, because in a political landscape of intense partisanship and perceived danger his presidency provides a living laboratory for the study of intentional humor in our time.

By way of context for a discussion of highly pointed and partisan humor, it's worth noting that many of the most widely consumed jokes about politicians and politics are deliberately written and delivered only to amuse. For America's most-watched comedian, Jay Leno, avoiding the appearance of partisanship or political advocacy is a matter of marketing in a sharply divided and ideologically intense media environment. In response to questions posed during the 2004 presidential campaign by Nikki Finke, an *LA Weekly* columnist who had been critical of what she saw as the pro-right slant of his monologues, Leno claimed to be apprehensive about the war in Iraq and likely Bush appointees to the Supreme Court but then explained: "I always say comics make the mistake that they start off as comedians, then they become humorists, then they become satirists, then they become commentators, then they're out of show business. That's sort of the way it goes. I don't want to be preached to as a member of the audience. I like to hear a joke." In addition to his sense that comedy (and comedians) are funnier than satire (and satirists), that jokes by their very nature are neither didactic nor instructive—Leno has to deal with a mass audience of poorly informed viewers. Leaving ideology aside, for a joke to work with a significant percentage of uninformed viewers, they need to have in mind the ideas, facts, or images required in resolving the joke's incongruity (for instance, that Ted Kennedy is a lush, Bill Clinton a lecher, and George W. Bush an inarticulate dope). Leno meets what he may see as a fair representation of his audience during his famous jay-walking interviews with random people on the street who, though they probably know the names of Michael Jackson's gardeners, generally cannot come up with the name of a Supreme Court justice or one of their own senators. Building a joke around an obscure news story (for instance, mass murder in Africa or the details of global climate change) seems as self-destructive to Leno as building it as part of a directed satirical campaign. For this reason, what Leno calls a comedian will focus with unparalleled reiteration on Bill Clinton's infamous assertion that he "didn't have sex with that woman, Monica Lewinsky," while only a humorist, satirist or, worse, a commentator would relentlessly slam George W. Bush for having manipulated intelligence to drag the country to war—this in spite of the eloquent poignancy of the bumper sticker that appeared in response to news stories about the postinvasion failure to find weapons of mass destruction in Iraq:

Clinton Lied
No One Died[2]

More than two millennia before the second Iraq War, the Roman satirist Juvenal famously noted that it was "difficult not to write satire." In overcoming this difficulty by serving up scattershot and apolitical political jokes about politicians as celebrities with well-known flaws or by balancing jokes against conservative ideas and figures with jokes about progressive ones—where does the Leno impulse widely reflected in network comedy fit on the spectrum of American humor that runs from killing jokes to healing laughter? In not addressing and seeking to alleviate human suffering by holding those responsible up to ridicule, does it serve Freddy-like ends, leaving abuses unmocked, unexposed, and unimpeded? Or in stepping back from potentially stressful problems and finding amusement anywhere it can, does it provide healing or at least distracting laughter?

Away from the world of what Leno calls "the comedian," the great political struggles of our time aim to affirm contested sets of values by addressing questions about the problems we face and potential solutions. In following the role of humor in these raucous, often overheated debates, different observers will naturally have their own takes. But we should remember that on Giddens's juggernaut world—in which the profit of multinational corporations is often privileged over both civil rights and the rights of workers, in which actual weapons of mass destruction are proliferating, in which military spending takes priority over reducing poverty and preventing disease, and in which the weather is becoming stranger (and more dangerous) all the time—the stakes are high enough to make us wonder about the role of humor in undermining or supporting specific decisions, policy directions, and ideologies. And if the decisions, policies, and ideologies are detrimental—if they advance the interests of the few over those of the many, if they promote injustice, misery, and death—should they be considered Kruegersque? Conversely, if they are sensitive but still satirical, intended to expose destructive acts and ideas to ridicule and in this way advance social justice, can political jokes help society at large find what healing laughers seek for themselves: solutions and cures?

Questions like these about the virtue and efficacy of satire underpinned Jon Stewart's responses in a July 11, 2003, exchange with Bill Moyers on the PBS program *Now*. After denying that he was either a "social critic" or a "media critic," Stewart continued:

> I think of myself as a comedian who has the pleasure of writing jokes about things that I actually care about. And that's really it. You know, if I really wanted to enact social change ... I have great respect for people who are in the front lines and the trenches of trying to enact social change. I am far lazier than that. I am a tiny, neurotic man, standing in the back of the room throwing tomatoes at the chalk board. And that's really it. And what we do is we come in in the morning and we go, "Did you see that thing last night? Aahh!" And then we spend the next eight or nine hours trying to take this and make it into something funny.

It's one thing for Jay Leno, who epitomizes the commercialization of humor, to eschew satirical commentary; it's another thing to hear Stewart, regarded by many as the greatest American satirist of our time, say that his own material has no social force or impact. And this before the (re?)election in 2004 of a president *The Daily Show* butted up against throughout the campaign in revised news stories about the Iraq War (which Stewart called the "Mess-o-potamia"), regular features on arrogant, contradictory, hypocritical, stumbling, or erroneous comments made by George W. Bush, Donald Rumsfeld, John Ashcroft, and numerous other administration figures, and off-site pieces on conservative (and frequently clueless) movements and people done by comic reporters like Samantha Bee and Stephen Colbert—all of which were only slightly offset by jokes about John Kerry's timidity as a campaigner or lack of conviction. Regular *Daily Show* viewers during the months leading up to the Bush/Kerry election understood the implied editorial slant of the program, as explained by Colbert on NPR's *Talk of the Nation* on March 4, 2004:

> I 100% have an editorial stance: I desperately want our president to lose the next election, but it doesn't keep me from attacking the Democrats on the show too. Listen, you're going to attack, or mock, or make fun of anybody who is in power right now, and the Republicans control, the judicial, the legislative, the executive branches. So there's hardly another target. And during the entire primary season we were just throwing the biggest haymakers we could find at all the Democratic candidates. We weren't kind to them on any level, but most of the time there's really only one game in town, and that's the Republicans.

After the election (on April 6, 2005) at a seminar that I attended at Harvard's Institute of Politics, David Javerbaum, the head writer on *The Daily Show,* took up the subject of satire and politics when he said "I don't think our show makes a difference. Aristophanes didn't make a difference, Swift didn't make a difference." But then Javerbaum, thinking for a second before moving onto another question, wondered aloud about whether Thomas Nast just might have made a difference in the undoing of New York's infamous Boss Tweed. This claim, widely made at the time of the Nast-Tweed conflict, has been repeated frequently since. If it's true, is Nast the exception that proves the rule (that satire is generally impotent) or a model for the effective use of humor in political advocacy?

The role of cartoonist Thomas Nast (1840–1902) in bringing down one of America's first entrenched political rings (the Tammany Hall group led by William Marcy Tweed that ruled New York City from 1866 to 1871) is not only legendary but also worthy of a detour back to the nineteenth century devoted to highlighting connections to the current state of political satire in the United States. Alarmed by the corruption of Tweed and his cronies, by their use of government to serve the interests not of the people but a corrupt few, and by the encroachment of religion into public policy—Nast triumphed through the use of vivid and imaginative images that expressed his consistent point of view: a moral vision that allowed him to starkly contrast good and evil. By drawing Tweed and his colleagues both as decadent, lowbrow hedonists and as predatory animals, Nast conveyed the idea that they were using public funds to enrich themselves. In "A Group of Vultures Waiting for a Storm to Blow Over," for instance, members of the ring are depicted as bloated predators who have grown fat by feasting on the flesh and bones of New York City and whose exclamation, "Let us prey," puns about their self-serving manipulation of religion. In "The Tammany Tiger Loose," Tweed appears as an obese Roman Emperor cheering as a large cat savages the female body of murdered Liberty in the Coliseum. And in "Can the Law Reach Him?" (fig. 19), Tweed towers over a policeman whose left hand cannot quite reach the boss's waist and whose right hand firmly holds a miniature criminal, ball, chain and all. Contrasts between caricatures like these of Tweed and his cohorts and representations of suffering, neglected, ill-served citizens shown sinking into poverty, miseducation, and intemperance define the stark clarity of Nast's vision: his use of exaggeration and incongruity to slam home his points. And the impact of his work was apparent. During the Civil War Lincoln called Nast "our best recruiting officer." Grant saw "the pencil of Nast" as a force in his 1868 victory. The *Nation* noted his

CAN THE LAW REACH HIM!—THE DWARF AND THE GIANT THIEF.

FIGURE NINETEEN. Thomas Nast, "Can the Law Reach Him?" *Harper's Weekly*, January 6, 1872

"unprecedented influence of opinion," while Tweed himself railed against his "damned cartoons." Not only was the Tweed group successfully prosecuted for corruption, Tweed himself, who managed to escape and flee to Europe, was caught in Spain by policemen who used one of Nast's cartoons to identify and arrest the fugitive.[3]

Questions raised by Nast's success concern the efficacy of satire and ridicule, of humor as a force in political contestation. Its relevance to understanding the current state of American satire is brought home by the comparison between Tweed and Bush lurking in the astonishment expressed by an early Nast biographer, Albert Bigelow Paine, who could barely contain his sense of bewilderment about how the citizens of New York in the postbellum period managed to support Tweed's misrule of incompetence, corruption, and greed:

It is difficult to understand the moral and patriotic impulses of a community in which such a condition could endure. It would almost seem that some dire influence of the planets was operating upon the lives and minds of those who, under normal conditions, would be expected to represent and to preserve the city's moral, political and financial integrity. As an example of the Ring's supremacy, one has but to refer to the files of that period to learn that, for a time, the great majority of the metropolitan daily press was frankly for the municipal government, while the remainder—to pervert an old line—praised it with faint condemnation, when silence itself was akin to crime.

Beyond the fascinatingly timely reference to the complicity of the press, Paine's incredulity about the public's response to Tammany abuses is based on the seemingly obvious cronyism, corruption, and criminality of the Ring (and as I tick them off, I invite you to be alert to precursors of the politics of the Bush/Rove/Cheney administration): running up $30 million in municipal debt in a few years that would take the city thirty years to pay off; enriching insiders and supporters while staging acts of charitable (think "compassionate conservative") giving to the poor; undermining church-state separation by giving municipal funds to parochial schools; and rigging elections.[4]

In the hurly-burly world of recent American politics—in which many of the issues that animated Nast are all too alive and vexing—the nineteenth-century cartoonist not only offers lessons to progressive humorists and satirists about techniques that can give their work what Nast came to see as the "terrible power" of his cartoons but also identifies specific abuses as worthy as ever of exposing. A review of presidential humor—efforts to use jokes both offensively and defensively—especially in and around the George W. Bush administration and in the 2004 presidential campaign—should allow us to unpack questions about the efficacy of satire and highlight an ironic juxtaposition: that conservative advocates of positions Nast assailed have in recent decades done a better job than progressives in adapting his techniques. To put this another way, Nast's focus on unambiguously negative traits illustrates by way of counterexample a point Mark Crispin Miller reaches in *The Bush Dyslexicon:* that less clearly negative portrayals, so far from hurting the president, may have contributed to his success. Though Bush and company have arguably presented the most succulent target for satire since the Tammany Hall Ring, and though many shafts have been aimed at them, no fatal hits have been landed. A review of Bush jokes and joking, set in relation to other recent political humor, should allow us to follow his apparent triumph as the last and, therefore, best laugher in the greatest butt war of our time.[5]

In the run-up to and the months following the 2004 presidential race, Democrats scrambled to understand their ongoing descent into what was beginning to feel like a permanent minority party. Two books out in 2004 that sold well and were widely discussed—Thomas Frank's *What's the Matter with Kansas* and George Lakoff's *Don't Think of an Elephant*—surveyed strategies of persuasion to show how cultural deception and linguistic cunning supported the rising Republican movement. Treating Kansas as a microcosm of red-state America, Frank shows how conservatives have used social issues (abortion, gay marriage) to draw majorities of voters to the side of candidates who then work against the majority interest. Reflecting on responses to such trends as outsourcing, the consolidation of agriculture, the Wal-Martization of retailing with its attendant lowering of wages, reduction of benefits, and destruction of Main Streets, Frank shows how Kansas has misdirected its anger away from Republican leaders whose policies support these trends onto liberal supporters of abortion rights, gay rights, and church-state separation.

Frank emphasizes the role of rhetorical evasions that obscure the relevance of class interest: labeling all contrary arguments "class warfare"; promoting a culture of misdirected complaints and grievances (for instance, blaming liberals for the moral excesses of mass culture produced by corporations); fostering anger and fear (about the "murder of unborn children," the undermining of "family values," and the secularization of America); and generally obscuring the role of corporate power and influence in politics. Though he occasionally takes note of conservative humor—like the bumper sticker he saw at a Kansas City gun show ("A working person who supports Democrats is like a chicken that supports Col. Sanders!") and David Brook's pillorying of Vermont latte liberals—Frank concentrates on the right's performance of indignation, not of indignation's tendentious comic twin: ridicule.[6]

The same emphasis on serious strategies of persuasion runs through Lakoff's analysis of conservative linguistic frames. Noting how resonant words and phrases (for instance, tax relief, partial birth abortion, death tax, clear skies) structure entire debates by evoking myriad positive and/or negative associations, Lakoff calls on progressives to define their own opposing values and then find their own more compelling linguistic frames. For instance, where conservatives refer to their support for a "strong defense, free markets, lower taxes, smaller government, and family values," progressives, Lakoff argues, should assert the importance of a "stronger

America, broad prosperity, better future, effective government, and mutual responsibility."[7]

Both Frank and Lakoff note how the intellectual and communications infrastructure the right has built up over the past three or four decades has allowed it to wield influence and advance its causes. As its subtitle suggests, this is also the focus of Richard Viguerie and David Franke's *America's Right Turn: How Conservatives Used New and Alternative Media to Take Power,* which both celebrates and seeks to explain the rise of the Republican right. Comparing this triumph to earlier media- and technology-driven power shifts, including (with the immodesty that characterizes their movement) the Protestant Reformation and the American Revolution—Viguerie and Franke describe how bulk mail, talk radio, think tanks, and cable news were used to transform conservatives from a warring set of fringe figures into a disciplined, well-funded, and persuasive fighting force. Central to this has been talent, most significantly, the talent of Rush Limbaugh whose increasingly popular talk show has discomforted Democrats and given Republicans an unwavering booster and model. In taking note of Limbaugh's abilities, *America's Right Turn* emphasizes what it sees as his command of fact and detail. Indeed, these authors bask in what they see as the weakness of liberal arguments that collapse when exposed to forceful opposition. The fact that the right's media stars rarely engage in open and fair debates with credible moderates and progressives does not seem to have kept these authors from arriving at this view.[8]

That said, taking Limbaugh as a, perhaps the, prime example of triumphant Republican rhetoric, it is instructive to consider the nature of his persuasive force and the role of intentional humor in it. When I introduce the subject of Limbaugh's sense of humor to my blue-state friends, they seem perplexed and invariably say something like, "Limbaugh? Rush Limbaugh? I don't think he's at all funny." Of course they don't, and yet if you peruse the archived materials on his Web site (http://www.rushlimbaugh.com/), you will find it loaded with a wide range of mocking song parodies and news "updates," like the ones on environmental topics discussed in chapter 3, directed at issues that Limbaugh needed to explain, opinions he needed to pillory, and, of course, lib-er-als whose characters he needed to assassinate. In addition to three dozen anti-Clinton routines—including "Road to Perversion," "Hey Paula," "Mrs. Jones You've Got a Lovely Daughter," "I Saw Her Derriere," and "Had Myself a Scary Little Intern"—Limbaugh goes after what he calls "Assorted Wackos" that include Howard Dean, Saddam Hussein, Senator Byrd, and Osama bin Laden, a list that revitalizes the concept of guilt by association.

Beyond these prerecorded satirical sermons, one need not listen all that closely to Limbaugh's daily patter to see that its tone is an artful combination of outrage and ridicule that can fairly be called "rage-icule." While the "Great One" claims that he strives for "a good entertaining program that has controversy without spitting on people," great gobs of his saliva, barely concealed in banter, are routinely expectorated at anyone assumed to be stupid, arrogant, elitist, ignorant, or (worst of all) politically correct enough to disagree with him in any way. Indeed, because this mood of anger mixed with contemptuous humor is Limbaugh's trademark, a feature of his brand, one can find it any day of the week by dropping in on his show. Whatever the issues are during Limbaugh's daily three-hour diatribe, they admit only one side, one unequivocal position: no gray tones, shades, or nuances allowed. For example, in his discussion of global climate change broadcast on May 6, 2005, while I was drafting this chapter, Limbaugh held forth, ridiculing the notion that manmade pollution could possibly cause global warming, insisting that environmental wackos were telling us that we would either "boil or fry," deriding the notion that only experts can be trusted to understand the underlying science, and spitting verbal bullets at the idea that regulatory policies needed to be changed. Cunningly, in tandem with his unfaltering conviction, his passionately defended sense that it would be absolutely absurd to do anything to try to affect climate—Limbaugh used tone shifts as satiric rapiers to deride scientists who claimed to have evidence that contradicted his views by saying words like "experts" and "policies" in an upper-class, snotty, almost-British accent. One needs to hear the way Limbaugh speaks these words to get a clear sense of their snarling intensity, their barely concealed hostility.[9]

Though progressives deplore Limbaugh's choice of butts, everyone who studies his work knows that he is often (if rarely ever just) kidding. Early on Stephen Talbot, writing in *Mother Jones,* described what he called Rush's "bad-boy jokes," his way of "playing the angry white guy with a sense of humor." Molly Ivins sounds as though she is talking about Freddy Krueger when she castigates Limbaugh for using his media power to aim satirical barbs at the powerless: "dead people, little girls, the homeless, and animals—none of whom are in a particularly good position to respond." Rush's tendency to ridicule "helpless targets" strikes Ivins as "profoundly vulgar . . . very much like kicking a corpse." That such jokes can also be appealing should alarm humor boosters by suggesting that sadistic jokers have brought cruel levity not only to our gothic subculture but to the politics of greed, moral posturing, militarism, and division abroad in the land.[10]

The mean-spiritedness of Limbaugh's ridicule is obvious in specific jokes he told about the physical appearance of Clinton's secretary of labor Robert Reich (short), Attorney General Janet Reno (frumpy), and Texas Governor Ann Richards (old). Ivins describes a particularly nasty example: "On his TV show in 1993, he put up a picture of Socks, the White House cat, and said: 'Did you know there's a White House dog?' And then he put up a picture of Chelsea Clinton, who was 13 years old." In snarling put-downs like these, Limbaugh has from time to time flashed the razor claws he generally conceals behind his distorted factoids, fallacious arguments, and more ingratiating jibes.[11]

Applying Karl Rove's method of turning political weaknesses into strengths (and vice versa for opponents) to the production of pointed satire, Limbaugh has elaborated the defense-of-torture humor motif in rightwing discourse. In the spring and summer of 2005, for instance, he extended his earlier defense of the Abu Ghraib guards to similar stories of abuse at the Guantanamo Bay (G'itmo) prison where the U.S. military had imprisoned hundreds of people labeled "enemy combatants" by the president without bringing them to trial. A 2002 investigation by the FBI, disclosed in the spring of 2005 as a result of a legal action brought by the American Civil Liberties Union, contained allegations not only of Koran abuse but of widespread beating and sexual humiliation. According to a May 25, 2005, story in the *Washington Post*, "One prisoner [told FBI investigators that] he and other detainees had been 'beaten, spit upon and treated worse than a dog,'" while "the records also include numerous allegations that guards or interrogators . . . used sexually suggestive techniques designed to humiliate Muslim men." Just as this report was made public, Amnesty International called Guantanamo "the gulag of our time," accused the United States of practicing torture, and called for an international investigation of U.S. conduct in the war on terror. In response to an earlier controversial story about the desecration of Korans at the prison that appeared in *Newsweek,* Scott Ott, the conservative satirist who runs scrappleface.com, ran a mock story called "Red Cross: Al Qaeda May Violate Geneva Conventions." In it, a *New York Times* story about Red Cross claims that the treatment of detainees at Guantanamo Bay was "tantamount to torture" is juxtaposed with "a second story alleging that Al-Qaeda-linked terrorists in Iraq conduct interrogations that are 'tantamount to beheading.'" In a similarly playful spirit, Limbaugh launched a Club G'itmo humor campaign on his Web site. (Hey, the going got tough!) An EIB parody commercial promotes Club G'itmo as a "one-of-a-kind-Muslim resort paradise" where "Diet Korans and free prayer rugs" are distributed, and "Muslim extremists get together for relaxation." Pictures of the club show orange-clad terrorists enjoying "in-room ethnically sensitive snacks," panoramic oceanfront views, and water sports. If you look carefully, you'll see Richard Reid, the shoe bomber, munching on a "complimentary Islamist break-fast" and Osama bin Laden stretching out in a spa mud bath. Invidiously, a weather report, updated daily, contrasts overheated Baghdad with cooler Club G'itmo. Products like the G'itmo baseball cap ($19.95), the Jihad Java Café Club G'itmo coffee mug ($16.95), and the Club G'itmo T-shirt ($19.95) that reads "I got my free Koran and prayer rug at G'itmo" were just a mouse click away when I visited the Limbaugh Web site on July 7, 2005. Lost, indeed deliberately removed from sight, in this hilarity is the anguish of prisoners whose guilt has never been proven.[12]

Building on early exposés of Limbaugh's inaccurate and/or deceitful mode of argumentation by Fairness and Accuracy in Reporting (FAIR)—in its 1994 report on "Limbaugh's Reign of Error" and the follow-up 1995 book, *The Way Things Aren't*—a watch group called Media Matters for America (http://mediamatters.org/) that tracks conservative news and talk media regularly posts examples of what it regards as Limbaugh's errors of fact and logic. It's interesting to note how many of these might actually have been intended as comic exaggeration. Intended or not, "I was only kidding" is a defense strategy deployed by Limbaugh when his accuracy is challenged. Criticized by FAIR for incorrectly stating that "most Canadian physicians who are themselves in need of surgery . . . scurry across the border to get it done right: the American way," Limbaugh defended the comment as "an obvious[ly] humorous exaggeration." The authors of *The Way Things Aren't* insist that the original statement in Limbaugh's 1993 book, *See, I Told You So* was a "perfectly straightforward assertion." Though Limbaugh's claim that the assertion is "obviously" humorous is dubious, the critic's counterclaim that it is "perfectly straightforward" is also a stretch insofar as it ignores the verb "scurry," which associates potentially amusing images of small rapidly moving animals rushing toward better care in the United States with Canadian doctors traveling south for surgery. Factually, of course, Limbaugh was wrong, as the FAIR authors demonstrated and as he so often is, but the interwoven subradar comic undertone illustrates one of Limbaugh's most effective (that is, insidiously fallacious) rhetorical strategies: the use of a veneer of comedy to lower resistance to his arguments and provide cover when they are assailed. Much to the detriment of clear thinking, Limbaugh's cavalcade of fallacies—his art of evoking irritation, anger, resentment, entitlement, and amusement—has been effective. With all of these emotions swirling about, how can listeners be expected to attend to the coherence, logic, and evidentiary solidity of the Great One's arguments?[13]

The answer is obvious: Limbaugh's fans are not expected to notice his illogical detours and factual distortions. They are supposed to be mesmerized by what passes for anger, charm, righteousness, and humor on the Excellence in Broadcasting network. Only this explains Limbaugh's repetitive self-congratulatory riffs: his claims about having "talent on loan from God," being "the epitome of morality and virtue," "saying more in five seconds than most talk show hosts say in a whole show," or being able to "demolish" liberals "with half [his] brain tied behind [his] back." Taken seriously, such utterances would give arrogance a bad name. But Rush's self-conscious exaggeration and elbow-in-the-ribs-give-us-a-wink tone legitimate his absurdly self-aggrandizing and boastful self-characterizations. Progressives who have been alarmed and dismayed (shocked and clawed?) by Rush's popularity have found it easy to focus on his anger and ignore his humor, but it is the Freddy-like combination of aggression and wit that has allowed him to advance the causes he holds dear.[14]

Whether expressed in Nast's caricatures or Limbaugh's self-adulation, it seems as though humor, or some versions of it in some situations, has persuasive force. I say "seems" because empirical studies of persuasion in advertising, education, and public speaking have not yet provided firm answers to questions about the role of humor in shaping and changing opinions and habits. Though millions of dollars are spent each year crafting and distributing comic ads, especially on TV and radio, the number of variables involved in designing useful experiments has slowed progress in evaluating how and what kind of humor will have the greatest impact. Still, since the process of getting a joke moves quickly through an often unconscious flow of analysis or interpretation of its images and ideas to a burst of affect (delight, amusement) and bodily activity (smiling, groaning, laughing), it should come as no surprise that humor can lure listeners away from the comprehensive, thoughtful evaluation of questionable assertions, that it can operate (like appeals to pity, fear, revulsion, etc.) as a distortion of and distraction from rational reflection.

According to Marc G. Weinberger and Charles S. Gulas, who reviewed research on humor and persuasion in 1992, though rife in the industry, "generalizations about the effect of humor [in advertising] are fraught with pitfalls." Rod A. Martin, who updated this review in 2005, notes that "research on this topic indicates that there is no simple relationship between humor and persuasion" and that there is no reason to think that "simply making a message humorous . . . [makes] it more persuasive" than a serious message on the subject would be. At the same time, Martin follows a line of cognitive research that seeks to understand and describe how humor persuades when it succeeds. According to the "elaboration-likelihood" model of persuasion, developed by Richard E. Petty and Joan T. Cacioppo, arguments are processed in more or less detail and with greater or less attention to their facts and logic. If the issue seems urgent, if receivers are more involved with it, they will subject it to careful evaluation. If, on the contrary, receivers are less involved, they will allow themselves to arrive at conclusions on the basis of such peripheral factors as their impressions about the source: is the presenter likable, believable, objective? In this analysis, humor can promote intellectual relaxation or distraction, opening audiences up to illogical and factually insufficient forms of persuasion. Jim Lyttle, who studied humor and persuasion in a business-instruction context, hypothesized that humor could advance persuasion by establishing a sense of values shared by the presenter and receiver (based on their shared amusement or laughter) and by boosting the receiver's sense that the presenter can be liked and, therefore, trusted (because she or he is amusing). All of this would tend to reduce the receiver's resistance to new ideas in part by interfering with the "rehearsal of subvocal counterarguments." Though Lyttle's research only begins to establish these patterns, it appears to highlight the potentially fallacious role of humor in advancing ideas that might not be equally acceptable when presented seriously.[15]

Bush Butt: 2000 to 9/11 to 2004

Undaunted by the possibility that humor can mislead and misdirect public opinion, in an interview broadcast on NPR on President's Day, February 17, 2001, Malcolm Kushner, co-creator of an exhibit on humor at the Ronald Reagan Library, asked what he intended to be a rhetorical question: "Would you want a president who didn't have a sense of humor?" Because in other contexts Kushner describes himself as "America's Favorite Humor Consultant," that is, because he sees himself as a Norman prince, he distinguishes between "being funny" and having a "sense of humor," the former being the preserve of comedians (whom we don't elect to high office) and the latter providing a "balanced perspective." After all of the cruel and one-sided joking highlighted here, it should be clear that only some humor nudges toward balance. While humor can, no doubt, promote detachment or counter bias, it does rather well in promoting extreme and downright stupid ideas as well. Arguably, the stupider the idea is, the more one might need to harness the fallacious power of comic persuasion to put it across, using humor to wink listeners into letting go of their tendency to construct counter arguments. Nothing says "chill out, dude" better than a joke.

Should we, then, want a president to have a sense of humor? Kushner is far from alone in considering the answer obvious. John Morreall uses the example of Reagan, whom he calls "a lifelong avoider of bad news," who could "make us laugh" to illustrate the value of humor in leadership without noting that empowering leaders who fail to confront pressing problems seriously can be disastrous. Paul E. McGhee praises Reagan's use of humor to defuse the issue of his advancing age during one of his debates with Walter Mondale without noting that the deteriorating state of Reagan's brain function should have been an important issue during the 1986 campaign, one that ought not to have been defused and dismissed from serious consideration. The same point is worth making about George W. Bush's apparently self-mocking laugh line in the second of his 2000 debates with Al Gore. Responding to a question about whether it was fair to criticize Gore for exaggerating and misspeaking, candidate Bush quipped, "Well, we all make mistakes. I've been known to mangle a syl-la-ble or two myself, you know." Amusing? Maybe. Disarming? Probably. But the question begged, the weakness skimmed over was worth taking seriously for at least two reasons. First, the leader of the free world, especially one who insists on regularly testing the language skills of grade school children, should be able to navigate an unscripted sentence. And, second, discounting the problem blocked consideration of the possibility that, like Reagan, Bush may have been suffering from a specific condition called presenile dementia: the early onset of Alzheimer's disease. Bush's handlers did so well in taking this off the table as a serious campaign issue in 2000, relegating it to realm of endless joke-fodder, that virtually no one has paid attention to the possibility that there may be a clinical explanation for the conspicuous decline in Bush's verbal ability. Does it matter that the man whose finger is on the nuclear trigger, who has the power to take the country to war may be sliding into senility? If so, was the attempt to obscure this a service to democracy?[16]

When political candidates tell jokes, especially as a way of introducing themselves to voters, the strategy is designed to convey far more than their sense of humor. Research on humor and attractiveness suggests that when we conclude that someone we meet has a good sense of humor, we are also likely to assume that he or she is interesting, considerate, imaginative, creative, impulsive, and perceptive, all highly desirable traits. Moreover, sharing humor with a stranger is more likely to promote closeness than the perception of shared values. It is, then, reasonable to wonder whether the informed and rational evaluation of candidates can be undermined by an artful joke. And, if so, whether voters may find that they feel like a woman who, after a few drinks, goes home from a bar with a guy she thought was funny and, therefore, smart and playful, only to realize the next morning or a week later that he's a jerk.[17]

Consider, then, an alternative to the pat response to Kushner's question: that whether we want the president to have a sense of humor should depend on who the president is and what you mean by humor. To the extent that humor persuades by making the salesman, presenter, or politician seem more like our kind of guy, progressives might be wise to prefer their FDRs, JFKs, and Clintons with humor, but their Nixons, Reagans, and anyone named Bush straight up. Conservatives already tend to reverse this. Though the ability to laugh at oneself is a rare and admirable trait—performances of which are often planned by staff writers and then delivered with feigned spontaneity by presidents trying to sway public opinion or mood—shared amusement frequently breaks along party lines. Indeed, the experience of hearing a political figure one disapproves of tell a joke—Clinton on his dalliances, Reagan on nuking the USSR—and finding its humor resistible suggests that political humor is far from always welcomed or appreciated. To doubt this one must have both feet planted in the positive humor movement, rather than one foot there and one in Freddy's dark realm.

The idea of the resisting partisan nonlaugher sets the stage for a discussion of that most polarizing figure, a man whose political power has been shadowed by his ability to attract and deflect ridicule: George W. Bush. The rise, fall, and reemergence of Bush-bashing humor, framed by two elections and slammed into quiescence by the September 11 attacks, did not simply happen; the contours of the process were shaped by deliberately crafted satire and public reactions to events. One need not question the official explanation of 9/11, as David Ray Griffin and others in the 9/11 Truth Movement have done, to see that the terrorist attacks in New York and Washington, DC, functioned as Pearl Harbors that rallied public opinion to the president's side and inoculated him from both serious and comedic challenges to his authority. The story of how one of the weakest, most personally deficient presidents in U.S. history became one of the strongest is at the least reflected in what may well be the greatest butt shift (from goat to hero) in the history of American humor.

During the 2000 campaign, candidate Bush was regularly mocked in late-night monologues. In the rough hands of network joke writers, then-Governor Bush was assailed for his sketchy war record—"Senator John

McCain recently compared the situation in Iraq to the Vietnam era—to which President Bush replied, 'What does Iraq have in common with drinking beer in Texas?'" (Craig Kilborn); his lack of intelligence and past reliance on nepotism—"Bush has a new campaign slogan. It's 'Reformer with Results,' which I think is a big improvement on the old one: 'A Dumb Guy with Connections'" (David Letterman); and his history of drinking, as when Jay Leno referred to him and Dick Cheney as "Drunk and Drunker" in reference to the news that they had accumulated three citations for driving under the influence between them. Leno's suggestion was simple: that the Republicans should be elected "just to get them off the road."[18]

Though qualified and offset by jokes told about Bush opponents—first Senator McCain, later Bill Bradley and Al Gore, and finally just Gore—the critique implicit in these early national Bush jokes is consistent with the substantive analysis served up by Molly Ivins and her coauthor Lou Dubose in their witty 2000 unauthorized campaign biography: *Shrub: The Short but Happy Political Life of George W. Bush*. In pointed detail, Ivins and Dubose devote chapters to Bush's (1) time in (and out of) the Texas National Guard, (2) nepotism-driven career as a crony capitalist in both the oil and baseball industries, and (3) ineffective, unenergetic, detached, and reactionary work as the governor of a weak-governor state. In its review of Governor Bush, *Shrub* focuses on his failures in dealing with education, the environment, and criminal justice, while calling attention to his underlying priorities, as in the following discussion of how the governor weighed the public interest against private, corporate goals:

You don't need a Ph.D. from the LBJ School [to know that] Dubya takes care of bidness. While he was fighting to deny children health care at the beginning of the 1999 session, he was personally flogging the only bill he designated "emergency legislation": his $45 million tax break for owners of marginally productive oil and gas wells. "There's a lot of people hurting," said Bush, the bleeding heart. Bush sold this tax break as one that would benefit only the owners of itty-bitty oil wells. Turned out that most of the marginal wells were owned by Exxon.[19]

Following the contested 2000 presidential election, during the first hundred days of his term, Bush acquired two new comic attributes: his ignominious status as a minority, appointed president and a leadership style that seemed to surrender authority to others, including Vice President Cheney and Campaign Director Rove. Representative of the many, many jokes about the way the election ended up in the Supreme Court is Jon Stewart's quip: "On Saturday, amidst pomp and extenuating circumstance, [Bush] will be sworn in as leader of the free world. The only non-traditional element in this inauguration is that the winner will be watching it from Carthage, Tennessee." The following Jay Leno joke captures the spirit of the weak-leader gags: "Dick Cheney has been on TV everywhere. He's doing press conferences, he's setting up the transition team back in Washington. What's Bush doing? Bush is relaxing on the ranch. Which guy had the heart attack?" Whether they provided comfort to wound-licking Democrats or served as ironic tributes to the more cunning, ruthless Republicans, these postelection joke motifs took their place in the Bush canon beside the already familiar put-downs based on the president's perceived intelligence and linguistic deficits. "If you're just waking up," David Letterman said, "the election is over and we have a president, George W. Bush. This is nice, for everyone who wondered what it would be like if Dan Quayle was president, well, here you go."

Meanwhile, during the first few months of his first term, Bushisms circulated widely via e-mail and on specific Web sites. Because they were associated with significant early presidential events or decisions, the following unintended self-parodies drew attention:

It's very important for folks to understand that when there's more trade, there's more commerce.
(At the Summit of the Americas in Quebec City, April 21, 2001)

First, we would not accept a treaty that would not have been ratified, nor a treaty that I thought made sense for the country.
(On the Kyoto Accord, April 24, 2001)

Particularly ironic (if not poignant) in retrospect is the following quip offered by Darrel Hammond on *Saturday Night Live* as an explanation of why he didn't vote for Bush: "I think that if you are the leader of planet Earth, you should be smarter than me. You just get the feeling, don't you, in the Oval Office that Dick Cheney is working behind the big desk. And then off to the right there is a little collapsible card table where George has like airplanes and stuff. Then every once in a while he looks up and says, 'I've discovered that if I shut my eyes, I can disappear.'" In early September of 2001—when jokes like these were the staple of late-night humor, when Bush's standing as America's Most Wanted Butt seemed secure, according to the Washington Post/ABC News Poll, the president's approval ratings fell to their lowest pre-9/11 levels of 55 percent (with 26 percent of respondents saying they strongly approved and 29 percent saying they somewhat approved). Two days after the attacks, 86 percent of Americans approved of Bush's performance (63 percent strongly; 23 percent somewhat); four weeks after (on October 9, 2001) 92 percent approved (76 percent strongly; 16 percent somewhat)—numbers that would recede from these stratospheric heights to just under 60 percent over the following year and a half (that is, in January, 2003).[20]

Whether the 9/11 attacks "changed everything," as people have been wont to suggest, they certainly scrambled American humor, first by sucking the oxygen out of public joking, then by reshuffling the order of butts: whom we joked about and how. A search of the AMU Reprints database of the eleven editorial and twenty-four noneditorial cartoons distributed by Universal Press Syndicate for strips that ran in the two weeks leading up to 9/11 and the two weeks that began on September 19, 2001, using the keywords "President Bush" and the politics and government subject filter showed a decline from a total of nineteen (before) to twelve (after). Beyond this, the before cartoons were uniformly critical—focusing on such then-current issues as stem-cell research and relations with Mexico and relying heavily, regardless of the specific issue, on the stupidity motif. For instance, on September 5, 2001, Tom Toles showed Bush as a squirming schoolboy being taught the three branches of the U.S. government from a schoolmarm with a pointer; in spite of the simple diagram she has drawn on the blackboard, the president is unable to "get it." Similarly, on September 7, 2001, Stuart Carlson ironically has Bush claim to have come up with a "brilliant compromise" on stem-cell research based on the use of "64 existing lines." In a series of panels, the president first admits that "There might be slightly less than that" and then that "Awright—It's one cell, ok? But it's a real beaut!!" Lalo Alcaraz's August 30, 2001, cartoon shows Bush as one of two passengers in a raft labeled "U.S. Economy." To reassure his obviously worried companion, Bush says, "Things are looking up," but this claim is visually undercut by the three large shark heads swimming at the raft from below. And Trudeau directly engages the low-intelligence motif in his Sunday, September 2, 2001, strip. In it, Bush (as floating cowboy hat) is shocked to learn that a study of the intelligence of recent presidents has placed him at the bottom with a score of just 91 while Bill Clinton is rated twice as bright with a score of 182. "How," the tongue-tied leader wonders, "is this possibilistic"?[21]

Several of the Bush cartoons that ran in the post-9/11 weeks were positive, featuring heroic attributes. On October 2, 2001, Glenn McCoy has Bush carrying the whole world into a private room in the White House where Laura Bush stops sipping from a cup long enough to say, "Tough day at the office, dear?" In his September 29, 2001, strip, Bill DeOre shows

Bush dressed as a cowboy and rough riding a commercial jetliner. Inside the cockpit below the pilot is speaking to the copilot: "I think he's tryin' to get folks flying again." In his September 27, 2001, cartoon, Toles Alcaraz took a break from anti-Bush satire to show the president forcefully instructing Israeli Prime Minister Sharon to "reach an agreement in the Middle East." And, after suspending *Doonesbury* for seven days (September 17–23, 2001), Trudeau spent the first week back (September 24–30, 2001) dealing with the personal responses to 9/11 of characters in Walden, especially Boopsie who is seen struggling with her loss of interest in pop culture. On October 1, 2001, she is sad to report that she "no longer care[s about] what Madonna had for breakfast." Four weeks post-9/11 *Doonesbury* returned to criticizing the president, though not for his response to the attacks, when it took up the issue of stem-cell research. After a scientist explains that the policy is flawed and in need of review, Bush (heard in a speech bubble coming from within the Oval Office) says, "But I don't want to put my thinking cap back on." Alone in this group of cartoonists, Aaron McGruder's *The Boondocks* (October 2, 2001) praised Congresswoman Barbara Lee (D-CA) for "opposing Bush's warmongering." And both McGruder and Ted Rall were in a then-tiny minority when they mocked the way many former Bush critics were now rallying to his side (*The Boondocks,* September 28, 2001; Rall, September 27, 2001).

Because humor seemed conspicuously absent in the hours and days following the attacks, commentators and pundits retreated from coverage of emergency- and disaster-response stories to ponder a question about the national mood: Would there be jokes about this latest, most spectacular tragedy? With both Jay Leno and David Letterman off air and in no mood for humor, with the *Onion* suspending publication, the *New Yorker* running an issue without cartoons on September 24, many comedy clubs, The Capital Steps and a DC comedy troupe called Gross National Product that had been performing a play called *Son of a Bush* canceling performances—a moratorium on joking seemed to have been declared. *Vanity Fair* editor Graydon Carter achieved his fifteen minutes of fame by asserting that we had reached "the end of the age of irony," while George Schlatter, a television producer best known for his work with the 1960s comedy show *Laugh-In,* opined, "This may be an event which historians look back to as the beginning of a new era of sensitivity, introspection and growth."[22]

Writing about the first post-9/11 broadcast of *Saturday Night Live* in the *Washington Post,* Tom Shales noted that while the show "went smoothly," "Ferrell's popular impression of George W. Bush as a confused bumbler, something that turned up on nearly every 'SNL' last season, was nowhere to be seen" and wondered how long it would remain "in mothballs." Belying his own assertion, Jay Leno captured the mood of hesitation when he noted, "We can't do Bush jokes anymore; he's smart now." Around this time, James Poniewozik, writing in *Time* magazine, observed that "a country where it is forbidden to mock the president by popular consensus is no freer than a country where it is forbidden to mock the president by law," and Tony Norman, a columnist for the *Pittsburgh Post-Dispatch,* wrote, "I look forward to the day we'll be able to make fun of the president again without being charged with sedition."[23]

At an international humor studies conference held in June of 2002 at which I chaired a panel on terrorism and humor, I learned that jokes about the suffering of 9/11 victims and mourners began to circulate in Europe and elsewhere shortly after the attacks, but my searches of U.S.-based joke Web pages during the days, weeks, and months following the attacks suggested that American humor after 9/11 was remarkable for its avoidance of these targets. In a culture defined by its transgressive audacity particularly in the area of violence-based humor, this restraint in itself was unusual enough to suggest questions. How were the 9/11 victims different from, say, the astronauts who died in the fiery explosion of the space shuttle Challenger in 1986 and were said to have vacationed "all over Florida" as their *blue* eyes *blew* this way and that way in jokes that conjured up images of their spectacular deaths and that circulated widely within twenty-four hours of the disaster? Did the loss of humor following 9/11 suggest a narrowing of response to the hostility- and fear-based options of fight or flight? Is there a correlation between the perceived severity of a public calamity and the length of time it takes for jokes to appear and circulate? Or was the sense of connection to or affiliation with the 9/11 victims more personal than the connection to the dead astronauts? One may have fantasized about becoming an astronaut; many Americans admired the crew and even adored Christa Macauliff, the teacher in space. But the degrees of separation to the victims of the two events were different, insofar as most Americans have flown in airplanes and/or been up to high floors in skyscrapers, while virtually none have been in spaceships. And almost everyone knew someone who knew someone who died on 9/11. At Boston College, the medium-size university where I teach, sixteen alumni, including Joseph Visciano who had graduated in the spring of 2001, died that day, four current students lost a parent, while forty-five friends and relatives of current students, faculty, and staff were killed. A sense of connection to these people (living and dead), combined with confusion and insecurity, was palpable at the solemn service held on campus at noon on the day of the carnage.[24]

Perhaps because earlier disasters, going back in then-present memory to the Challenger and the Ethiopian famine of the early 1980s, inspired joke cycles that seemed edgy at the time, perhaps because the conventions of both the healing laughter and killing joke cultures had direct applicability to the post-9/11 mood of danger, fear, and loss, the humor hiatus was increasingly discussed. On September 27, just sixteen days after the attacks, *Saturday Night Live* came back on-air for its season premier and opened with a shot of Rudolph Guiliani standing with New York City police and firemen. After a brief tribute to these "heroes" and a performance by Paul Simon of "The Boxer," the following exchange provided official cover for the resuscitation of American humor:

LORNE MICHAELS: On behalf of everyone here, I just want to thank you all for being here tonight, especially you, sir.

MAYOR RUDOLPH GUILIANI: Thank you, Lorne. Thank you very much. Having our city's institutions up and running sends a message that New York City is open for business. *Saturday Night Live* is one of our great New York City institutions, and that's why it's important for you to do your show tonight.

LORNE MICHAELS: Can we be funny?

MAYOR RUDOLPH GUILIANI: Why start now? Live, from New York! It's Saturday Night!

Perhaps empowered by this permission, a week later Malcolm Kushner, writing in *USA Today,* called on the country to "unleash humor," our "secret weapon." Kushner went further, suggesting that the terrorists hate us because we have humor and they "lack it":

The current conflict has been characterized as good vs. evil; right vs. wrong; freedom lovers vs. freedom haters; and the list goes on. But [there's] another way of looking at it: the humorous vs. the humorless. Just think about it. The freedom to laugh at each other and ourselves encompasses most of the other freedoms that we cherish so dearly. . . .

America is the country that gave the world the one-liner, the light-bulb joke and the top 10 list. . . . What have our enemies offered in the way of humor? The answer is found in another indigenous American joke form, the list of the world's shortest books. It must certainly include *The Wit and Wisdom of Fundamentalist Islamic Extremists.*

Carried away by the urgency of restoring lost laughter, as if the process required midwifery, Kushner probably went too far in contrasting heroic American humor with the humorlessness of Islamic extremists—since our jokes express a wide range of impulses, some of which are positive, others mean-spirited—and since even Osama bin Laden has been heard laughing on tape and sometimes appears to be smirking triumphantly on his taunting videos. Beyond these signs, responsible claims about the humor of "our enemies" require more than implied appeals to common sense or general knowledge. Indeed, wouldn't the idea that a particular group is humorless contradict that other claim of the positive humor movement: that humor is a universal human attribute? Still, in spite of the weakness of this part of Kushner's argument, he deserves credit for calling the country to its most noble use of laughter, urging us to exercise "the freedom to laugh at each other and ourselves," to enjoy inner-directed and, perhaps, self-critical humor, rather than hostile and outward-targeted joking. Unfortunately, in the run-up to the invasion of Afghanistan this advice went largely unheeded.[25]

To get a sense of the way the cultural shockwave set off by 9/11 affected U.S. humor in general and President Bush's standing as a butt in particular—stirring up anxiety, xenophobia, patriotism, and hostility—consider the rather different experiences of three unconnected humorists, one British and two American, whose work in comedy or satire changed at the time: stand-up comic Shazia Mirza, political Web designer David Counts, and amateur songwriter Ron Piechota. In the weeks following September 11, Britain's first Muslim woman stand-up comic, Shazia Mirza, who had, about nine months before, stopped working as a high school physics teacher and begun working full time as a performer, was dealing with a personal problem rather similar to the struggle to return to laughter in the United States. On September 22, she was quoted in a *Daily Telegraph* story about why she had cancelled her scheduled gigs post-9/11. Prior to 9/11 she had worried about being assaulted by Muslim men in comedy club audiences; just after the attacks, she was concerned about the ongoing "backlash against Muslims." Because it addressed and disarmed both of these concerns, the joke she wrote to reopen her act made news on both sides of the Atlantic: "Hello. I'm Shazia Mirza, or at least that's what it says on my pilot's license."[26]

Mirza insists that she has never been particularly interested in politics, that her goal from the start has been to be funny. In an interview following a performance at The Comedy Store in Picadilly Circus on June 11, 2005, she emphasized this, saying, "to be honest, I never wanted to be [seen as] a novelty. Reporters got it wrong after 9/11 when they said that I was breaking down barriers. No comedy act can do this." And yet, Mirza's political views are complex, and the jokes she crafts from her transcultural experiences show, at the least, how barriers can be crossed. Soon after 9/11 she insisted that "there [was] no justification for the attacks on

America," but also that Islam was widely misunderstood both by the terrorists and in the West: "My act took off because no one had really heard what it's like to be a Muslim woman here. . . . You have to attack ignorance with humor. We're not all fanatics." As a moderate, devout Muslim, Mirza said, she was "placed between two cultures and able to cast a critical, as well as a forgiving, eye on both."[27]

During an interview with Mirza on February 13, 2005, after a gig in Northampton, Massachusetts, when I suggested that her combination of mockery and acceptance about both of her cultures pointed to an answer, a way out of the global conflict of the decade between radical Islam and a militant U.S. foreign policy, and that people in America were "hungry for her material"—she pointed out that to be effective in reaching beyond the converted, one has to avoid hostility and rage: "I think you have to be likable. There are some Muslim male comics I can't imagine white Americans going to see because they ram their beliefs down Americans throats. They say this is what we believe in, what we are. If you really want to change people, to be a great comedian, your comedy has to be for everyone." As with Kushner's call for self-directed laughter, Mirza's sense of cultural balance, of comic material "for everyone," was conspicuously missing from America's post-9/11 return to humor. Indeed, the turn away from mockery of our own public figures to a more warlike, other-directed humor was apparent in the overnight shift from the treatment of President Bush as butt to a reverence or ambivalence that halted satire and for a time seemed to preclude it.

David Counts—the Web designer and animator who created the toostupidtobepresident.com Web site in March of 2001 in an effort to demonstrate (according to its original mission statement) that of "all the smug, duplicitous, rich whelps who have served as President of the United States, . . . none [has] been quite as dumb [and, therefore, unfit to serve] as George W. Bush"—got into the on-line satire business after seeing how the Bush campaign "savaged John McCain" in the South Carolina primary." For the 2000 presidential race, Counts produced a number of animations including a version of *Jeopardy*, "National Jeopardy," that features Bush, Sean Connery, and Al Gore as contestants. In a series of responses to answers under the category of Potent Potables, Bush demonstrates his familiarity not only with illegal recreational drugs but also with such beverages as the Midland Martini and the New Haven Riot, while guessing correctly under the category of Political Philosophers (which he pronounces in a number of startling ways including phil-os-o-cators) that, insofar as Jesus created everything, he can be said to have written assorted statements by such actual political theorists as John Locke and Sir Thomas

More. And well before 9/11 Counts was developing a talent for posting "top 11" lists on a range of satiric subjects, including top 11 reasons: "Dubya and Rumsfeld are shaking-up the Department of Defense"; "Dick Cheney helped Saddam Hussein restore Iraq's oil production capacity in the late 1990s"; "Dubya 'corrected' the impression that he blamed Clinton for the current level of violence in the Middle East"; and "Bush waved to Stevie Wonder."[28]

At the time of the 9/11 attacks Counts was working on what would have been his most ambitious project for the site: an anti-Bush version of "The Sorcerer's Apprentice" with the president in the out-of-control Mickey Mouse role, guns carrying barrels of oil (in place of Disney's broomsticks carrying pails of water) and missiles streaming across the heavens (instead of stars). "Within a half hour of watching the second plane fly into the World Trade Center," Counts recalls, "I took down the site." Caught in uncertainty, and determined to do the right thing, he left it down until December of 2001 when Bush started to invoke 9/11 as part of the midterm election campaign. "I thought, if he could do that, it was time to get the site back up."

Unaware of the possibility that he would contribute to what turned out to be a dramatic butt shift, Ron Piechota, by day the editor of a small technology magazine, by night (and as a hobby) a musician and songwriter, soon after 9/11 began to express his feelings about terrorism by writing, recording, and posting anti–bin Laden and anti-Taliban song parodies on-line. Sitting in an all-but-deserted café in the Javits Center in Manhattan having a cup of coffee a week after 9/11, Piechota recalls that he "saw a USA Today article that said people were trying to relieve their attack-related stress through comedy." His account of this process written for the 9/11 Digital Archive, continues:

It said that a couple of morning show DJs in Tucson, AZ were even putting together a tribute CD for the twin trade tower survivors, with all of the proceeds going to them. So I contacted this DJ and asked if he wanted any submissions and he said, "sure!" So, I sent him a variation of a Paul Simon song, I call "50 Ways to Kill Bin Laden." I did it originally for my own amusement and played it for people at work and they said that I should send it in to a radio station. But I didn't really know who to send it to until I saw the . . . article and contacted the DJ, JohnJay Vanes. That was my first parody and the first song I sent to him. He liked it, so I ended up recording four more and sending them in also.

The gee-whiz sense of opportunity is palpable here. Experienced with working from his living room with just a digital audio workstation

(DAW) and audio-processing technology, Piechota knew that he could produce "radio quality material" without using a professional studio. In short order, he wrote, recorded, and dispatched (to the DJs) and uploaded onto the Web four other song parodies called "The Christmas Song" ("Bin Laden's Head Roasting on an Open Fire"), "Dance All Night, Osama," "Hey! Mr. Taliban Man," and "Sitting on a Box in a Cave." Stunned by the rapid dissemination of these songs, especially "Fifty Ways" and "Sitting on a Box"—by the numerous Web sites that posted links to them, the news stories that included them in discussions of responses to 9/11, and the sense that an idea can begin as "a kernel of imagination" and be "dispersed worldwide" in no time, Piechota was "fascinated" by the "democratizing" power of the Web. Looking back, in 2005, at post-9/11 humor, he suggested that "collectively we needed to find a way past the shock" and noted that his songs fit into a wider effort to "reduce" bin Laden's status and, therefore, menace by imaginatively "blowing up, shooting or otherwise disemboweling" him. Piechota was particularly imaginative when it came to elaborating this "otherwise"; among the fifty ways to kill bin Laden are the following suggestions:

You know, it's really not my habit to be rude,
But battery acid enema would surely kill this dude,
Underneath a shuttle blastoff would not really be too crude,
There must be 50 ways to kill Bin Laden,
50 million ways to kill Bin Laden.

Chorus:
Just rip off his balls, Paul, with a rusty fork, Mork,
Drown him in oil, and boil, and set his skin free,
Lop off his face, Grace, you don't need to use mace spray,
Pop open his heart, with a dart and set his blood free.

In his version of the Nat King Cole classic, Piechota serves up images of "Bin Laden's head roasting on an open fire / Brains are dripping out his nose," and in the Otis Redding–based ditty "special forces" relentlessly pursue and "won't leave" the obviously worried terrorist alone.[29]

Though he got into bin Laden bashing early, Piechota had company, as wish-fulfilling images of the enemy running, dodging, cornered, and exterminated rapidly became conventions of bin Laden fake news stories and animations that appeared on the Internet and can still be found at about.com's political humor Web site devoted to cartoons and song parodies produced after 9/11. For example, on December 12, 2001, the *Onion*

ran a story called "Starving, Bandaged Bin Laden Offers U.S. One Last Chance to Surrender" that features a picture of a wounded and bleeding bin Laden. Similarly, in the animated "Osama bin Laden: Nowhere to Run, Nowhere to Hide," President Bush plays the bongos, Colin Powell sings "Hey Mr. Taliban, turn over bin Laden, / Daylight come and we drop de bomb," and a diminutive, frightened version of the terrorist king-pin flees from one bombed out cave to another until he is trapped in a hole with a U.S. missile and utterly eradicated, while in the animated "Osama Got Run over by a Reindeer," he ends up with a "reindeer antler up his . . . Ho Ho Ho Ho Ho Ho Ho!" If only it had been so easy. Like the propa-gandistic tags cable news networks used in covering the U.S. response to the attacks (for instance, "America at War," "America Strikes Back") that Aaron McGruder mocked in his September 27, 2001, *Boondocks* strip (fig. 20), the bin Laden and Taliban jokes did little to promote introspection about why we were hated so much around the world that people were willing to die in the process of committing mass murder while others ap-plauded them for doing so.[30]

Less obvious than the frustration about the failure to find the culprit President Bush said six days after 9/11 he "Wanted Dead or Alive," below the surface of these parodies lurked resentment about the unexpected in-flowing of unfamiliar images and ideas from the alien culture of funda-mentalist Islam. For, as the country absorbed information about al Qaeda and the Taliban, Afghanistan and its warlords, burkas and jihads, a coun-terbalancing desire for cultural hegemony or isolation found at least tem-porary satisfaction in jokes that shifted bin Laden and the Taliban into contexts that reasserted America's domination. The use of familiar American songs begins to suggest this frame shift, as do references specific to U.S. popular culture, including Santa Claus, the Flintstones, and, among Piechota's fifty ways, a monster that had been haunting American nightmares for years: "I said no grieving is allowed if he's in pain. / I wish

FIGURE TWENTY-ONE. Taliban Barbie, posted anonymously at http://www.funlol .com/pictures/taliban-barbie.html; http:// politicalhumor.about.com/library/images/ bltalibanbarbie.htm.

there was some way Hannibal Lecter could even eat his Brain." Other examples of this impulse include the *Taliban TV Guide* that circulated via e-mail and featured such shows as *Talibantubbies* and *Mad about Everything;* the on-line ad parody *The Taliban on Broadway* that began, "If you liked *Iraq on Ice,* you'll love *The Taliban on Broadway*" and featured such lyrics as "Veil me a lady tonight" and "Osama, I just met a man named Osama, and suddenly I see what a terrorist he would be"; and parodic ads for toys like Jihad Joe, the Taliban Barbie doll (fig. 21), and Mr. Osama (Potato) Head.

Two of the best examples of the hegemonic yearning expressed through jokes, lyrics, and parodies like these can be found in seemingly unrelated places: the teen-talk expression "Osama yo mama" and the *New Yorker* cover of December 10, 2002, that featured a map of New York City with Afghanistanized names of geographic areas. Fitting bin Laden into the context of an urban African American insult game that usually conjures up images of mothers who have hairy arm pits or wear combat boots seeks to bring him inside a familiar set of associations in which the insulted traits involve unconventional grooming or dressing habits rather than megalomania and mass murder. Similarly, the "New Yorkistan" *New Yorker* cover (fig. 22)—featuring such neighborhoods as Lowrentistan,

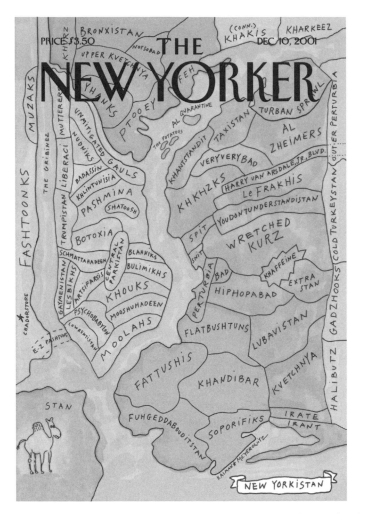

FIGURE TWENTY-TWO. "New Yorkistan" cover art by Maria Kalman and Rick Meyerowitz
© 2001 Conde Nast Publications, Inc. All Rights Reserved.

Turban Sprawl, Khantstandit, and Fattushis—acknowledges but also
re-Americanizes (or re–New York–icizes) the invasion of Islamic and
Afghani cultural terms. Though the area names look Afghani, they allude
to such diverse New York groups as commuters (Kharkeez), gays
(Gaymenistan), cab drivers (Taxistan), Chinese (Mooshuhadeen), Jews
(Kvetchnya), Wasps (Khakis), Yuppies (Boxtoxia), and financiers (Moo-
lahs). This cover achieved its instant notoriety by exposing the widely
shared uneasiness that underpins much of American antiterrorist humor:
anxiety about our sudden vulnerability, our openness not only to violent

attack but to new and unwelcome images of a hostile and culturally different enemy. Just as the new Brooklyn neighborhood of Fuhgeddabouditstan implies a yearning to move on, so turning Kandihar into Khandibar and all the Stans into Youdontunderstandistan offers a brief sense of control by bringing the unfamiliar and menacing landscape of the war on terrorism into comfortably familiar frames of reference. In the brittle moments of amusement these jokes provide—when Osama (now just) yo mama, has been run over by a reindeer or bombed out of his cave—we are laughing at the image of a monster transformed into a stooge.

While the bin Laden and Taliban jokes worked toward a national consensus based on the detestation of a common enemy, preparing for and even promoting the invasion of Afghanistan, their implied assumption of U.S. cultural supremacy raises questions about public attitudes and brings us back to the dramatic shifts in comedic treatments of President Bush. The overnight improvement in Bush's approval rating following 9/11 and the suspension of joking about him suggests that his standing as a butt benefited considerably from the way the first major attack on the U.S. homeland left many Americans not only angry and upset but also yearning for a strong leader who would affirm their sense of national belonging and security. That the guy at the top had until then seemed illegitimate and/or ridiculous to roughly half the electorate ceased to matter for a time, as the enemy-of-your-enemy principle took hold. Indeed, one ironic effect of the stories about pre-9/11 intelligence failures reported after the attacks was the downgrading of concern about the importance of intelligence as a presidential attribute. Miller argues, in *The Bush Dyslexicon,* that, like earlier politicians going back at least to Andrew Jackson, Bush benefited from the way accusations of stupidity and ignorance, whether serious or satirical, can appear to be expressions of an unattractive intellectual snobbery, and this certainly seems to have been operative in the Bush-as-dope and Gore-as-Brainiac contrast that carried through the 2000 campaign. But after 9/11, the denial or obscuring of Bush's manifest verbal and intellectual weaknesses gained a new intensity and source. During the weeks and months of vulnerability and outrage, satire took a vacation in part because focusing on the inadequacies of the previously mocked president would have been excruciating. As Miller notes, "the national trauma blew the President sky-high, transforming him . . . from a very easy punchline to something like a God." And, though the suspension was brief, its effects were long-lasting: three years later, just after the 2004 election, a scant 7 percent of voters polled by CNN said that they thought intelligence was the most important quality for a president; of these 91 percent voted for John Kerry and only 9 percent for Bush. So it came to this: at a time when the keenest minds were needed to deal with the complex security, economic, environmental, and political challenges of the post–Cold War period, as many as 90 percent of Americans came to think that we were well served by George W. Bush, a number that hovered around 50 percent during the run-up to the presidential election in which, by a slim majority, 50.73 percent of voters returned Bush to the White House in 2004.[31]

Because the adversarial nature of partisan argument moves advocates on both sides to lash out with whatever weapons they command especially around elections, not even the group-think that set in following 9/11 could long suppress political humor. In a cartoon that ran on September 20, 2001, called "America: Standing Firm," Ted Rall attempted to reintroduce Bush bashing into the postattack mood. In separate panels, Rall shows groups of people under such captions as "We accept that everything has changed" and "We're willing to wallow in cheesy patriotism." And yet, the cartoon concludes, "there's one truth we will always know: Our 'President' is a twit." The October 26, 2001, cartoon by Toles shows a weary but determined Republican elephant (ironically called "Our Hero") that has navigated a dizzying game board of events—including the terrorist attacks, the declaration of war, the anthrax scare, the squandering of the surplus, and the shut down of the U.S. capital—all to deliver a tax cut to the feet of a fat cat that represents corporations. The transparent way the Bush administration and its congressional allies exploited the calamity to advance unrelated and backlogged goals jolted progressive satirists to life. In the Dan Wasserman cartoon that ran on September 28, 2001, in the Boston Globe, two well-fed Republican lawmakers are in conversation, one asking the other, "Which should we pass first, the antiterrorist capital gains tax cut or the antiterrorist ANWAR oil drilling bill?" Similarly, two months after the attacks and in time for early action in the 2002 midterm election campaigns, in response to what he saw as Bush's exploitation of 9/11 during a partisan trip to Florida, David Counts put his Web site back up. And in the long run-up to the 2004 presidential election—that is, from the fall of 2003 on—the butt wars of Bush versus Democrats and then versus Kerry raged.

One particularly striking battle was waged between white.house.org (on the left) and scrappleface.com (on the right), both of which use parodic documents to make sharply partisan points. Written primarily by Scott Ott, the author also of Axis of Weasels, scrappleface functions as a low-graphic, Republican version of the Onion, that is, it makes its points by way of fake news stories that call attention to undesirable characteristics of progressive politicians and programs and to the virtues of conservative figures and ideas. During the 2004 campaign, many of these focused offensively on attacking Kerry and defensively on responding to questions about and criticisms of the president. Anti-Kerry headlines posted early on include ones that feature the Democrat as flip-flopping ("Bush Offers 'Clear Choice,' Kerry to Decide Soon" [February 24, 2004]) and as naive about defense ("Kerry Calls for Bin Laden to Testify" [March 28, 2004]). In the former, Kerry is said to have "initially supported the President's 'No Child Left Behind' education plan, the use of force to overthrow Saddam Hussein and USA Patriot Act"—only to later flip-flop into "a critic of all three initiatives." The story concludes: "'If I continue to stand on my principles,' said the Vietnam veteran war-protestor, 'I will likely support President Bush for reelection until the second week of November.'"[32]

On the positive side, Ott turned Bush campaign missteps into virtues. When viewers and pundits noticed a bump under Bush's jacket in the first 2004 presidential debate on October 11, scrappleface posted a story called "Object under Bush Jacket Identified: 'It's a Spine.'" Deflecting speculation that Bush was wearing a device through which Karl Rove was putting words in his mouth, Ott contrasted the protuberance with Kerry's lack of backbone, as is clear in the mock-comment Kerry offers: "I had a spine when I defended this country as a young man, and I will have one again when I defend her as president of the United States."[33]

Carrying water for the other team, whitehouse.org, whose domain name was designed to give Karl Rove fits, also played both offense and defense during the campaign. In response to Kerry's comment about Mary Cheney's sexual orientation in the second debate, widely seen as unfortunate at least because it opened the democratic standard bearer up to accusations of political exploitation, whitehouse.org ran a story called "Mrs. Cheney's Irate Response to Senator John Kerry's Cheap Debate Reference to Her Beloved Daughter's Vile and Repulsive Lifestyle Choice," which leads with Mrs. Cheney's prepared statement: "Good morning. As everyone knows by now, last night, during the final presidential debate, Senator John Kerry proved beyond a shadow of a doubt that he is not a good man. Specifically, he said that my daughter was a . . . he accused her of . . . he called whatsername a . . . one of those . . . um . . . 'L Words.' And by making such a cheap and tawdry political reference to my little girl, he has made me a pretty indignant mom!" Adopting the format of official White House statements, press releases and news conferences, whitehouse.org exaggerates what might actually be said by administration officials into embarrassing revelations, often using obscenities to highlight the contrast between a veneer of piety and a concealed special-interest agenda and narrow-minded worldview. Typical of these is "Matt Drudge: Fair and Balanced Blogger: Ask the White House" (September 9, 2004), "Defusing the Flu Vaccine: President Unveils Patriotic Three Point Virus Survival Plan for America's Disease-Infested Geriatrics" (October 19, 2004), and a mock press conference under the headline "President Holds Prime Time Press Conference to Rekindle America's Fast-Declining Faith in Conspicuous Ineptitude and Planetary Chaos" (April 13, 2004) that opens as follows: "Good evening. In the next 45 minutes, I will utter the words "FREEDOM," "FREE," and "TERROR!!!" a total of 21, 29, and 28 times, respectively. That's once every 35 seconds. It's a tight schedule, but thank the Lord we're a FREEDOM-loving country of FREE people who hate TERROR!!! So let's get started with the questions." In all of this, anti–Bush Web site designers have one eye on the man they see as opponent number one, Rush Limbaugh, who, during the 2004 campaign, added thirteen anti-Kerry parodies with titles like "Just a Gigolo," "Dawn of the Brain Dead Candidate," "I Was in Nam," "Bad Vibrations," and "DNC Eye for a Dull Guy" to an archive that had already banked three dozen anti-Clinton routines. In general, Limbaugh depicts Kerry as boring, indecisive, unprincipled, affluent, uninspiring, and sluggish.[34]

Visual satire featuring unflattering pictures of the candidates in editorial cartoons, campaign advertising, and advocacy Web sites represented another butt-war battlefield. Mallard Fillmore, Bruce Tinsley's far-right syndicated cartoon, predictably spent the two weeks just before the election ridiculing Kerry by drawing him with buck teeth, implausibly protruding temples, and an impossibly long chin. In a series that ran during the week of October 26, Tinsley's protagonist, a duck who sees liberal bias everywhere, recounts a nightmare he had. In it, John Kerry, having won the presidency, gives a postelection speech in which he promises to tax the rich, "the almost rich, those who want to be rich, those who know a guy named rich, [and] those who watch 'The O'Reilly Factor.'" Meanwhile, pro-Bush "Webtoonists" outdid each other in coming up with depictions of Kerry as an indecisive, flip-flopping waffler.[35]

Although allowing Kerry to be photographed and filmed while windsurfing and then interviewed about it was undoubtedly intended as part of the familiar campaign strategy of showing (off) a candidate's strength and youthfulness, this turned out to be a blunder. First, unlike baseball or basketball, windsurfing was not that popular or common a sport: according to a New York Times story that ran a month before the election, "The latest survey by the National Sporting Goods Association showed that 400,000 people participated in windsurfing at least once in 2001." Beyond this, so much about the sport—from its association with wealthy beach commu-

FIGURE TWENTY-THREE. "Kerry's Anti-Terrorism Plan," Jay D. Dyson, http://www
.sacredcowburgers.com/, by permission.

nities to the $1,200 cost of a "basic startup kit"—confirmed the association
of Kerry with affluence and privilege. Even worse, when the Bush team
put together an ad that used unappealingly clownish music and grainy
images of Kerry tacking first in one and then in the opposite direction, it
reinforced the impression of him as indecisively lacking in conviction.[36]

Satire played a role in the depiction of Kerry as an unpatriotic, weak-on-
defense, antimilitary liberal more interested in serving the perceived global
interests of the United Nations than the national interests of the United
States. At the sacredcowburgers.com site, Kerry appears as a "lunatic" eager to mouth ideas advanced by Kofi Anan, the advocate of a "Terrorist-
Approved" "Global Defense Plan" outlined on a parodic version of a
pregnancy-test kit and committed to the idea of letting "other nations decide how the US should surrender." Even more striking is Jay D. Dyson's
"Kerry's Anti-Terrorism Plan AKA Operation Infinite Appeasement" (fig.
23), a composite that combined a few news photos to dress the Democratic
candidate in the outfit of a Muslim (Palestinian?) protester in a crowd of
hooded terrorists and angry Islamic demonstrators.[37]

Anti-Bush send-ups have, arguably, tended to lack both this level of
focus (Nast's clarity) and Lakoff's clearly progressive framing. In the
Stuart Carlson cartoon (fig. 24) that ran just after the 2000 election (on
November 7, 2000), the familiar image of Bush as cowboy, in this case
sheriff, is a study in ambiguity, setting the future president—goofy expression, large ears, elevated waist line, oversized badge, overly dramatic
gesture, and all—in one of the mythic postures of the Old West. Is this a
costumed pretender, or will he clean up that stink hole of hostility and
dysfunction: the DC Saloon? Still weakened by ambiguity but moving in

the direction of a sharper attack is the Oliphant cartoon (fig. 25) that ran on July 20, 2004 in which Bush appears in the familiar "all-hat-and-no-cattle" style: a tiny man with a pointy chin and a liar's nose. The effort to emphasize the evasiveness of the president's campaign rhetoric, his use of key phrases about war, god, family, and patriotism, and his determination not to discuss his own war record, indeed to deflect attention from it by talking about gay marriage, was undoubtedly apparent to like-minded viewers of the cartoon. The problem is that Bush's repetition here, though intended to come across as an evasive, shifty campaign tactic, might also have evoked the idea of focus and even conviction, just as the cowboy hat, though humorously super-sized, is not all that different from images of Bush wearing or waving a large white cowboy hat on the ranch served up regularly by the White House publicity operation. As in other cartoons in which Oliphant represents Cowboy Bush as a little boy demanding attention from adults, most notably his father, the president here gesticulates childishly, struggling to defend himself. One wonders whether cartoons like this were pointed enough to shake the support of readers who saw the president's focus on these themes and the image of him as a cowboy at the worst as mixed and at the best positive.[38]

7/20

By way of contrast, consider the work of Marc Forest, the creator of theworriedshrimp.com Web site devoted incongruously to Nastian images of Bush and discussions of fly fishing. Though Forest sees himself as "club handed and drawing challenged," he has produced a portfolio of unambiguously reductive and negative caricatures. By manipulating photographs he downloads from Yahoo, Forest places his ominously bemused, distracted, goofy, and/or insane Bush in familiar settings in which the emphasized traits are wildly, often alarmingly, inappropriate. In Forest's "Mad Cowboy Disease" picture (fig. 26), for instance, Bush appears to be demented: his nostrils flared, his ears oversized, his eyes beady, and his expression stupid, irritated, and untrustworthy to say the least. By exploding whatever sense of well-aimed determination or admirable ruggedness might be associated with the Marlboro president, unlike many of the Bush-as-cowboy parodies, this one loses little if any of its derogatory force. But this may well be the exception that highlights the rule: like the stupidity motif, as Miller noted early on, the cowboy barbs, that work so well in reducing Bush to an American stereotype abroad, have in general had a mixed resonance that has weakened their impact at home.[39]

After the election the inevitable gloating and groaning found comic expression. Ann Coulter threw one of Kerry's campaign lines back at him when she posted the following comment almost as soon as the winner was

FIGURE TWENTY-SIX. "Mad Cowboy Disease" © 2003 Marc Forest, with permission

determined: "I guess John Kerry went into the primary without a plan to win the election." Jibjab produced an animation about Bush's second-term agenda; e-mails containing a ragingly detailed screed called "Fuck the South" and others linked to maps of a postsecessionist America divided between blue states that were joined to a United States of Canada and red states called either Jesusland or Dumfuckistan circulated. Meanwhile, by way of Monday morning review, humor creators looked back and mulled their impact. Rush Limbaugh must have felt that his characterization of liberal radio talk shows as an ineffective reaction to the success of conservatives was accurate. David Counts came at least partially to regret his domain name (toostupidtobepresident) because he no longer saw stupidity (in the sense of failures of thought and expression) as an entirely negative attribute as far as voters were concerned. R. J. Crane, the creative force behind topplebush.com, maintained his opinion that, in a culture where the reading of books and newspapers is down, "humor might be the best or only way to reach most people with political information." While Barry Crimmins, the author of *Never Shake Hands with a War Criminal* and a joke writer for Air America Radio, insisted in a post-election interview that "the greatest tyrant can be brought down by ridicule," Daniel Kurtzman more cautiously noted, looking back a month after the election from his viewing point at About.com's political humor Web site, that "the effect that political satire has on people can be difficult to gauge." Kurtzman continued:

Political humor that has a real partisan edge is more likely to simply make like-minded people laugh than it is to convert anyone to a new way of thinking. At the same time, using humor to communicate a political message can enable people to reach an audience that might otherwise be hostile to that message. A sharp-edged joke or incisive parody may be more likely to penetrate than, say, a newspaper editorial or a campaign ad trying to communicate the same point because it catches people with their defenses down.

When seen in relation to recent work on humor and persuasion, Kurtzman's points seem both valid and significant. Incisive parodies are unlikely to be more persuasive than incisive editorials, though there is some reason to suppose that they can reach a more diverse audience. As Ford and Ferguson's work suggests, hostile humor is likely to exert influence on listeners already unsympathetic to the butt. For this reason, as Kurtzman notes, it may be that political satire exerts influence less by changing than by strengthening opinion. By providing experiences of shared amusement (the Kerry windsurfing ad; the endless circulation of Bushisms), it can foster and solidify communities of like-minded thinkers, some of whom may be more likely to vote because they more strongly identify with the part of themselves that has found others with whom to laugh. Some voters may feel a greater urgency about getting to the polls to oppose a candidate they find utterly ridiculous. At the same time, it can be easier to back a candidate whose personal defects and/or potentially destructive ideas are occasionally dressed up in self-deprecating comedy. Though unlikely to sway many elections, the tendency of campaign humor to promote group thinking and relax logical thought makes its contribution to democratic process mixed at best, unfortunate at worst.[40]

Conclusion

Given the weak effect of humor as a means of persuasion, the intensity and intentionality of recent political satire can seem a bit delusional, not altogether different from the inflated sense of efficacy that seems to motivate advocates of healing laughter and disputants quarreling over the propriety of particular jokes or joke cycles. Though focused, unambiguous, and repetitive put-downs like those used by Thomas Nast against his targets are more likely to strike home, even their impact seems generally to be marginal, perhaps because receiving a joke in the spirit intended requires a sense of fellow feeling with the joker as well as receptivity to the point being made. Amid the hubbub of recent intentional political joke writing, it's worth remembering that humor neither hurt bin Laden nor prevented George W. Bush from being elected—at least once.

And yet, since even marginal influences can be important in close elections and other decision-making processes, political humor matters enough that its intended recipients (citizens, voters, and politicians) should pay attention to how it is meant to affect them. Because at no time in human history has our species been so technologically enabled to execute its decisions, the level of fact and logic used in deciding what it would be best to do has never mattered so much. It was one thing to conclude erroneously that Socrates was immortal (even though he was a man and all men are mortal); it's another thing to conclude that global climate change is beyond human influence because Rush Limbaugh says so repeatedly, sometimes in a serious, sometimes in a comic, tone.

So even if you like a joke as much as the next person, even if you think that what the world needs now is laughter, sweet laughter, there are times when wisdom dictates a reflective, rather than reflexive, reception of political humor. Stimulating this reflective approach can begin by complicating our response to the assumption that, of course, we want a president with a sense of humor. The more obviously true this seems, the more it feels like common sense, the more it probably needs to be qualified or at least challenged by specific examples. And so this chapter will conclude with three final instances of presidential joke telling—involving Reagan, Clinton, and George W. Bush—that collectively raise questions about how humor can seek to support ruinous policies and obscure personal defects. Call this: "When Bad Things Happen to Good Jokes, or Vice Versa. You Be the Judge!"

Beginning with Reagan: Was the fortieth president just kidding when, according to Kitty Kelley, he shared a favorite joke about the treatment of AIDS patients with friends? In her 1992 unauthorized biography of

Nancy Reagan, Kelley focuses on the years of inaction on AIDS by an administration that squandered precious time by not supporting research and frank public education, a case that was made in greater detail by Randy Shilts in *And The Band Played On*. It is startling to learn that Reagan's inaction on the issue was accompanied by jokes that targeted AIDS victims. Reagan laughed at jokes about giving AIDS to Moamar Quaddafi, and, Kelley writes, "Reagan, who enjoyed mimicking homosexuals, . . . added AIDS jokes to his repertoire. He loved to tell the one about two doctors at the medical convention talking about treating AIDS patients. . . . One doctor said to the other: 'I've got the solution. I serve them a special dinner of crepes and filet of sole.' 'What does that do, [said the other doctor], it's not a cure.' 'No it's not,' said the [first] doctor, 'but the advantage is that I can just slide it under the door and I don't have to touch them.'" Though at the time of his death in June 2004 he was highly praised, indeed virtually canonized, by members of the party he helped bring to power, and lauded in particular for the wit and humor he brought to the presidency, this joke reminds us of the downside of presidential humor, its ability to promote relaxation and indifference where concentration, effort, and caring are required. Nor is this the only example of Reagan's use of humor to minimize the importance of pressing issues. Joking about his veto of a clean air bill in January of 1987, the Gipper said, "I just said no." Ridiculing the Dukakis campaign in June of 1988, Reagan quipped, "You know, if I listened to him long enough, I would be convinced . . . that people are homeless, and people are going without food and medical attention, and that we've got to do something about the unemployed." If this was a joke, the antijoke might have gone something like this: during the Reagan presidency, the dramatic increase in the number of people living beneath the federal poverty line (from 24.5 million in 1978 to 32.5 million in 1988) drove people onto the streets. As Peter Dreier, director of the Urban and Environmental Policy program at Occidental College, put it, "One of Reagan's most enduring legacies is the steep increase in homeless people. By the late 1980s, the number of homeless had swollen to 600,000 on any given night and 1.2 million over the course of a year." Nor is Reagan's image enhanced, by recalling, as Professor Dreier does, that "in 1984 on 'Good Morning America' he said that people sleeping on the streets 'are homeless, you might say, by choice.'" Roger Wilkins may well have had the contrast between Reagan's general affability and the cruelty of his political program in mind when he described him as "a nasty man whose major talent is to make us feel good about being creepy and who lets us pretend that tomorrow will never come." Sound familiar?[41]

As little as progressives appreciate jokes told at the expense of AIDS sufferers and the homeless, conservatives have always recoiled from what they have seen as Bill Clinton's smarmy, smirking allure. Clinton for his part thought that humor mattered, and he counted on specific writers— Al Franken on occasion, Mark Katz regularly—to craft strategic jokes and routines. To push back against the well-funded Harry and Louise campaign mounted in 1994 by the insurance industry in opposition to health care reforms, Bill and Hillary taped their own "mockumercial" in which they played the parts of a middle-aged, middle-class couple worried about health care costs and spotty coverage. As part of the ritual performances associated with both the annual White House Correspondents and Gridiron Club dinners, Clinton joked about such then-current stories as the Whitewater investigations and the embarrassment caused by the answer he gave to a question on MTV about the kind of underwear he wore. All of this seemed routine, though the underwear episode, jokes and all, certainly struck many observers as characteristically undignified. But the sex scandal—involving marital infidelity, oral sex, and dishonest denials— pushed the comedic envelope. Like an anxious court jester, even Clinton's joke writer, Mark Katz, agonized over the use of humor in defusing the problem. Angry enough to consider quitting his post, Katz was talked out of this by his brother who urged him to get over himself and "write the poor bastard [Clinton] some fucking jokes." Telling himself that he was working for the presidency, Katz wrote "a series of humor speeches [in the spring 1998] that set the backdrop of [the] fevered, sordid scandal." A specific joke Katz wrote and Clinton delivered at the Gridiron Dinner took off on the way newspapers, driven by 24/7 cable news reporting, were printing poorly sourced (but possibly true) stories about the president's sex life and then having to print retractions soon after: "Now I'm at a little bit of a disadvantage this year. I've been so busy I haven't read a newspaper or a magazine or even watched the evening news since the Pope went to Cuba. What have you been writing about since then? I hardly have time to read news anymore. Mostly I just skim the retractions." As he reflected on jokes like this that Clinton used not to support besieged policies but to "reinforce lies," Katz wallowed in self-doubt: "I didn't realize it at the time, but this was a joke that took me over a threshold I had hoped not to cross. . . . Now I was using humor to paint a picture of a plausible story on behalf of a client whom I did not myself believe. Had Bill Clinton succeeded where my parents, my girlfriends' parents and my guidance counselor had failed? With writing these semantic jokes that were narrowly construed to fortify falsehoods, had I finally turned into a goddamn lawyer?" If a supporter as ardent as Katz could find jokes like this disturbing, imagine what the president's political opponents, who believed the stories and doubted the retractions, made of humor as crassly exploitative and self-serving as, well, as having nonsexual sex with an intern young enough to be your daughter.[42]

Finally, at the 2005 White House Correspondents Dinner, the Bushes planned a surprise. At the start of his presentation, as he was launching into a joke he had often told on the campaign trail, the president was interrupted by the First Lady who brushed him aside and took over the podium—much to the hilarity of the assembled press. Some of the joking revolved around the idea that Laura Bush was a "desperate housewife," abandoned by a man who falls asleep by 9 P.M.; some of it poked fun at familiar administration figures like Barbara Bush (whom she compared to Don Corleone of *Godfather* fame) and Dick Cheney (whose morning exercise consists of a "twenty- to thirty-foot walk"). Even Bush policies came in for some tangential ribbing when she said, "George's approach to any problem at the ranch is to cut it down with a chain saw, which is why I think he and Cheney and Rumsfeld get along so well." According to a reporter for the *New York Times,* the First Lady "brought down a very tough house" in laughter.[43]

In the spirit of Malcolm Kushner, we could celebrate this levity, go along with the joking, congratulate ourselves on having chosen a president who has a sense of humor, who can laugh at himself. But then we would need to overlook the event as theater, as a performance that reveals far less about the performers themselves—about what they think is funny—than about their intentions. Of course, slowing down long enough to consider Mrs. Bush's jokes will make it less likely that we'll find them amusing, but this seems a small price to pay for not being drawn inside this circle of shared delight. Written by Landon Parvin, who also wrote jokes for President and Mrs. Reagan, the desperate housewife gags were obviously intended to convey a sense of (ever so slightly) off color, pop culture edginess, just as the jokes about the president were meant to show his softer (I can take it) side. As the *Times* reporter put it, the effect was "to humanize her husband whose poll numbers [were] no match for [hers]."

At the time of this affair in early May 2005, why might the recently reelected president's poll numbers (below 50 percent for the first time) have been sagging? Could it have been his transparently deceptive attempt to undermine Social Security? The ongoing onslaught in Iraq where insurgents had intensified their violent resistance? The fact that the U.S. military was having trouble meeting enlistment quotas? Stories about the abuse of Islamic prisoners that were circulating worldwide? Or could it have been a sense of impending financial calamity based on the increasingly ominous growth of the federal debt primarily attributable to faith in the counterintuitive proposition that reducing revenue decreases deficits? Or the recent efforts to open up wilderness areas in national forests in general and drilling in the Arctic National Wildlife Refuge in particular? Or was it the Republican intrusion into the death of Terri Schiavo, the effort to force far right judges onto the federal bench, or the nagging feeling that whatever the administration was doing would not protect us from the next big terrorist attack? It's one thing to live on Gidden's juggernaut world; it's another to look up and see your president using his power (and wit?) to move things toward disaster in every possible way. If you bring this awareness to stories about the First Lady's night of fun—seeing images of this cavalcade of impending doom while reading news accounts or watching her performance on CNN—even though you know, or maybe because you know, that laughing would be pleasant and relaxing, you may not be willing to go along. Like a guest at the Macbeth's dinner party, once the ghost appears you may not care about the quality of the meal.

Conclusion

Do you know what week this is in our public schools? I'm not making this up: this week is National No Name-Calling Week. They don't want any name-calling in our public schools. What stupid dork came up with this idea?

JAY LENO, *Tonight Show* monologue, January 24, 2005

Results from 2004 bullying surveys in schools indicated that students reported a significant decrease in the amount of bullying and harassment in school after taking part in the first *No Name-Calling Week* and its activities. More than 5,000 educators and administrators have officially registered to take part in the [2005] week.

Press release issued by the No Name-Calling Week Coalition, January 24, 2005

Joke and antijoke: one last example. No doubt staying with his fixed role not as a satirist but a comedian, Jay Leno sent this joke flying, along with tried and true observations about Michael Jackson, Tom Cruise, Jessica Simpson, and Paris Hilton. Anything to avoid "preaching" to his audience, anything for a joke, a laugh. Leno may begin his routine by asking "Did you see *X* or *Y*," but affecting how viewers see anything is the last thing he intends. It appears not to matter that, however ridiculous it sounds or can be made to seem, National No Name-Calling Week might just be a good idea. A step away from a culture that leads the world not just in gun violence but specifically in school shootings. Not taken into account by *Tonight Show* gag smiths was the fact that there were twenty-three fatal shootings and six fatal stabbings in American schools during the 2004–5 school year, climaxing in the Minnesota Red Lake High School murder/suicide that left nine people dead and thirteen others wounded a mere two months after Leno enjoyed his dork putdown. Does it matter that Jeff Weise, the junior who began this killing spree by murdering his grandparents and ended it by killing himself was, as Red Lake students told MSNBC, "regularly picked on for his odd behavior," that he was "terrorized a lot by others who called him names"?[1]

"Hey," I can hear you thinking, "take it easy. Lighten up. It's just a bleepin' monologue." It's the "just" part that gives me pause. The Red Lake teen jokers, the ones who found, perhaps, an outlet for their aggressive instincts or were also, perhaps, just enjoying a joke or two at Jeff Weise's expense: should we lighten up about them too? Unlike Jay Leno, their humor was spontaneous, an expression of what was running through their twisted little adolescent brains. Perhaps they were feeling anxious, insecure, depressed, stressed out; perhaps the ridicule they served up was therapeutic, not for their target obviously, who would eventually acquire a more lethal weapon but, in the moment of laughing, for them. That the overlap of healing and hostile impulses, the morphing of Norman into Freddy in cases of adolescent name calling, can be fatal appears not to have factored into the creative process followed by the *Tonight Show* staff. As Leno told the *Los Angeles Times,* members of his audience have a simple desire: they "want to hear a joke."

This study of intentional humor—of jokers who set out to do more than amuse and who rely on the potentially subtle operations of humor to achieve specific effects—has sought both to describe recent trends and to use striking examples of them to awaken moral sensibilities. Because humor is delightful, because it provides breaks from the constraints of logic and restraints of conscience, nudging us into the moral lassitude implicit in the expression "it's only a joke," we need to see that some jokes and jokers can do harm. Throughout I have chosen edgy and purposive examples and shared my own ethical perspectives in an effort to encourage you to take sides, to prefer some of the humorists discussed here to others, and to respect both your ability to find some jokes funny and others beyond the pale. Where you draw the line is less important than knowing that it needs at times to be drawn, since there are important differences between the four "players" of Cornell and their many outraged detractors; the tree-loving and tree-cutting singer songwriters; the laughing ministers and their unsmiling critics; the hospital clowns who bring moments of comic empowerment to sick children and the clowns and critters who sell kids junk food, alcohol, and tobacco; the talk show host who thinks torture is funny and the soldier who was both appalled and captivated by the killing jokers he encountered; the anti-Bush blog masters and the pro-Bush joke writers.

Taken from the ongoing cavalcade of American humor, these typical but far from exhaustive examples suggest that we need to get beyond the distinction Leno offers between "preaching" and "a joke" to an awareness of the possibility that humor can have an impact, make a difference, have consequences. Beyond the detached world of professional comedy where performers and writers measure success by the volume of the laughter they elicit, where the subject is "yada yada" and the worldview is "whatever," we need to move past Leno's preaching/joke distinction by becoming aware of how humor is being used around us. The point would be the activation not of humor-killing self-consciousness but of humor-motivating and filtering conscience: a contrast that can be illustrated by comparing the Leno dork joke with a convention-exploding performance of Jon Stewart's.

At the more responsible and frequently funnier end of late-night television, thinking about the consequences of joking and specific jokes is surely what gave the *Daily Show* host pause when, on October 15, 2004, a little more than two weeks before the election that would return George W. Bush to office, he appeared on CNN's *Crossfire* and mixed it up with its two hosts: Paul Begala and Tucker Carlson. An Emmy Award winner and the coauthor of the best-seller *America (The Book): A Citizen's Guide to Democracy Inaction,* Stewart refused, contrary to expectation, to be their "monkey," that is to be funny about everything and nothing. Instead, he confronted his hosts, arguing forcefully that they were staging fake debates that were cheapening political discourse. Afraid that they will be attacked on shows "such as *Crossfire, Hardball* or 'I'm Going to Kick Your Ass,'" Stewart argued, candidates avoid speaking clearly. When Stewart implored his interlocutors to "stop hurting the country" by serving the interests of politicians and corporations, it set up the following exchange:

BEGALA: By beating up on them? You just said we're too rough on them when they make mistakes.

STEWART: No, no, no, you're not too rough on them. You're part of their strategies. You are partisan, what do you call it, hacks.

When Carlson tried to go on the offensive by accusing Stewart of asking liberal guests—including John Kerry who had recently appeared on *The Daily Show* but declined invitations from *Crossfire*—easy questions, Stewart responded by highlighting the distinction between a news program/ network and a comedy program/network:

STEWART: You know, it's interesting to hear you talk about my responsibility.
CARLSON: I felt the sparks between you.
STEWART: I didn't realize that—and maybe this explains quite a bit.
CARLSON: No, the opportunity to . . .
[Crosstalk]
STEWART: . . . is that the news organizations look to Comedy Central for their cues on integrity.

By developing this unusually candid critique of the treatment of the election on cable TV, Stewart clearly startled his hosts. The generally irrepressible Begala was almost speechless; the generally witty Carlson was reduced to crude insults: noting, for instance, that Stewart was John Kerry's "butt boy" and saying that he (Carlson) would not enjoy having Stewart over to his house. Though this might seem like just another celebrity shout fest, you can see why the CNN hosts were shaken. Having introduced Stewart as the "funniest smart guy on TV," the last thing they expected was direct, heartfelt criticism. That his critique employed both serious assertions ("You're part of their strategies") and comic thrusts ("I'm Going to Kick Your Ass," "what do you call it, hacks") suggests that Stewart, unwilling to be randomly amusing, was determined to use humor to make a point he seriously believed. Insofar as it encourages us to bring our full selves, conscience and all, to humor, this habit, fundamental to satire as opposed to stand-up, is well worth cultivating.

Because we value humor so much, a common move in the art of denigration is the assertion that one's opponent or enemy is "humorless." As discussed in chapter 4, a few weeks after 9/11, humor consultant Malcolm Kushner argued that the struggle between the United States and Islamic terrorists could be characterized as a conflict "between the humorous and the humorless." By way of ironic counterexample, consider this: months before 9/11, Bush critic Mark Crispin Miller called the president's team a "deeply humorless cabal of rightist pols." Or this: that both of Bush's Democratic presidential opponents, Al Gore and John Kerry, were characterized this way. As a check of the blogosphere can demonstrate, *Boston Globe* columnist Joan Vennochi spoke for many Republicans when she attributed Gore's ineffectiveness to his "humorless, self-righteous liberalism," while Mark Steyn stated a common criticism of Kerry when he called him "grimly humorless, touchy, [and] self-regarding." Just to round this out, in a *Washington Post* interview, Gene Weingarten asked

Ralph Nader to respond to the view that he is a "friendless, humorless killjoy," while no less a student of American culture than Hunter S. Thompson described Nixon as "absolutely humorless." Coming from radically divergent perspectives, these accusations have in common disapproval (and perhaps limited knowledge) of the people so characterized and an idealized view of humor. Unstated but nonetheless operative is a syllogism that assumes an upbeat characterization of humor as its major premise (humor is positive, beneficial; it provides balance, irony, perspective, humanity), a negative characterization of a detested person or group (terrorists are hostile and violent; conservatives are hateful and narrow minded, progressives are smug and hyperintellectual) and a seemingly logical conclusion (the person or group is humorless). Moving Freddy back into the exclusively Norman major premise where he belongs explodes the foundation of this argument, since it is naive to suppose that only people who think and act as we do have, use, and enjoy humor.[2]

Contrary to what many in the positive humor movement in general and the laughter club movement in particular believe, humor is not a universal experience that necessarily draws humankind together but a malleable force in communication: a source of delight brought by puns, jokes, comic genres, and spontaneous wit, a cue to relax, a way of reaching out to others, and a sign of intelligence, to be sure, but also an effective tool of denigration, misdirection, and attack. None of these negative functions requires humor, obviously, but the discordant addition of incongruity, surprise, and play to aggression can intensify, even as it makes light of, suffering—just as the use of humor in the promotion of harmful products and ruinous policies is ultimately not that funny. While no PC formula or list of permissible topics can provide useful guidance, and while rules regulating comic speech are absurd and self-defeating, we have much to gain by avoiding both cruelty and deception in joking.

In conclusion, the good news about American humor over the past thirty years is that much of it has been not just enjoyable but relaxing and distracting as well; the bad news is the same insofar as we need to inhabit our anxieties, feel the danger, and motivate to recognize problems and find solutions. At its most insidious, humor can put us into a nonserious frame of mind about matters we urgently need to take seriously. The yearning for evasion, as Giddens and Macy observe, can develop out of or in resistance to a sense of overwhelming vulnerability. When denial of this magnitude morphs into a political program based on a rejection of empathy, the consequences can be fatal.

To put it another way, the healing laughter/killing joke distinction not only characterizes two trends in recent American culture, it provides angles of insight into arguments waged with and about humor. The yearning for detachment served by sadistic jokes and the yearning for recovery sought by healing laughers highlight underlying insecurities—feelings of entrapment in a world and/or body at risk. Among the many overgeneralizations bandied about by consultants and practitioners are claims that humor is a way of coping with suffering, that in a world free of fear and pain there would be no need for laughter. But to the extent that this is true, it begs the question at issue here about how particular jokes and jokers respond to the feelings evoked by dire conditions. Both denial and activism are forms of coping—a difference that matters in a world in which globalization, with its attendant risks of global genocide and humanicide, raises the level of threat. As the anti-PC backlash demonstrated, positing a morality of humor by interposing questions between comic creativity and amusement or by juxtaposing jokes with antijokes is about as welcome as a corpse at a birthday party. But in a time of crucial decisions, how we cope will determine whether we achieve our species potential or succumb to our worst impulses.

Acknowledgments

Among the humor scholars whose ideas have provided frames of reference and points of departure for this study, I am particularly grateful to Mahadev L. Apte, Joseph Boskin, Christie Davies, Alan Dundes, Rhoda L. Fisher, Seymour Fisher, Lawrence E. Mintz, Elliott Oring, and Victor Raskin. During the 2004–5 academic year when I was actively drafting chapters, Rod A. Martin, professor of psychology at the University of Western Ontario, was writing a book about the current state of research in the psychology of humor. Though our projects were different, my various citations here of Martin's work indicate how richly I made use of the summaries he shared with me as we exchanged chapters via e-mail and offered mutual support and occasional suggestions for revision. In a similar act of generosity, John Morreall shared the chapter he wrote for a book on humor studies and applications forthcoming from Mouton de Gruyter in 2006.

I am indebted to Boston College—specifically to the chair of my department, Mary Crane, the deans of the College and Graduate School of Arts and Sciences, Joseph F. Quinn and Michael A. Smyer, the academic vice president, John J. Neuhauser, and the interim associate vice president for research, Michael J. Naughton—for support and encouragement made tangible in the form of subvention funding and research expense and incentive grants. While Stephen E. Vedder and Darren M. Herlihy provided help with images used as illustrations, Brendan A. Rapple assisted in late-stage citation checking.

During the long period of thinking about post-1980 humor in the United States that preceded the writing of this book, I benefited from discussions with colleagues at Boston College, friends, relatives, and students. At the outset, Carlo Rotella read a draft of the introduction and helped me think about the direction I would take; toward the end Lad Tobin and Mark Byers read the manuscript and offered suggestions. While the book was at the press being copyedited and I was obsessing about what to call it, my colleague Caroline Bicks spent thirty seconds listening to me rant about alternatives and came up with the main title. For their support and encouragement, I am grateful to Treseanne Ainsworth, Amy Boesky, Melissa Cote, Adele Dalsimer, Audrey Friedman, Elizabeth Kowaleski Wallace, Tom Kaplan-Maxfield, John L. Mahoney, John McDargh, Bonnie Rudner, Susan Roberts, Dennis Shirley, Jackie Skolnik, Robert Stanton, Laura Tanner, Christopher Wilson, and Judith Wilt.

For several years, starting in the mid-1980s, I regularly taught a course on humor writing. Discussions that began in those classes with highly motivated, intelligent, and talented students have reached fruition here. To those students and to others I came to know through their participation in My Mother's Fleabag, Boston College's student improv comedy troupe, I am profoundly grateful.

Having benefited from the accessibility of materials on-line, one of the great pleasures of working on recent culture, I encourage readers to follow my notes to Web sites devoted to humor or humorous advocacy that I found useful. I am grateful to a number of people who generously either responded to questions sent by e-mail or agreed to be interviewed: Darryl Cherney, David Counts, R. J. Crane, Barry Crimmins, Marc Forest, Joyce Friedman, Daniel E. Kurtzman, Paul E. McGhee, Shazia Mirza, John Morreall, and Deborah Price. For invitations to share ideas in early stages of their development, I am grateful to Moses Znaimer of IdeaCity (Toronto) and Wil Verhoeven and Hans Krabbendam of the Netherlands American Studies Association.

At the University of Chicago Press, while Robert Devens brought enthusiasm and energy to the work of editing the manuscript and guiding it through internal and external reviews, Elizabeth Branch Dyson helped solve problems at every stage of the project, and Yvonne Zipter copyedited the book with both skill and sensitivity.

One's sense of humor and how one makes sense of it develop over years in response to everyday experiences and reflections on them. For their contributions to this process, I am grateful to Bob Begiebing, Tony Byers, Susan Cammer, Harvey Cohen, Joanna Colwell, Fivel Eisenberg, Cora Greenberg, Gerry Hotaling, Nic Johnson, Jonathan Katz, Joan Lewis, Louis Lewis, Mary Lewis, Lois Licht, Linda Lurie, Michael Lurie, Martin

Obin, Yvette Pollack, Ed Reckford, Paul Roberge, Peggy Scott, Nancy Seidman, Terri Seligman, Emma Sichterman, Peter Thomas, Judy Weiner, Gabrielle Wellman, and Deborah Wiggs. Finally, I am above all grateful to Wendy and Clara Lewis for their interest in and enthusiasm about the project. Without their support I would still have finished this book, but it would have taken longer and been much less fun.

Notes

Introduction

1. For an introduction to the work of these and other early humor theorists, see John Morreall, ed., *The Philosophy of Humor and Laughter* (Albany: State University of New York Press, 1987).

2. "Fox News Threatened to Sue 'The Simpsons,'" October 28, 2003, http://politicalhumor.about.com/b/a/038486.htm (accessed July 20, 2005).

3. Jan Freeman, "The Word," *Boston Globe,* sec. H, November 16, 2003.

4. "Testi-Lying to the Senate and the People: The Janice Brown/Orrin Hatch Cartoon Furor," http://www.blackcommentator.com/62/62_cover_brown_cartoon_pf.html (accessed October 9, 2005).

5. Jane Weaver, "Comedy Is King in Super Bowl Ads: But Did Advertisers Get Their Money's Worth," February 3, 2004, http://www.msnbc.msn.com/id/4132154/ (accessed July 20, 2005); George Konig, "SuperBowl," Christian Internet Forum, February 15, 2004, http://www.konig.org/wc48.htm (accessed July 20, 2005). Al Franken, *Rush Limbaugh Is a Big Fat Idiot and Other Observations* (New York: Delacorte Press, 1996); David T. Hardy and Jason Clark, *Michael Moore Is a Big Fat Stupid White Man* (New York: Harper Collins, 2004); Ann Coulter, *Treason: Liberal Treachery from the Cold War to the War on Terrorism* (New York: Random House, Inc., 2003); Clint Willis, ed., *The I Hate Ann Coulter, Bill O'Reilly, Rush Limbaugh, Michael Savage, Sean Hannity . . . Reader* (New York: Thunder's Mouth Press, 2004); Rush Limbaugh, *The Way Things Ought to Be* (New York: Simon & Schuster, 1992); Steven Rendall, Jim Naureckas, and Jeff Cohen's *The Way Things Aren't* (New York: W. W. Norton & Co., 1995).

6. In *The End of Comedy: The Sit-Com and the Comedic Tradition* (Hamden, CT: Archon Books, 1983), David Grote contrasts traditional comedies, in which social

change occurs, with sit-coms, in which the preservation of an established "family unit" or core group of characters works against change.

7. On the current state of research on humor and physical health, see Rod A. Martin, "Humor, Laughter, and Physical Health: Methodological Issues and Research Findings," *Psychological Bulletin* 122, no. 4 (2001): 504–19; Martin, "Sense of Humor and Physical Health: Theoretical Issues, Recent Findings, and Future Directions," *Humor: International Journal of Humor Research* 17, nos. 1/2 (2004): 1–19; and Martin, *The Psychology of Humor: An Integrative Approach* (New York: Elsevier, forthcoming). On humor and stress, see Millicent H. Abel, "Humor, Stress, and Coping Strategies," *Humor: International Journal of Humor Research* 15, no. 4 (2002): 365–81; Arnie Cann, Lawrence G. Calhoun, and Jamey T. Nance, "Exposure to Humor Before and After an Unpleasant Stimulus: Humor as a Preventative or a Cure," *Humor: International Journal of Humor Research* 13, no. 2 (2000): 177–91. On humor and attraction, see Arnie Cann and Lawrence G. Calhoun, "Perceived Personality Associations with Differences in Sense of Humor: Stereotypes of Hypothetical Others with High or Low Senses of Humor," *Humor: International Journal of Humor Research* 14, no. 2 (2001): 117–30; Arnie Cann, Lawrence G. Calhoun, and Janet S. Banks, "On the Role of Humor Appreciation in Interpersonal Attraction: It's No Joking Matter," *Humor: International Journal of Humor Research* 10, no. 1(1997): 77–89.

8. On "Gilligan," see "Soldiers and Detainees Tell Stories behind the Pictures," *Washington Post,* May 22, 2004, A1. For the other quotes, see "Report: Sivits Describes Laughing Abusers," *Yahoo! News,* May 14, 2004; and Evan Thomas, "Explaining Lynndie England: How Did a Wispy Tomboy Behave Like a Monster at Abu Ghraib?" *Newsweek,* May 15, 2004, http://msnbc.msn.com/id/4987304/%20Graner%20 (accessed August 9, 2005).

9. T. A. Badger, "Graner Found Guilty in Iraq Prisoner Abuse," Associated Press, January 14, 2005.

10. Adam Nagourney, "Bush Planning August Attack against Kerry," *New York Times,* August 1, 2004, sec. A.

11. For an early treatment of the idea of the antijoke, see Paul Lewis, "Three Jews and a Blindfold: The Politics of Gallows Humor," in *Semites and Stereotypes: Aspects of Jewish Humor,* ed. Avner Ziv and Anat Zajdman (Westport, CT: Greenwood Press, 1993), 47–58.

12. E. B. White, "Some Remarks on Humor," in *Essays of E. B. White* (New York: HarperCollins Publishers, 1977), 303–11, quote on 303.

13. Thomas E. Ford and Mark A. Ferguson, "Social Consequences of Disparagement Humor: A Prejudiced Norm Theory," *Personality and Social Psychology Review* 8, no. 1 (2004): 79–94, 82.

14. Abel, "Humor, Stress, and Coping," 376. On the dismissive potential of humor, see Christopher P. Wilson, *Jokes: Form, Content, Use, and Function* (New York: Academic Press, 1979).

15. "FrogWeb: Amphibian Declines," National Biological Information Infrastructure, http://frogweb.nbii.gov/declines/ (accessed July 20, 2005); "Photos of De-

formed Frogs," Minnesota Pollution Control Agency, http://www.pca.state
.mn.us/hot/frogphotos.html (accessed July 20, 2005).

16. Tracing this position to its source has proven difficult. Ben Ewen-Campen, a student enrolled in a course on environmental policy taught by Professor E. Carr Everbach at Swarthmore College, attributed it to "a teacher [he] studied with in Vermont" ("Pascal's Wager and Global Warming," http://fubini.swarthmore .edu/~ENVS2/Bewenca1/bens_fourth_essay.htm [accessed August 8, 2005]). In a follow-up e-mail forwarded to me by Everbach, Ewen-Campen identified the teacher as Pat Barnes and the institution where he teaches as the Mountain School in Vershire, VT. Professor Barnes passed an inquiring e-mail I sent him along to a colleague, Jack Kruse, from whom he got the climate change/Pascal's Wager association; Professor Kruse traced it back through another colleague, Kevin Mattingly, to Mattingly's former teacher: Craig Nelson, professor of biology at Indiana University. Though Professor Nelson could not recall how he came up with the idea, given the way global climate debates turn on two possible futures (one infinitely worse than the other), the appeal to Pascal is virtually implicit in both risk assessments and the pro-active positions they tend to support.

17. On the anonymity of joke cycles, see Christie Davies, *Ethnic Humor around the World* (Bloomington: University of Indiana Press, 1990), 9, 3. For an overview of studies of American humor that focuses on efforts to define essential national characters and themes, see Nancy A. Walker's introduction to *What's So Funny: American Humor and Culture* (Wilmington, DE: Scholarly Resources, Inc. 1998). For studies of American humor based on the assumption that jokes reveal and express widely shared concerns, see Alan Dundes, *Cracking Jokes: Studies of Sick Humor and Stereotypes* (Berkeley, CA: Ten Speed Press, 1987); Joseph Boskin, *Rebellious Laughter: People's Humor in American Culture* (Syracuse, NY: Syracuse University Press, 2004); Joseph Boskin, ed., *The Humor Prism in Twentieth-Century America* (Detroit: Wayne State University Press, 1997); Nancy A. Walker, *A Very Serious Thing: Women's Humor and American Culture* (Minneapolis: University of Minnesota Press, 1988); and Lawrence E. Mintz, "American Humor as Unifying and Divisive," *Humor* 12, no. 3 (1999): 237–52.

18. For a different take on the relation of jokes to the ideas they appear to convey, see Elliott Oring, *Engaging Humor* (Chicago: University of Illinois Press, 2003), 37–39.

Chapter One

1. Roger Ebert, "Why Movie Audiences Aren't Safe Anymore," *American Film,* March, 1981, 54–56, quote on 54; Philip Brophy, "Horrality—the Textuality of Contemporary Horror Films," *Screen* 27(1986): 5.

2. William Schoell, "A Talk with Robert Englund," http://nightmareonelmstreet films.com/nightmareinterviewsrobert.html (accessed August 9, 2005).

3. Richard Corliss, "Did You Ever See a Dream Stalking?" *Time,* September 5, 1988, 66. According to Richard Harrington, "Forever Freddy," *Washington Post,*

September 13, 1991, C1, prior to the opening of *Freddy's Dead: The Final Night-mare,* New Line had earned over $460 million on *NES I–V.* On the marketing of Freddy Krueger, see also Aljean Harmetz, "Waking from a New 'Nightmare' to New Profits," *New York Times,* July 13, 1989, C17.

4. Ebert, "Why Movie Audiences," 56.

5. "America Loves Freddy Vision," *Business Wire,* September 16, 1991, retrieved through Factiva database on December 13, 2005; Corliss, "Did You Ever," 66; figures for *Batman* and *Silence of the Lambs* from http:boxofficemojo.com (accessed December 13, 2005).

6. For a collection of representative Joker tales from the 1940s on, see Mike Gold, ed., *The Greatest Joker Stories Ever Told* (New York: Warner Books, 1988).

7. Alan Moore, *The Killing Joke* (New York: DC Comics Inc., 1988), 14.

8. Grant Morrison, *Arkham Asylum* (New York: DC Comics Inc., 1989), 25.

9. Moore, *Killing Joke,* 44.

10. Paul M. Sammon, ed., *Splatterpunks: Extreme Horror* (New York: St. Martin's Press, 1990), xv–xvi.

11. Ibid., 11, 122, 266, 271.

12. Thomas Harris, *The Silence of the Lambs* (New York: St. Martin's Press, 1988), 21, 54–55, 331.

13. On joke structure and interpretation as functions of incongruity resolution, see Jerry M. Suls, "Cognitive Processes in Humor Appreciation," in *Handbook of Humor Research,* ed. Jeffrey H. Goldstein and Paul E. McGhee (New York: Springer-Verlag, 1983) 1:39–58. For a more comprehensive approach based on the idea of script opposition, see Victor Raskin, *Semantic Mechanisms of Humor* (Dordrecht: D. Reidel, 1985).

14. Blanche Knott, *Truly Tasteless Jokes* (New York: St. Martin's Press, 1982), 2, 3, 68, 56; *The Worst of Truly Tasteless Jokes* (New York: St. Martin's Press, 1986), 11, 14–15, 10, 14, 11–12.

15. This typical characterization of Clay comes from Ellen Goodman, "Live from New York, It's the Bigot in a Comic Mask," *Boston Globe,* May 17, 1990.

16. Jay Carr, "Child's Play," *Boston Globe,* November 9, 1988.

17. Mark Edmundson, *Nightmare on Main Street: Angels, Sadomasochism, and the Culture of the Gothic* (Cambridge, MA: Harvard University Press, 1997), 5, 77.

18. Jim Collins, *Uncommon Cultures: Popular Culture and Post-Modernism* (New York: Routledge), 1989.

19. On the subjectivity of responses to humor and the importance of context in joke interpretation, see Lawrence La Fave, Jay Haddad, and NancyMarshall, "Humor Judgments as a Function of Identification Classes," *Sociology and Social Research* 58, no. 2 (1974): 184–94; Norman Holland, *A Psychology of Humor* (Ithaca, NY: Cornell University Press, 1981); Mahadev L. Apte, *Humor and Laughter: An Anthropological Approach* (Ithaca, NY: Cornell University Press, 1985); Harvey Mindess, Carolyn Miller, Joy Turek, Amanda Bender, and Suzanne Corbin, *The Antioch Humor Test: Making Sense of Humor* (New York: Avon Books, 1985); Paul Lewis, *Comic Effects: Interdisciplinary Approaches to Humor in Literature* (Albany:

State University of New York Press, 1989), x–xi; and Elliott Oring, *Engaging Humor,* 30, 37–39.

20. For Baudelaire on laughter, see "The Essence of Laughter" in *The Essence of Laughter and Other Essays, Journals, and Letters by Charles Baudelaire,* ed. Peter Quennell, trans. Gerard Hopkins (New York: Meridian Books, 1956); for Baudelaire on Melmoth, see 117.

21. Sigmund Freud, *Jokes and Their Relation to the Unconscious* (1905), trans. James Strachey (New York: Norton, 1960), 102–3.

22. Elliott Oring, "Humor and the Suppression of Sentiment," *Humor: International Journal of Humor Research* 7, no. 1 (1994): 7–26, esp. 7. On humor and anxiety, see Abel, "Humor, Stress, and Coping"; Cann et al., "Exposure to Humor."

23. For Twitchell's take on pop violence as a force in the maturation of teenage boys, see *Preposterous Violence: Fables of Aggression in Modern Culture* (New York: Oxford University Press, 1989), and *Dreadful Pleasures: An Anatomy of Modern Horror* (New York: Oxford University Press, 1985). Thomas Doherty, *Teenagers and Teenpics: The Juvenilization of American Movies in the 1950s* (Boston: Unwin Hyman, 1988).

24. On the fear of being ridiculed, see Jeremy P. Shapiro, Roy F. Baumesiter, and Jane W. Kessler, "A Three-Component Model of Children's Teasing: Aggression, Humor, and Ambiguity," *Journal of Social and Clinical Psychology* 10, no. 4 (1991): 459–72. On "jeer pressure," see Leslie M. Janes and James M. Olson, "Jeer Pressure: The Behavioral Effects of Observing Ridicule of Others," *Personality and Social Psychology Bulletin* 26, no. 4 (2000): 474–85.

25. On the role of disposition in humor appreciation, see La Fave, et al., "Humor Judgments"; Frank W. Wicker, William L. Barron, and Amy C. Willis, "Disparagement Humor: Dispositions and Resolutions," *Journal of Personality and Social Psychology* 39, no. 4 (1980): 701–9; Dolf Zillman and Joanne R. Cantor, "A Disposition Theory of Humour and Mirth," in *Humour and Laughter: Theory, Research, and Applications,* ed. Antony J. Chapman and Hugh C. Foot (London: John Wiley & Sons, 1976), 93–115; and Dolf Zillman, "Disparagement Humor," in *Handbook of Humor Research,* ed. Goldstein and McGhee 1:85–108. On the responses of adolescents to disgusting humor, see Patrice A. Opplinger and Dolf Zillmann, "Disgust in Humor: Its Appeal to Adolescents," *Humor: International Journal of Humor Research* 10, no. 4 (1977): 421–37. On responses to cruel jokes, see Thomas R. Herzog and Joseph Karafa, "Preferences for Sick versus Non-sick Humor," *Humor: International Journal of humor Research* 11, no. 3 (1998): 291–312; and Thomas R. Herzog and Maegan R. Anderson, "Joke Cruelty, Emotional Responsiveness, and Joke Appreciation," *Humor: International Journal of Humor Research* 13, no. 3 (2000): 333–51.

26. On the rising rate of adolescent suicide in the United States between 1955 and 1985, see Judith M. Stilton, Eugene E. McDowell, and Jacque H. May, *Suicide across the Life Span—Premature Exits* (New York: Hemisphere Publishing Corp., 1989). On nuances of affiliation that factor in humor appreciation, see Zillmann, "Disparagement Humor," 90–95, quotes on 91, 95.

27. Simon Wiesenthal, *The Sunflower* (London: W. H. Allen, 1970), 60.
28. Anthony Giddens, *The Consequences of Modernity* (Stanford, CA: Stanford University Press, 1990), 131, 137. Giddens has been criticized for positing essential ideas and feelings as components of contemporary consciousness; the connection I seek to establish is more modest: not that Giddens's runaway world defines modernity but that something very like it has been widely shared in the United States between the cold war–antienvironmentalism presidency of Ronald Reagan and the terrorism war–antienvironmentalism presidency of G. W. Bush.
29. Laura Mulvey, *Visual and Other Pleasures* (1975; reprint, Bloomington: Indiana University Press, 1989), 20.
30. Davies, *Ethnic Humor,* 232.
31. Andrew Tudor, *Monsters and Mad Scientists: A Cultural History of the Horror Movie* (Oxford: Basil Blackwell Ltd., 1989), 211–23, quote on 222.
32. Gregory A. Waller, *American Horrors: Essays on the Modern American Horror Film* (Chicago: University of Chicago Press, 1987), 12; Tudor, *Monsters,* 217.
33. Edmundson, *Nightmare,* 29.
34. Andrew Ross, *No Respect: Intellectuals and Popular Culture* (New York: Routledge, 1989), 237, 231, 13, 231.
35. The possibility that popular works can both satisfy and contain the impulses that attract audiences has been explored by several critics. It is close to Roland Barthes's account of the inoculating function and rhetoric of some modern myths; to Frederic Jameson's sense of the way popular works can both arouse and contain potentially damaging desires; and to the view of reader responses to popular romances described by feminist critics like Tania Modeleski and Janice Radway. Just as killing jokes can allow audiences to enjoy brief fantasies of human destruction, so—Modeleski argues—women who read romances can move through a fictive experience of sexual attack to an imagined triumph over their anxieties about rape. Radway makes a similar point in observing that "the act of constructing the romantic tale . . . enables a woman to achieve a kind of mastery over her fear of rape because the fantasy evokes her fear and subsequently convinces her that rape is either an illusion or something that she can control easily" (*Reading the Romance: Women, Patriarchy, and Popular Literature* [Chapel Hill: University of North Carolina Press, 1984], 214.). Frederic Jameson. "Reification and Utopia in Mass Culture," *Social Text* 1 (1979): 130–48; Tania Modeleski, *Loving with a Vengeance: Mass-Produced Fantasies for Women* (Hamden, CT: Archon Books, 1982).
36. Anne Rice, *Interview with the Vampire* (New York: Ballantine Books, 1976), 71, 79, 80, 83, 296.
37. Ibid., 217, 219, 221, 224–25.
38. Stephen King, *Carrie* (New York: Doubleday & Co., 1974), 8–9, 22, quote on 168.
39. Ibid., 168, 188.
40. Paul Slansky, *The Clothes Have No Emperor: A Chronicle of the American 80s* (New York: Simon & Schuster, 1989), 238.

41. "James C. McKinley, "Officials Say Youths Admit Role in Attack," *New York Times,* April 24, 1989, B1.

42. Kim Curtis, "After 24 Years on Death Row, Convicted Murderer Says He's Changed," Associated Press, December 3, 2005, http://www.mercurynews.com/mld/mercurynews/news/local/states/california/northern_california/13320620.htm (accessed December 21, 2005).

43. For an early account of *Beavis and Butt-Head,* see Rick Marin, "Sooner or Later Beavis and Butt-Head Had to Happen," *New York Times,* July 11, 2003, sec. 9, 8. For Chief Siegler's comment, see "Cartoon on MTV Blamed for Fire," *New York Times,* October 10, 1993, sec. 1, 30.

44. Tom Shales, "Tweedledumb and Tweedledumber: The Absolutely Positively Last word on 'Beavis and Butt-Head'" *Washington Post,* October 10, 1993, G1.

45. On sales of the *Bumfights* video, see Ray Delgado, "'BumFights' Online Video Producers Charged," *San Francisco Chronicle,* September 26, 2002, A2.

46. For this account of the sentencing, see Greg Moran, "Three Receive Probation for Video Brawling," *San Diego Union-Tribune,* June 21, 2003, B-1. For Hannah's comment, see Michael Stetz, "Former Bum Beats the Bottle," *San Diego Union-Tribune,* July 17, 2004, B1. On the copycats, see James Madden, "Film Spurred Fatal Attack," *Australian,* December 21, 2004, 3.

47. Jameson, "Reification," 141; Philip Fisher, *Hard Facts: Setting and Form in the American Novel* (New York: Oxford University Press, 1987), 19.

48. Joanna Macy, *Despair and Personal Power in the Nuclear Age* (Philadelphia: New Society Publishers, 1983), xiii.

Chapter Two

1. David Granirer, "Laughter: The Best Medicine," http://www.granirer.com/ART-0007.htm (accessed August 10, 2005). Allen Klein, *The Healing Power of Humor: Techniques for Getting through Loss, Setbacks, Upsets, Disappointments, Difficulties, Trials, Tribulations, and All That Not-So-Funny Stuff* (New York: Penguin Putnam Inc., 1989), 12. Jack Shea, e-mail to Humor Project discussion forum, November 5, 1999, http://www.humorproject.com/discussion/index.php?mode=replys&id=10 (accessed August 10, 2005). For overviews of the humor consulting business, see Donald E. Gibson, "Humor Consulting: Laughs for Power and Profit in Organizations," *Humor: International Journal of Humor Research* 7, no. 4 (1994): 403–28; and John Morreall, "Applications of Humor: Health, the Workplace, and Education," in *The Primer of Humor Research,* ed. Victor Raskin (Berlin: Mouton de Gruyter, forthcoming).

2. Klein, *Healing Power of Humor,* 153, 33, 34; Annette Goodheart, *Laughter Therapy: How to Laugh about Everything in Your Life That Isn't Really Funny* (Santa Barbara, CA: Less Stress Press, 1994), 44, 45.

3. "Humor," *Humor: International Journal of Humor Research* 1, no. 1 (1988), back cover. William F. Fry, "The Biology of Humor," *Humor: International Journal of Humor Research* 7, no. 2 (1994): 112, 114, 114, 116–17, 117.

4. Rod A. Martin, "Humor, Laughter, and Physical Health," 516; Martin, "Sense of Humor," 2; Leslie A. Martin, Howard S. Friedman, Joan S. Tucker, Carol Tomlinson-Keasey, Michael H. Criqui, Joseph E. Schwartz, "A Life Course Perspective on Childhood Cheerfulness and Its Relation to Mortality Risk," *Personality and Social Psychology Bulletin* 28, no. 9 (2002), 1155–65, esp. 1157, 1155; Gillian A. Kirsh and Nicholas A. Kuiper, "Positive and Negative Aspects of Sense of Humor: Associations with the Constructs of Individualism and Relatedness," *Humor: International Journal of Humor Research* 16, no. 1 (2003): 33–62; Nicholas A. Kuiper, Melissa Grimshaw, Catherine Leite, and Gillian A. Kirsh, "Humor Is Not Always the Best Medicine: Specific Components of Sense of Humor and Psychological Well Being," *Humor: International Journal of Humor Research* 17, nos. 1–2 (2004): 135–68.

5. Kuiper et al., "Humor Is Not Always the Best," 137, 139, 164.

6. Dan Gascon, "Humor for Your Health," http://www.humorforyourhealth .com/meet_dan_gascon.html (accessed August 10, 2005); Steven M. Sultanoff, "Survival of the Witty-est: Creating Resilience through Humor," http://www .humormatters.com/articles/resilience.htm (accessed August 10, 2005); Larry Wilde, "Laughter: Rx for Healing, Health, and Happiness," http://www.larry-wilde.com/LaughterForHealingProgram.htm (accessed August 10, 2005).

7. Phrases from *Laughing Matters* quoted in text appear in multiple issues; longer passages are from vol. 3, no. 1, p. 27 and vol. 2, no. 3, p. 124.

8. Norman Cousins, *Anatomy of an Illness as Perceived by the Patient* (New York: Norton, 1979), 39, 146.

9. Norman Cousins, *Head First: The Biology of Hope and the Healing Power of the Human Spirit* (New York: Dutton, 1989), 126, 104, 140; Martin, "Humor, Laughter, and Physical Health," 508–9.

10. Patch Adams and Maureen Mylander, *Gesundheit! Bringing Good Health to You, the Medical System, and Society through Physician Service, Complementary Therapies, Humor, and Joy* (Rochester, VT: Healing Arts Press, 1993), 65, 83.

11. Patty Wooten, "Humor Skills for Surviving Managed Care," http://www .jesthealth.com/arthmrskills.html (accessed August 10, 2005).

12. Martin, "Humor, Laughter, and Physical Health," 511, 514; Jackie Silberg, *The Learning Power of Laughter* (Beltsville, MD: Gryphon House, 2004), 11, 12; Granirer, "Laughter: The Best Medicine"; Goodheart, *Laughter Therapy*, 32, 75.

13. Martin, "Humor, Laughter, and Physical Health," 511, 514, 509; Madan Kataria, "About US: Benefits," http://www.laughteryoga.org/stress-management.htm (accessed August 10, 2005); "Therapeutic Benefits of Laughter," http://www .holistic-online.com/Humor_Therapy/humor_therapy_benefits.htm (accessed December 15, 2005).

14. Adams and Mylander, *Geshundheit*, 19; Klein *Healing Power of Humor*, xx; Steven M. Sultanoff, "What Is Humor?" http://www.aath.org/articles/art _sultanoff01.html (accessed October 7, 2005).

15. Goodheart, *Laughter Therapy*, 19–22, 120; Klein, *Healing Power of Humor*, 182–83, 185–86.

16. Klein, *Healing Power of Humor,* 50, emphasis mine; Judy Long, "Nursing Professor Enhances Healing through Humor," http://pr.baylor.edu/story.php?id=003593 (accessed August 7, 2005).

17. David M. Jacobson, "Appropriate vs. Inappropriate Humor," http://www.humorhorizons.com/app.html (accessed August 10, 2005).

18. Goodheart, *Laughter Therapy,* 82.

19. Keynote Presentations and Workshops by Michael Kerr, http://www.mikekerr.com (accessed December 21, 2005); http://www.discoverfun.com/ (accessed December 21, 2005); Mike Moore, "Five Ways to Sharpen Your Sense of Humor and Improve Your Relationships," http://www.e-syndicate.net/a10453.htm (accessed December 21, 2005); Christian Hagaseth, "The Twelve Affirmations of Positive Humor," http://www.learnwell.org/positivehumor.htm (accessed December 21, 2005); Granirer, "Laughter: The Best Medicine."

20. Joel Goodman, *Laffirmations: 1001 Ways to Add Humor to Your Life and Work* (Deerfield Beach, FL: Health Communications, Inc., 1995), 182, 292. Yvonne Francine Conte, *Serious Laughter: A Guide Book to a Happier, Healthier, More Productive Life* (Rochester, NY: Amsterdam Berwick Publishing, 1998), 77.

21. Paul E. McGhee, *Health, Healing and the Amuse System* (Dubuque, IA: Kendall/Hunt Publishing Co., 1996), 53, 58, 198, 72.

22. Ibid., 178.

23. Paul E. McGhee, interview by the author, October 23, 2004.

24. John Morreall, *Humor Works* (Amherst, MA: HRD Press, Inc., 1997), 255.

25. Ibid., 129, 74–75, 135.

26. Joyce Friedman, interview by the author, October 28, 2004.

27. Kirsh and Kuiper, "Positive and Negative," 35.

28. Forest Wheeler, *Using the Power of Humor to Improve Your Life* (Wilsonville, OR: BestSeller Books, 2004).

29. Herman Melville, *Moby-Dick; or, The Whale* (1851; reprint, London: Penguin Books, 1972), 684.

30. Ibid., 550–51, 612, 329, 295, 527.

Chapter Three

1. Sigmund Freud, "Humour," in *The Standard Edition of the Complete Psychological Works of Sigmund Freud,* James Strachey (1927; reprint, London: Hogarth Press, 1961), xxii, 161–66; 161, 163, 163; Giddens, *The Consequences of Modernity.*

2. For a discussion of the dark side of gallows humor, see my "Three Jews"; and Giddens, *Consequences of Modernity.*

3. Kirsh and Kuiper, "Positive and Negative," 33.

4. For Boskin on joke wars, see *Rebellious Laughter,* 145–57, esp. 145; Oring, 38–39, 65. For Christie Davies's take on the relation between ethnic joke cycles and their ostensible subjects/butts, see *Ethnic Humor.*

5. Paul Lewis, organizer and ed., "Debate: Humor and Political Correctness," *Humor: International Journal of Humor Research* 10 (1997): 453–513, 457, 461–62, 493.

6. Ibid., 457, 457, 461, 462, 493.

7. "Cornell Charges 4 Students in E-Mail Prank," *New York Times,* November 15, 1995, B11.

8. Michael Grunwald, "List of Sexist Jokes about Women Sparks an On-line Outrage," *Boston Globe,* November 10, 1995, B25.

9. Online Freedom Fighters Anarchist Liberation, press release, http://www .petting-zoo.net/~deadbeef/archive/629.html (accessed on June 4, 2005); Ellen Goodman, "The Envelope Please . . . ," *Boston Globe,* August 26, 1996, Nation/ World, 11.

10. Lewis, ed., "Humor and Political Correctness," 463.

11. Ibid.; Online Freedom Fighters Anarchist Liberation; David Brock, *The Republican Noise Machine: Right-Wing Media and How It Corrupts Democracy* (New York: Random House, 2004). See the chapter on "Political Correctness and the Coming of the Thought Police," in Rush Limbaugh, *See I Told You So* (New York: Simon & Schuster, 1993), 227–38, 227.

12. Boskin, *Rebellious Laughter,* 125; Oring, *Engaging Humor,* both quotes on 66.

13. On the effects of telling disparaging jokes, see James M. Olson, Gregory R. Maio, and Karen L. Hobden, "The (Null) Effects of Exposure to Disparagement Humor on Stereotypes and Attitudes," *Humor: International Journal of Humor Research* 12, no. 2 (1999): 195–219, 216; Karen L. Hobden and James M. Olson, "From Jest to Antipathy: Disparagement Humor as a Source of Dissonance-Motivated Attitude Change," *Basic and Applied Psychology* 15, no. 2 (1994): 239–49; Gregory R. Maio, James M. Olson, and Jacqueline. E. Bush, "Telling Jokes That Disparage Social Groups: Effects on the Joke Teller's Stereotypes," *Journal of Applied Social Psychology* 27 (1997): 1986–2000; Thomas E. Ford, "Effects of Sexist Humor on Tolerance of Sexist Events," *Personality and Social Psychology Bulletin* 16, no. 9 (2000): 1094–1107; Thomas E. Ford, E. R. Wentzel, and J. Lorion, "Effects of Exposure to Sexist Humor on Perceptions of Normative Tolerance of Sexism," *European Journal of Social Psychology* 31, no. 6 (2001): 677–91.

14. Ford, "Effects of Sexist Humor," 1105; Ford and Ferguson, "Social Consequences," 79; Martin, *The Psychology of Humor,* 5.7.

15. Gary Spencer, "An Analysis of JAP-Baiting Humor on the College Campus," *Humor: International Journal of Humor Research* 2, no. 4 (1989): 329–48; quoted material on, respectively, 331, 340, 343, 330.

16. Bryan Robinson, "Five Years Ago, Matthew Shepard's Killing Changed the Dialogue on Gay Life—but Did It Change America's Heart?" ABC News Original Report, May 10, 2005, http://abcnews.go.com/US/story?id=96832&page=1 (accessed August 10, 2005).

17. Michael Taylor, "North Coast Loggers in War of Nerves with the 'Enviros,'" *New York Times,* July 10, 1990, A4.

18. Judi Bari, "The PALCO Papers," March 27, 1991, http://www.things.org/ ~jym/ef/the-palco-papers.html (accessed September 12, 2005).

19. "Spike a Tree for Jesus," words and music © 1988, 2004 by Darryl Cherney, by permission.

20. Darryl Cherney, interviews by the author, February 2–5, 2005.

21. John Dias, interview by the author, March 9, 2005.

22. Limbaugh, *The Way Things Ought,* 160.

23. Ibid.

24. Ibid., 296, 58, 154, 152, 152–53, 152.

25. For a monthly access fee, Limbaugh's parodies can be found at http://www .rushlimbaugh.com/home/today.member.html.

26. Paul Slansky, *The Clothes Have No Emperor,* 18, 48.

27. *Doonesbury* cartoons can be accessed on line at http://www.amureprints.com/.

28. Goodheart, *Laughter Therapy,* 120; Morreall, *Humor Works,* 103; McGhee, *Health, Healing,* 103; Klein, *Healing Power,* 13.

29. Edward Epstein, "American History Brims with Gaffes of Politicians," *San Francisco Chronicle,* December 18, 2002. Note that the first *Washington Post* story, which ran on page 1 of the December 6, 2002, edition, did not quote or discuss these sentences. Roy Douglas Malonson, at http://www.aframnews.com/html/archives/2002-12-25/lead2.htm (accessed August 12, 2005).

30. Christine Stansell, "What Stuff!" *New Republic,* January 17, 2005, 21; David Greenberg, "The Gay Emancipator? What's Wrong with *The Intimate World of Abraham Lincoln,*" January 14, 2005, http://slate.com/id/2112313.

31. Letters, *Nation,* February 14, 2005, 2.

32. Ibid.; Janet Bing and Dana Heller, "How Many Lesbians Does It Take to Screw in a Light Bulb?" *Humor: International Journal of Humor Research* 16, no. 2 (2003): 157–82, quotes on 157, 167, 166.

33. The editors, "Our Readers and Robert Grossman" and "Grossman Replies," *Nation,* February 14, 2005, 2.

34. Stuart Elliott, "Outcry over Commercials Joking about Mental Illness," *New York Times,* April 23, 1992, D21.

35. Matt Sutkoski, "Teddy Bear President Quits Hospital Board," *Burlington Free Press,* February 10, 2005.

36. Max Nardini, "Vermont Teddy Bears Gone Crazy in Love: Midd Alum CEO at Odds with Mental Health Groups," February 10, 2005, http://www .middleburycampus.com/media/paper446/news/2005/02/10/Features/Vermont. Teddy.Bears.Gone.Crazy.In.Love-861959.shtml (accessed May 28, 2005).

37. Scott Plous, "More about Joe," http://www.joechemo.org/about.htm (accessed May 28, 2005).

38. J. R. DiFranza, J. W. Richards, Jr., P. M. Paulman, N. Wolf-Gillespie, C. Fletcher, R. D. Jaffe, and D. Murray, "RJR Nabisco's Cartoon Camel Promotes Camel Cigarettes to Children," *JAMA* 266 (1991): 3149–53, quote on 3149.

39. Dotsey Welliver, *Laughing Together: The Value of Humor in Family Life* (Elgin, IL: Brethren Press, 1986), ix; Cal Samra, *The Joyful Christ: The Healing Power of Humor* (New York: Harper Collins, 1985), 7; Elton Trueblood, *The Humor of*

Christ (New York: Harper & Row, 1964), 15, 19. The many Web stores featuring laughing Jesus merchandise include Stephen S. Sawyer's "Art for God," http://www.art4god.com/ (accessed September 24, 2005); "Laughingjesus.com: All the Best Resources on the Net," http://www.jesuslaughing.com/ (accessed September 24, 2005), which specializes in marketing the work of Ralph Kozak; and "ChristArt: Free Christian Clipart," http://www.cafepress.com/christart/ 130890 (accessed September 24, 2005), which features T-shirts festooned with a laughing version of the early Christian fish symbol.

40. Charles Hunter and Frances Hunter, *Healing through Humor* (Lake Mary, FL: Strang Communications Co., 2003); "Revival Ministries International," http:// revival.com/revapp/index.asp (accessed April 15, 2005).

41. Albert James Dager, "Holy Laughter: Rodney Howard-Browne and the Toronto Blessing," Biblical Discernment Ministries, March 1996, http://www .rapidnet.com/~jbeard/bdm/Psychology/holylaugh.htm (accessed June 4, 2005); "Laughter in the Bible," MacGregor Ministries: A Christian Outreach to Those Trapped in Cult Groups, http://www.macgregorministries.org/cult_groups/ laughter.html (accessed June 4, 2005).

Chapter Four

1. There appear to be problems with the common attribution of this famous quote to Mark Twain. Beyond the fact that the comment is included in a character's speech that may or may not represent what Twain himself believed at the time of its composition, it appears in an early version of a manuscript called *The Chronicle of Young Satan* that was unpublished at the time of Twain's death in 1910 and that was reworked into a now-discredited version of the text published as *The Mysterious Stranger.* The passage can be found in the version of *Stranger* that appears in *The Complete Short Stories of Mark Twain,* ed. Charles Neider (Garden City, NY: Doubleday, 1985), 671, but not in the more authoritative text called *No. 44, The Mysterious Stranger* (Berkeley, CA: University of California Press, 1969). Charles Churchill, "Ghost," bk. 2, line 943, in *The Poetical Works of Charles Churchill,* ed. Douglas Grant (Oxford: Clarendon Press, 1956), 130; Jonathan Swift, "The Battle of the Books" in *A Tale of a Tub, to Which Is Added the Battle of the Books, and the Mechanical Operation of the Spirit. Together with the History of Martin, Wotton's Observations upon the Tale of a Tub, Curll's Complete Key, Etc.,* ed. A. C. Guthkelch and D. Nichol Smith, 2d ed. (Oxford: Clarendon Press, 1958), 215; Ambrose Bierce, *The Devil's Dictionary* (New York: Dover Publications, Inc, 1993), 113; William Cowper, "The Task" in *The Poems of William Cowper,* ed. John D. Baird and Charles Ryskamp (Oxford: Clarendon Press, 1995), 2:147.

2. Nikki Finke, "Does Mr. Middle of the Road Lean Left?" *LA Weekly,* September 17, 2004.

3. The cartoons discussed here, which can be found in *Thomas Nast: Cartoons and Illustrations* (New York: Dover Publications, 1974), appeared originally in the fol-

lowing editions of *Harper's Weekly:* "A Group of Vultures," September 23, 1871; "The Tammany Tiger," November 11, 1971; "Can the Law Reach Him?" January 6, 1872. For the comments about Nast's work, see Morton Keller, *The Art and Politics of Thomas Nast* (New York: Oxford University Press, 1968), 13, 45, 181, 181, 76.

4. Albert Bigelow Paine, *Thomas Nast: His Period and His Pictures* (New York: Macmillan, 1904), 141.

5. Mark Crispin Miller, *The Bush Dyslexicon* (New York: W. W. Norton & Co., 2002), 34–35; 39–40.

6. Thomas Frank, *What's the Matter with Kansas* (New York: Metropolitan Books, 2004), 67–68.

7. George Lakoff, *Don't Think of an Elephant* (White River Junction, VT: Chelsea Green Publishing Co., 2004), 94.

8. Richard Viguerie and David Franke, *America's Right Turn: How Conservatives Used New and Alternative Media to Take Power* (Chicago: Bonus Books, 2004). On Limbaugh's influence, see Eric Alterman, in Willis, ed., *I Hate Ann Coulter,* 72–75.

9. Viguerie and Franke, *America's Right Turn,* 180.

10. Stephen Talbot, in Willis, *The I Hate Ann Coulter,* 75, 82; Molly Ivins, foreword to Steven Rendall, Jim Naureckas, and Jeff Cohen, eds., *The Way Things Aren't* (New York: W. W. Norton & Co., 1995), 5, 4.

11. Ibid., 5.

12. Dan Eggen and Josh White, "Inmates Allege Koran Abuse," *Washington Post,* May 25, 2005, A1; Scott Ott, "Red Cross: Al Qaeda May Violate Geneva Conventions," http://www.scrappleface.com/MT/archives/001956.html (accessed July 7, 2005).

13. Rendall, Naureckas, and Cohen, *The Way Things Aren't,* 66, 120; Limbaugh, *See I Told You,* 121.

14. Limbaugh, "The Limbaugh Lexicon," in *The Way Things Ought,* 294–99.

15. M. G. Weinberger and C. S. Gulas, "A Survey of the Nature and Extent of Bullying in Junior/Middle and Secondary Schools," *Educational Research,* 35 (1993): 3–25; Martin, *The Psychology of Humor,* 5.6, 5.6; Richard E. Petty and Joan Cacioppo, *Communication and Persuasion* (New York: Springer Verlag, 1986); Jim Lyttle, "The Effectiveness of Humor in Persuasion," *Journal of General Psychology* 128 (2001): 206–16, esp. 213.

16. Morreall, *Humor Works,* 144; McGhee, *Health, Healing,* 134. In a letter that ran in the *Atlantic Monthly*'s October 2004 issue, Dr. Joseph Price, a Midwestern physician, suggested that Bush's conspicuously declining verbal skills, his "'mangled' words are a demonstration of what physicians call 'confabulation' and are almost specific to the diagnosis of a true dementia." *Boston Globe* columnist Alex Beam, who had advance notice of Price's letter, called attention to the possible diagnosis in his September 14, 2004, column. After this, the issue dropped out of sight and played no role whatsoever in the 2004 campaign.

17. On the association of humor with other positive traits, see Cann and Calhoun,

"Perceived Personality Associations"; on the importance of shared humor in first encounters, see Barbara Fraley and Arthur Aron, "The Effect of a Shared Humorous Experience on Closeness in Initial Encounters," *Personal Relationships* 11, no. 1 (2001): 61–78.

18. These examples and the postelection jokes in the next paragraph were found in the collection "The 100 Best Bush Jokes, 2000–2004" at About.com's political humor Web site, http://politicalhumor.about.com/library/jokes/blbushjoke90 .htm (accessed June 23, 2005).

19. Molly Ivins, *Shrub: The Short but Happy Life of George W. Bush* (New York: Vintage Books, 2000), 101.

20. See, for example, "Bushisms: Adventures in George W. Bushspeak—Updated Frequently," http://politicalhumor.about.com/library/blbushisms.htm (accessed June 24, 2005). For Washington Post/ABC News poll data back to the start of the Bush presidency, see http://www.washingtonpost.com/wp-srv/politics/polls/ postpoll110305.htm (accessed December 15, 2005).

21. Toles, September 5, 2001; Alcaraz, August 30, 2001; *Doonesbury,* September 2, 2001—all at http://www.amureprints.com/ (accessed June 30, 2005).

22. See Alina Tugend, "Maybe Not," *American Journalism Review,* May 2000, for a six-month retrospective of 9/11 and American humor; see Daniel Kurtzman, "The Return of Irony," *San Francisco Chronicle,* September 9, 2002, for a one-year review.

23. Shales and Poniewozik quoted in Kurtzman, "The Return"; Tony Norman, "No Terrorist Should Steal Our Laughter," *Pittsburgh Post-Dispatch,* September 28, 2001, Lifestyle.

24. See Paul Lewis, "Disaster as a Laughing Matter," *Chicago Tribune,* March 25, 1986, for an early discussion of the shuttle-explosion jokes. See Emily Wax, "Times of Terror, Teens Talk the Talk: Boys Are 'Firefighter Cute,' Messy Room Is 'Ground Zero' in Sept. 11 Slang," *Washington Post,* March 19, 2002, A1; Michael Bruton, "A Funny Thing Happened: Academics Gather to Study Post–Sept. 11 Humor," *Time On-line,* July 15, 2002; and Kurtzman, "The Return," for news stories in which I offered early analyses of 9/11-based humor; on the impact of 9/11 on Boston College, see "Remembered," *Boston College Magazine,* Fall 2001, http://www.bc.edu/publications/bcm/fall_2001/ll_remembered.html (accessed June 24, 2005).

25. Malcolm Kushner, "Unleash USA's Secret Weapon: Humor," *USA Today,* October 4, 2001.

26. Nigel Reynolds, "Britain's Muslim Comedienne Finds Work Is No Joke," *Daily Telegraph,* September 22, 2001, 21.

27. Shazia Mirza, interview by the author, June 11, 2005. Tom Pilston, "War on Terrorism," *Independent,* October 5, 2001, 3; Dominic Cavendish, "Muslim Makes bin Laden a Laughing Matter," *Daily Telegraph,* October 18, 2001, 11.

28. David Counts, interview by the author, June 27, 2005. For Counts's Web site, go to http://www.toostupidtobepresident.com/.

29. "The September 11, Digital Archive: Saving the Histories of September 11,

2001" http://911digitalarchive.org/ (accessed June 28, 2005); all Ron Piechota quotes taken from an e-mail interview by the author on April 2, 2004.

30. "Osama bin Laden Videos and Animations: Funny Osama Videos, Animation Cartoons, and Song Parodies," http://politicalhumor.about.com/library/blbinladenanimations.htm (accessed June 26, 2005).

31. Miller, *Bush Dyslexicon,* xxiv.

32. For an early account of scrappleface and other political humor Web sites, see Bobbien Johnson, "Media: New Media: Clicking and Screaming," *Guardian,* April 28, 2003, 48.

33. Scott Ott, "Object under Bush Jacket Identified: 'It's a Spine,'" http://www.scrappleface.com/index.php?s=object+bush+jacket+spine (accessed December 15, 2005).

34. "Mrs. Cheney's Irate Response to Senator John Kerry's Cheap Debate Reference to Her Beloved Daughter's Vile and Repulsive Lifestyle Choice," http://www.whitehouse.org/news/2004/101404.asp (accessed July 7, 2005).

35. For examples of these cartoons, see "Kerry's Waffle House" at http://politicalhumor.about.com/library/images/blpic-kerrywafflehouse.htm; and "Kerry's When You're Serious about Flip-Flops" at http://politicalhumor.about.com/library/images/blpic-kerryflipflops.htm (both accessed September 23, 2005).

36. Karry Hurt III, "The Sport That Has Everything: Water, Wind and Politics," *New York Times,* October 3, 2004, sec. 3, p. 7. For an analysis of how this ad played into the Bush campaign strategy, see Nina J. Easton, Michael Kranish, Patrick Healy, Glen Johnson, Anne E. Kornblut, and Brian Mooney, "On the Trail of Kerry's Failed Dream," *Boston Globe,* November 14, 2004, National/Foreign, 24.

37. For these images and others like them, see Sacred Cow Burgers, http://www.sacredcowburgers.com/side_orders/2004_campaign_collection/ (accessed September 23, 2005).

38. The mixed impact of the Bush cowboy motif came up in conversations with my colleague Chris Wilson.

39. To see Marc Forest's portfolio of Bush caricatures, go to http://www.mind.net/basile/DeficitDubya133.html (accessed September 18, 2005). The Bush as mad cowboy picture is also available at http://politicalhumor.about.com/library/images/blbushmadcowboy.htm (accessed July 13, 2005).

40. Ann Coulter, "One Last Flip-Flop," http://www.anncoulter.org/cgi-local/article.cgi?article=13 (accessed July 13, 2005); for Limbaugh's take on liberal talk radio, see the full text of the interview he did with Richard Zoglin of *Time,* posted on the Limbaugh Web site (www.rushlimbaugh.com); the edited version of the interview ran as "Ten Questions for Rush Limbaugh (Interview)," *Time,* June 7, 2004, 17; David Counts, interview by the author, June 27, 2005; R. J. Crane, e-mail message to author, November 10, 2004; Barry Crimmins, interview by the author, May 26, 2005; Daniel Kurtzman, e-mail message to author, December 7, 2004.

41. Randy Shilts, *And the Band Played On: Politics, People, and the AIDS Epidemic*

(New York: St. Martin's Press, 2000); Kitty Kelley, *Nancy Reagan: The Unauthorized Biography* (New York: Pocket Star Books, 1992), 497; Peter Dreier, "Reagan's Legacy: Homelessness in America," *NHI Shelterforce Online,* no. 135 (May–June 2004) http://www.nhi.org/online/issues/135/reagan.html (accessed July 13, 2005); for Wilken's quote, see Slansky, *The Clothes Have No Emperor,* 172.

42. Mark Katz, *Clinton and Me: A Real Life in Political Comedy* (New York: Hyperion, 2003), 310, 330.

43. Elizabeth Bumiller, "Desperate White House Wife, Episode 1: The Ranch Hand," *New York Times,* May 2, 2005, A13.

Conclusion

1. No Name-Calling Week, http://www.nonamecallingweek.org/ (accessed October 14, 2005). For statistics on school violence, see "School-Related Deaths, School Shootings, and School Violence Incidents," National School Safety and Security Services, http://www.schoolsecurity.org/trends/school_violence04-05 .html (accessed August 10, 2005); on Red Lake, see "Officials: Student's Rampage Leaves Ten Dead: Witness Describes Gunman Grinning, Waving," http://www.cnn.com/2005/US/03/21/school.shooting/ (accessed August 10, 2005).

2. For an overview of attitudes about the importance of having a good sense of humor, see Cann and Calhoun, "Perceived Personality Associations," which reviews surveys in which "over 90 percent of respondents reported having an average or above average sense of humor" and "an ongoing survey of college students [that] indicated that 81 percent considered themselves to have an above average sense of humor relative to their peers" (118)." Miller, *Bush Dyslexicon,* 2. On Gore, see Joan Vennochi, "Being Al Gore," *Boston Globe,* May 28, 2004, http://www.boston.com/news/globe/editorial_opinion/oped/articles/2004/05/28/being_al_gore/ (accessed July 14, 2005); on Kerry, see Mark Steyn, "Kerry's Showing He Can't Take the Heat," *Chicago Sun-Times,* September 5, 2004, 33; on Nader, see "Gene Weingarten, "Unsafe from Any Screed: Ralph Nader Gets Invited to a Debate," *Washington Post Magazine,* August 29, 2004, W15; on Nixon, see Daniel Kurtzman, "Memorable Quotes by Hunter S. Thompson," http://politicalhumor.about.com/od/funnyquotes/a/huntersthompson .htm (accessed July 14, 2005).

Index

audience: anxiety reduction for, 43; autonomous responses of, 51–52, 117, 130, 148–49, 202–3; as disgust-tolerant or -sensitive, 45–46; disposition toward butts, 25, 45–49; as identified with villain, 28–29, 35, 112; jokes for uninformed, 157–58; playful detachment of, 35–36; reflective approach needed, 194; revulsion (gross out) of, 44; satisfying and containing impulses of, 216n35; transformational or cultural work of, 62. *See also* humor appreciation

Bandits (band), 130–31, 132, 140
Bandy, Stephen C., 142
Barbie doll, *183*
Bari, Judi: car bombing of, 126, 127; costume of, 130; lawsuit of, 129; on loggers' humor, 127–28; song about, 131, 132, 140
Barnes, Pat, 213n16
Barthes, Roland, 216n35
Basso, Bob, 76
Batman (1989 film), 31–34, 109–10, 112
Baudelaire, Charles, 41–42
Beam, Alex, 223n16
Beattie, James, 3
Beavis and Butt-Head (television series), 46, 58–60
Bee, Samantha, 159
Begala, Paul, 203–4
Bendib, Khalil, 4, 5
Benoit, Melissa, 57
Berendt, John, 142
Berg, Nick, 9
Bergson, Henri, 3
Berk, Lee S., 73, 77
Berle, Milton, 79
Biblical Discernment Ministries Web site, 151
Bierce, Ambrose, 156
Big Tee-Hee, 63, 111
Bill and Ted's Excellent Adventure (film), 59
Bing, Janet, 142–43
bin Laden, Osama: laughter of, 178; Limbaugh on, 164, 167; parodies about, 180–83

BlackCommentator.com, 4
Blix, Hans, 12
blond jokes, 121–22
Blumenfeld, Esther, 76
Bobbitt, Lorena, 23
Bonham, Tal D., 76
Boondocks (cartoon), 175, *182*
Boskin, Joseph, 115, 121–22
Boston College, 9/11 victims from, 176
Bradley, Bill, 172
Bradley, Tom, 26
Bradstreet, Anne, 75
Brennan, Donald, 61
Brock, David, 120
Brook, David, 163
Brooks, Mel, 79, 99, 104
Brophy, Philip, 24
Brown, Janice Rogers, 4, 5
Browne, Rodney Howard, 151
Browning, Tod, 104
Bryant, Edward, 34
Bubeck, Zachary, 60–61
Bud Light commercials, 146
Buford, Ann Gorsuch, 136
Bumfights (videos), 25, 59, 60–61
bumper stickers, 127, 158, 163
Burton, Tim, *Batman* film of, 31–34, 109–10, 112. See also *Nightmare on Elm Street (NES)* films
Bush, Barbara, 197
Bush, George H. W., 137, 155, 156
Bush, George W.: Abu Ghraib scandal and, 8–13; in bin Laden jokes, 182; caricatures of, 191, *192*; cartoons about, 137–38, 174–75, 186, 189–*91*; "compassionate conservatism" of, 18; contested election of, 172–73; *Daily Show* comments on, 159; decline of verbal ability of, 170, 223n16; deflecting missteps of, 187; fluctuating humor about, 156–57; global climate change and, 133; as humorless, 204; as *Jeopardy* (parody) contestant, 179–80; jokes about, 6, 171–73; joke telling of, 12, 170, 197; judicial nominee of, 4, *5*; opposition to stance of, 19; post-9/11 status of, 171, 173–76, 179, 185–86; sagging ratings of, 197–98; self-parodies of, 173; Tweed compared

Fry, William F., 65–66
Funny Times (periodical), 9
FUNsulting.com, 69

Galitz, David, 127–28
gallows humor, 11, 47–48, 111–12
Gard, Tim, 97–98
Gascon, Dan, 68
gay men: Lincoln alleged as, 142, *143,* 144; murder of, 124–25
Gehrman, Ed, 127
gender, disgust-tolerance and -sensitivity by, 45–46. *See also* men, jokes about; sexism; women
Gibson, Mel, 141, 150–51
Giddens, Anthony: approach of, 216n28; on environmental damage, 19; on humor and global risks, 25, 47–48, 50, 112, 158, 198, 205
Gingrich, Newt, 136–37
global climate change: humor and, 16–17; Limbaugh on, 133–34, 165; reality of, 194
global risks and dangers: Bush's role in, 133, 197–98; gallows humor in context of, 112; killing jokes in context of, 25, 47–48, 50–51, 62; other-directed humor and, 179, 185; realities of, 158. *See also* environment
God: on humor, 79, 149–50; laughter of, 151–52
Goessel, Jerry, 145
Goldberg, Whoopi, 6, 87
Goldman, Ronald, 23
Goodheart, Annette: Big Tee-Hee exercise of, 63, 111; heartwarming story of, 81; on joke telling, 64–65; on laughter's effects, 77, 139; on religion and laughter, 79
Goodman, Ellen, 119
Goodman, Joel: on exercises and practices, 83, 84; on humor and health, 64, 80, 102; Morreall on, 90–91, 101; writing of, 70–71
Gore, Al: on Abu Ghraib prisoner abuse, 8; debates of, 170; on environmental damage, 19; as humorless, 204; intelligence of, 185; as *Jeopardy* (parody) contestant, 179; jokes about, 172

Graner, Corp. Charles A., Jr., 10–11, *11*
Granirer, David, 63, 77, 82
Grant, Ulysses S., 160
Graveline, Capt. Chris, 11
Greenberg, David, 142
Gridiron Club dinners, 196
Griffin, David Ray, 171
Groening, Matt, 3, 6
Gross, Larry, 142
Grossman, Robert, 142, *143,* 144
Gross National Product (group), 175
Grote, David, 211–12n6
Guantanamo Bay, 8, 166–67
Guest, Christopher, 71
Guiliani, Rudolph, 177
Gulas, Charles S., 168–69

Hagaseth, Christian, III, 82
Halloween (film), 112
Hammond, Darrel, 173
Hannah, Rufus, 61
Hannity, Sean, 6
Harding, Tanya, 23–24
Hardy, David T., 6
Harman, Spec. Sabrina, 10, *11*
Harris, Eric, 57
Harris, Thomas, 34–35
Hatch, Orrin, 4
hate speech, 114–15
healing laughter, 17, 63–68, 71–74, 113. *See also* positive humor movement
Heathers (film), 52, 53–55
Heller, Dana, 142–43
Hellraiser series, 39
Hennard, George, 57
Hescht, Brian, 60
Higgins, Maggie, 146
Hightower, Jim, 18
Hobbes, Thomas, 2
Holistic Online Web site, 78
homeless people, 60–61, 195
horror fiction and films: audience response to, 24; nihilism and sadism in, 49–50; real-world perspective in sequels of, 56; search for more extreme, 34; special effects in, 41, *42;* transhuman life forms in, 49–50, 51–52. *See also* killing jokes; *specific films*

Internet: accessibility of, 20; Cornell University PC crisis and, 117–20, 121, 125–26; satire on, 156, 179–80; song parodies on, 180–81; Taliban parodies on, 183
Invasion of the Body Snatchers (film, 1978), 49
Iraq War, 12, 158, 172. *See also* Abu Ghraib prisoner abuse
Ireland, Doug, 144
ISHS. *See* International Society for Humor Studies
I Spit on Your Grave (film), 24, 41
Ivins, Molly, 165–66, 172

Jackass (television and film), 59–60
Jackson, Andrew, 185
Jackson, Janet, 5–6
Jackson, Michael, 23, 157
Jacobson, David M., 80
Jameson, Frederic, 62, 216n35
Janes, Leslie M., 45
Javerbaum, David, 160
Jaws (film), 110
Jeannie Lindheim Hospital Clown Troupe, 92
"jeer pressure" concept, 45
Jeopardy (television show), 179–80
Jesus Christ: film's depiction of, 150–51; humor controversies over, 141; jokes about, 152; joyful depictions of, 69, 149, *150*, 221–22n39
Jesus Laughing Web site, 69, 221–22n39
Jewish people, jokes about, 47, 123–24
Jibjab, 192
joke cycles: blond jokes, 121–22; dead babies, 36; disasters and, 176–77; ethnic, 48–49; history of, 75; Jewish American Princess (JAP), 123–24; killing jokes, 23–24; lawyers, 122; proliferation of, 114; relationships, 116–17; sick, 25–26; as weapon in public debate, 115
Joker (character): Freddy vs., 112; killing jokes of, 31–34, 109–10
jokes: books of, 36–37, 41; context of, 41; implications of, 19–21; practical, 97; reasons to like or not, 114; sick, 25–26; as sometimes beside the point, *199. See also* antijokes; hostile/critical/targeted jokes; humor; killing jokes; laughter

joke telling: as control mechanism, 64–65; innocent, 14; objectives of, 2–3, 6–7, 10, 21; of presidents, 12, 170, 171, 194–98
Judge, Mike, 58–59. See also *Beavis and Butt-Head* (television series)
Juvenal, 158

Kalman, Maria, *184*
Kataria, Madan, 68, 77–78, 96–97
Katz, Jonathan, 20
Katz, Mark, 196–97
Kaufman, Phil, 49
Keller, Dan, 76
Kelley, Kitty, 194–95
Kerr, Mike, 81
Kerry, John: cartoons about, 188; comic attack on, 12; *Daily Show* and, 159, 203–4; deflecting missteps of, 187–88; Democratic nomination of, 13; fund-raising event of, 6; as humorless, 204; parodies about, 186–87, 188, *189;* post-election jabs at, 191–92; votes for, 186; windsurfing by, 188–89
Kerry, Teresa Heinz, 6
Khan, Joseph P., 116
Kilborn, Craig, 172
killing jokes: abortion rights song as, 130; antecedents of, 25–26; apocalyptic gothicism linked to, 40–41; characteristics of, 24–25; of Chucky, 37–40; cigarette advertising as, 146, *147,* 148; conventionality of, 110–11; cultural significance of, 56–62, 113–14; cycles of, 23–24; diverse responses to and functions of, 51–52; emergence and acceptance of, 17, 41–43, 50–51; of the Joker, 31–34; joking criminals and criminal joking in, 56–61; mainstreaming of, 26, 35; positive humor movement compared with, 109–14; resistance to concept, 14; as response to anxiety, 25, 47–48, 50–51, 62; of splatterpunks and serial killers, 34–35; in stand-up comedy, 37; suspending species identification in response to, 44–49; taboos violated by, 43–44; in "tasteless" joke books, 35–37; tension and ambivalence in, 52–55. See also *Nightmare on Elm Street (NES)* films

King, Martin Luther, Jr., 37
King, Rodney, 57, 58
King, Stephen: killing jokes of, 25, 35; splatterpunks compared with, 34; works: *Carrie,* 52, 55–56, 61; *Sleepwalkers,* 35
Kinison, Sam, 37
Kirsh, Gillian, 66, 113
Klass, Polly, 23
Klebold, Dylan, 57
Klein, Allen, 63, 64, 76, 79, 140
Kloesk, Judi, 76
Koestler, Arthur, 3
Konig, George, 5
Kozak, Ralph, 221–22n39
Krause, Barbara, 118, 119
Krueger, Freddy (character), *27;* alternative response to, 63–64; anxieties exploited by, 48; development of, 26–28, 43; laughing at vs. with, 109–14; Limbaugh compared with, 134–35, 168; murderous humor of, 11, 18, 28–30; origin of, in sequels, 56–57; religious laughter compared with, 151–52; status of humor of, 103–4; taboos violated by, 44. See also *Nightmare on Elm Street (NES)* films
Kruse, Jack, 213n16
Kubrik, Stanley, 25
Kuiper, Nicholas A., 66, 67–68, 88, 113, 115
Kurtzman, Daniel, 12, 193
Kushner, Malcolm: credentials of, 69; on humorlessness of terrorists, 177–78, 204; on presidential humor, 169, 170, 171, 197; on self-directed humor, 179

Lakoff, George, 163–64, 189
Landon, Michael, 85
Langenkamp, Heather, 56
Lansdale, Joe R., 34
Laughing Matters (periodical), 70–71
Laughing Revival, 151
laughter: at vs. with, 109–14; clubs for, 68, 95–97; God's, 151–52; as healing force (or not), 17, 63–68, 71–74, 113; mechanical, 104, 110–11; physiological effects of, 65–67, 77–78, 85–86, 102; psychological effects of, 85–86, 139–40; in religion, 149–54; role of, 71–74; school

programs for, 100–101; as universal language, 96–97. See also humor; jokes
Laughter Club movement, 95–97
lawyer jokes, 122
Learnwell Institute, 82
Lecter, Hannibal. See *Silence of the Lambs, The* (book and film)
Lederer, Elizabeth, 57
Lee, Barbara, 175
Lehmann, Michael. See *Heathers* (film)
Leno, Jay: on Abu Ghraib prisoner abuse, 9; on Bush jokes, 155, 176; Bush jokes of, 172, 173; comedic intentions of, 157–58, 159, 203; on Lott's joke, 141; on National No Name-Calling Week, 201–2
lesbian humor, 142–43, 144
Less Stress Press, 77
Lethal Weapon (film), 35
Letterman, David, 141, 172, 173
Levin, Jennifer, 56
Lewinsky, Monica, 157–58, 196–97
Limbaugh, Rush: book about, 6; commercial parodies by, 135–36, 166–67; *Doonesbury's* parodies of, 136; on environment, 17, 133–35, 194; humor style of, 133, 140; Kerry parodies by, 188; media watch group on, 167–68; persuasive strategies of, 164–68; on political correctness, 120–21, 125; post-election reflections of, 192; on torture, 9–10, 12, 166–67
Lincoln, Abraham, 79, 141, 142–43, 144, 160
Little Mermaid, The (film), 111
Lott, Trent, 141–42
Lovecraft, H. P., 20
Lugosi, Bela, 104
Lyttle, Jim, 169

MacGregor Ministries Web site, 151–52
Macy, Joanna, 25, 62, 205
Malonson, Roy Douglas, 141–42
Mang, Anna, 76
Marshall, Thurgood, 4
Martin, Leslie R., 66–67
Martin, Robert, 57–58
Martin, Rod A.: on disparaging humor, 123; on humor's effects, 66, 67, 73–74, 77–78, 85–86; on persuasion and humor, 168–69

Marvel Comics, 49

Marx, Groucho, 20

Mattingly, Kevin, 213n16

Maturin, Charles Robert, 42

McAuliffe, Christa, 176

McBryde-Foster, Merry, 80

McCain, John, 172, 179

McCoy, Glenn, 174

McDevitt, James, 116

McDonald's Corporation, 4, 6, 146

McGhee, Paul E., *86;* on humor consultants, 87–88; humor enhancement program of, 85–87; on intellectual flexibility, 139, 140; on Reagan's humor, 170

McGruder, Aaron, 175, *182*

McJobs, 4, 6

McPherson, Ryan, 60–61

media: conservatives' use of, 164; criticism of, 116; propagandistic titles used in, 182; watch group of, 133, 167–68

Media Matters for America, 167–68

medical care: Adams's approach to, 74–75; Cousins's view of, 71–74. *See also* hospitals; patients

Meinholz, Henry L., 57

Melville, Herman, *Moby-Dick,* 105–7

men, jokes about, 122

mental illness, 144–46

Messner, Austin, 58

Messner, Jessica, 58

Meyerowitz, Rick, *184*

Michaels, Lorne, 177

Middlebury College, Vermont Teddy Bear controversy and, 145–46

Mikolashek, Lt. Col. Paul T., 8

Miller, Dennis, 9, 18

Miller, Mark Crispin, 162, 185, 191, 204

Mintz, Larry, 116–17

mirthmyopia concept, 140

Mirza, Shazia, 178–79

Modeleski, Tania, 216n35

Mondale, Walter, 170

monologues. *See* stand-up comedy and monologues

Montgomery, Brad, 97

Monty Python, 12, 17, 44

Moody, Raymond, Jr., 76

Moore, Alan, 31–32

Moore, Michael (filmmaker), 6, 12–13

Moore, Mike (humor consultant), 82

Morreall, John: background of, 85; credentials of, 88–89; on humor consultants, 75–76; on Humor Project and Goodman, 90–91, 101; on humor's positive functions, 89–90, 139–40; on Reagan's humor, 170

Morrison, Grant, 32–34

Morton, Thomas, 75

Mothers against Drunk Driving, 146

Moyers, Bill, 159

Mulvey, Laura, 48

Muslims, 178–79

Myers, Michael, 112

Nader, Ralph, 205

Nast, Thomas, 160–62, 194

Nation (periodical): "Babe Lincoln" cartoon in, 142, *143,* 144; on Nast, 160–61

National Alliance for the Mentally Ill, 145, 146

National No Name-Calling Week Coalition, 201–2

National Sporting Goods Association, 188–89

Naureckas, Jim, 6

Nelson, Craig, 213n16

New York City: Afghanistanized map of, 183–85; Tammany abuses in, 160–62

New Yorker (periodical): Afghanistanized map on, 183–85; bad joke payback cartoon in, *83;* cartoons absent in 9/24/01 issue, 175

New York State Lottery Crazy 8's game, 144–45

New York Times: on Kerry's windsurfing, 188–89; on mental illness terminology, 144–45

Nicholson, Jack, 31

Nightmare on Elm Street (NES) films: allusion to, in *Heathers,* 54; ambiguous responses to, 52; *Child's Play* compared with, 37; context in, 41; displaced vision in, 28–29; plot of first, 27–28; popularity of, 30–31; predictability of, 110; products and success of, 26, 213–14n4; sequels of, 26, 56–57; special effects in, *42. See also* Krueger, Freddy (character)

nihilistic gothicism: context of, 49–50, 112; doom and victimization in, 40, 50–51; killing jokes and, 40–41; New Age spirituality vs., 84–85

9/11 attacks: Bush's status strengthened after, 171, 173–76, 179, 185–86; cartoon references to, 174–75; European jokes about, 176; intelligence failures before, 158, 185; national mood for joking after, 175–81, 186; urge to restore U.S. hegemony after, 182–85

9/11 Digital Archives, 180

9/11 Truth Movement, 171

Nixon, Richard M., 205

Norman, Tony, 176

Oblongs (characters), 59

O'Brien, Conan, 9

Oliphant, Pat, 190, *191*

Olson, James M., 45, 122

O'Malley, Dave, 124–25

Onion (periodical), 175, 181–82

Online Freedom Fighters Anarchist Liberation, 119, 120

Opplinger, Patrice A., 45–46

O'Reilly, Bill, 6, 18

Oring, Elliott: on blond jokes, 121–22; on Freud and joke work, 43, 44; on jokes about African Americans, 117; on social function of humor, 115, 120, 124

"Osama yo mama" (expression), 183

Ott, Scott, 166, 186–87

Owens, Wayne, 57–58

Pacific Lumber, 127–28

Paine, Albert Bigelow, 161–62

Paine Webber joke, 116–17

parodies: of advertisements, 135–36, 166–67; anti–bin Laden and anti-Taliban, 180–83; in *Doonesbury*, 136–38; of *Jeopardy*, 179–80; of songs, 128–30, 131–32, 180–81

Parvin, Landon, 197

Pascal, 16–17, 213n16

Passion of the Christ, The (film), 150–51

patients: clown's approach to, 69, 74–75, 75, *91*, 91–94, 98, 105, 110; humor of, 100–101, 111–12

PC. *See* political correctness

Pearson, Jon, 102–4

persuasion: evasive strategies in, 163–68; humor's function in, 89, 90, 168–69

Peter, Laurence J., 76

Petty, Richard E., 169

Piechota, Ron, 180–81, 183

Pittsburgh Post-Dispatch, 176

playfulness: detachment in, 35–36; emphasis on, 89, 103; seriousness balanced with, 139–40

Plous, Scott, 146, *147,* 148

Poe, Edgar Allan, 20, 25

political campaigns: Abu Ghraib scandal and, 8–13; anger politics in, 120; anti-intellectualism in, 185–86; candidates' alleged humorlessness in, 204–5; candidates' joke telling in, 170–71; humor's and satire's effects on, 192–93; media's complicity in, 203–4; persuasion in, 163–69

political correctness: backlash against, 5, 119–20; conservatives' use of, 120–21; debates on, 114–16, 148; impetus behind, 117; university crisis over, 117–20, 121, 125–26. *See also* humor controversies

political humor: apolitical vs., 155–62; Bush's and Kerry's uses of, 186–93; controversies over, 6; efficacy of, 159–62, 192–93, 194; intentions of, 157–59; persuasion strategies in, 163–69; post-9/11 suspension of, 175–81, 186; professionalization of, 156; reflective approach to, 194; satire and, 155–56; uses of, 2, 156–57

politics: corruption in, 160–62; of denial, 17; hardening divisions in, 192–93. *See also* Democratic party; Republican party

Poniewozik, James, 176

Pontual, Jorge, 142

popular culture: contradictory messages of, 59; Cornell men's joke and, 119; gothicism vs. transcendence in, 40; intellectual elites' view of, 51–52; killing jokes diffused throughout, 41; names in, 52–53; post-9/11 parodies based in, 182–83;

Rothberg, Saranne, 100–101
Rove, Karl, 166, 172, 187
Rowson, Susanna, 44
Rumsfeld, Donald, 9–10, 159, 197
Russell, J. S., 34
Ryder, Winona, 53

sacredcowburgers.com, 189
sadism, 49–50. *See also* killing jokes; nihilistic gothicism
Sahara Club Newsletter, The (publication), 127–28
Sammon, Paul M., 34
Samra, Cal, 149
satire: comedy vs., 157–58; efficacy of, 159–62; on Internet, 156, 179–80; literary views of, 155–56; political campaigns and, 192–93; public opinion and, 13
Saturday Night Live (television show), 173, 175–76, 177
Savage, Michael, 6
Sawyer, Stephen S., *150*
Schiavo, Terri, 198
Schlatter, George, 175
Schumer, Charles, 4
scrappleface.com, 12, 166, 186–87
seriousness: of antijokes, 148–49; matters of, 16–17; play balanced with, 139–40; treatment for, 85–86
sexism, 123, 125–26
sexual harassment, 118, 119, 125
Shakespeare, William, 25, 28
Shales, Tom, 175–76
Sharon, Ariel, 175
Shepard, Matthew, 124–25
Shilts, Randy, 195
sick jokes, 25–26
Siers, Kevin, 9
Sigler, Harold, 58
Silberg, Jackie, 77
Silence of the Lambs, The (book and film), 31, 34–35, 112, 182
Silverglate, Harvey, 119
Simon, Paul, 177, 180
Simpson, Nicole, 23–24
Simpson, O. J., 23–24
Simpsons, The (television show), 3, 6, 59

Sinatra, Frank, 135
Singer, Melanie, 58
sitcoms: safe humor in, 7; traditional comedies compared with, 211–12n6
Sivits, Pvt. Jeremy, 10, 15
Slansky, Paul, 56
slasher films, 51–52
Slater, Christian, 53
Sleepwalkers (film), 35
Slyman, Michael, 60–61
Smirnoff, Yakov, 101, 102
social problems: humor and, 1–8; presidential joking about, 195
society, juvenilization of, 43
Socrates, 194
songs: anti–bin Laden and anti-Taliban parodies, 180–83; environmentalists' use of, 128–29; Limbaugh's parodies of, 164
Soros, George, 6
Spears, Britney, 141
Spencer, Gary, 123–24
Spiderman, 49, 92
Splatterpunks 1990 (anthology), 34
Springer, Jerry, 14
Stamaty, Mark Alan, *199*
stand-up comedy and monologues: extremely hostile jokes in, 37; function of, 14; growth of, 114; killing jokes in, 41; post-9/11 humor of, 178–79; safe humor in, 7
Stansell, Christine, 142
Stewart, Jon: Bush jokes of, 172–73; *Crossfire* appearance of, 203–4; on Lott's joke, 141; stance of, 149, 159–60
Stewart, Martha, 39
Steyn, Mark, 204
Stowe, Harriet Beecher, 44
stress reduction: Cornell University PC crisis and, 126; humor in, 85–86, 97–98; negative side of, 14–16, 90; realistic means of, 100
subgroups: disposition theory and, 25, 45–49; humanity of, 44; joke wars and intentions of, 115–16; stereotypes of, 48–49, 122, 124–26; vilification of, 117
suicides: gallows humor and, 47–48; identification with killing jokers and, 46–

47; ridicule linked to, 54–55. *See also* nihilistic gothicism

Sultanoff, Stephen M., 68

Super Bowl half-time show, 5–6

superiority theory, 41–42

Sutton, Ward, 9

Swift, Jonathan, 156

taboo violation, 43–44

Talbot, Stephen, 165

Taliban, 180–81, 182, *183*

Tanner, Daniel, 60–61

Taylor, Edward, 75

teachers, chat board of, 69

Terman Life-Cycle Study, 66–67

Terminator (films), 61–62

terrorists: alleged humorlessness of, 177–78; as improv subject, 1; Islam misunderstood by, 179; loggers and environmentalists as, 126–27; U.S. anxiety about, 184–85. *See also* 9/11 attacks

Texas Chainsaw Massacre, The (film), 112

Thelma and Louise (film), 41

theworriedshrimp.com, 12, 191, *192*

Thomas, Clarence, 4, 5

Thompson, Hunter S., 205

Thoreau, Henry David, 20

Three Stooges, 25

Thurber, James, 79

Thurmond, Strom, 141–42

ticklers and teasers, function of, 25

Tilly, Jennifer, 39

timber industry: environmental protesters and, 126–28; humor deployed by, 127–28, 130–31, 132; Limbaugh on, 135; song of, 131, 132, 140

Time magazine, 176

Tinsley, Bruce, 188

Toles, Tom, 174, 175, 186

Tolkein, J. R. R., 84

Tompkins, Jane, 44

TooStupidToBePresident.com, 12, 179, 180, 186, 192–93

Topplebush.com, 12, 193

Toronto Blessing (1994), 151

torture: Limbaugh on, 9–10, 12, 166–67; sadistic humor in, 8–13, 15, 89

Toxic Avenger (film), 49

toys, 183

transcendence, 40, 51–52

transhuman life forms: cyborg's death and, 61–62; imagining of, 49–50, 51–52

Traverse, Marshall, 146

Tripp, C. A., 142, 144

Trudeau, Garry: Bush cartoons of, 174; comic parodies by, 136–38; complex issues and humor of, 140; conflicting values considered by, 138–39; humor style of, 133, 136; on 9/11 attacks, 175

True, Herb, 76

Trueblood, Elton, 149, 150

Truly Tasteless Jokes (1982), 36, 41

T-shirts, 127, 149, 221–22n39

Tudor, Andrew, 49, 50

Twain, Mark, 155, 222n1

Tweed, William Marcy "Boss," 160–62

28 Days Later (film), 110

Twitchell, James B., 43

universities: JAP jokes in, 123–24; PC crisis at, 117–20, 121, 125–26; Vermont Teddy Bear controversy and, 145–46

U.N. weapons inspectors, 12

U.S. Senate Judiciary Committee, 4, 5

U.S. Supreme Court, 8, 172

Vanes, JohnJay, 180

Vanity Fair (periodical), 175

Vennochi, Joan, 204

Vermont Teddy Bear Company, 141, 145–46

victimization: degrees of separation and, 176–77; in nihilistic gothicism, 40, 50–51; politics of emotion and, 120

Viguerie, Richard, 164

villains: audience's identification with, 28–29, 35, 112; hero's identification with, 33–34; internalization of, 48–49. *See also* Krueger, Freddy (character)

violence: art and copycat crimes of, 60–61; climate of tolerance of, 153–54; preposterous, 43; real-world, 56–58, 60–61; in schools, 56, 57, 201–2; television and film violence blamed for, 56, 58

Visciano, Joseph, 176

Voltaire, 79